PARIS, PART TIME

Lisa Baker Morgan

published by *ciao yummy!*®
Los Angeles, California
Library of Congress Cataloging-in-Publication Data
available on request.
Identifier: LCCN 2020904829

ISBN: 978-0-9847443-2-9 (hardcover)
ISBN: 978-0-9847443-3-6 (softcover)
ISBN: 978-0-9847443-4-3 (ebook)

Cover photograph by Lisa Baker Morgan.
Cover Design by Lisa Baker Morgan and Ojai Digital.
All photographs and recipes are by Lisa Baker Morgan.
All photographs and recipes are the property of Lisa Baker Morgan.

Printed in the United States of America.

First Edition

For Ava and Julia

CONTENTS

PART III

PART IV

AUTHOR'S NOTE

This book is based upon true events as recorded in my daily journal. It is a snapshot of Paris and my travels in France from 2006 through 2012. Many events have been condensed or omitted for brevity. Photographs, documents, notes, and emails were consulted to refresh my memory when necessary. The majority of the names have been changed. I have included photographs in an attempt to show not only the aesthetic beauty of France and the differences in its regions, but its café society, the fraternity amongst those devoted to the culinary arts, and the French *joie de vivre*.

It is worth noting that Paris has changed since the writing of this book: some restaurants have closed or changed ownership or chefs; the U.S. dollar and euro conversion has varied; and acts of terrorism, immigration and the protests of the *gilets jaunes* have affected the city socially and economically. Security has become a part of Paris in a way it was not before. In fact, even my morning running route has changed; I can no longer run under the Eiffel Tower because its base is now surrounded by a bulletproof glass wall with turnstiles. Despite the changes, Paris endures and continues to evolve and reinvent itself.

I want to acknowledge two writers whom I greatly admire and also lived in Paris. Chapter 4, entitled "Paris is My Hometown, Too," is a nod to Gertrude Stein who famously said, "America is my country, and Paris is my hometown." I share that affection and duality. The final pages in this book allude to James Joyce, who wrote the last episode of *Ulysses* in a female voice, using the stream of consciousness style. Only this narrative device could accurately convey the gratitude and optimism I felt as I reflected upon the people and events which led us to Paris. However, instead of saying "yes" to a man, a woman can say "yes" to herself and be the one to write about it.

PARIS, PART TIME

PART I

CHAPTER ONE

The Paper Crown

MY BED, with its rails at attention, sits in the center of a room accompanied by flashing, beeping square machines and an IV stand with numerous hanging plastic bags of fluid. Large glass jars sit on the floor filling with liquids, the source of which comes from me. The bed faces a closed door; the large window to its right occasionally presents my still room with the distraction of shadowy figures passing by. Yet, in this sanitary and solitary confinement, there is a paper crown. It hangs from the corner of the frame of a lonely picture centered on an otherwise empty wall. Shiny gold on the outside, matte white on the inside. The scalloped edges on top give it a regal appearance. Light, presumably from a window behind my head, is recast from the crown's gold exterior, bestowing a warm glow to the stark room for a short time each day. My drowsy stare studies the glowing, light-diffusing crown, which maintains its shape despite its paper fabrication. It must be stronger than it appears, I think to myself. And, here we are, the paper crown and I, in the intensive-care unit at the Princess Grace Hospital in Monaco where I have been since December 29, 2007. My diagnosis changes daily. It is January 7, 2008.

The paper crown is a gift from an ICU nurse. It is the traditional garnish for *la galette des rois*, the cake made of two puff pastry layers enveloping a frangipane center and enjoyed on the Epiphany.

Her piece of cake must have hidden *la fève* (the bean). Despite my considerable consumption of these cakes over the years, my piece of cake has never contained *la fève*. This nurse, unknown to me, was the lucky one, and she gave her prize to me. Now, this previously elusive paper crown is the highlight in my sufentanil-clouded and hermitic ICU world.

Plastic tubes come and go from all body regions. I lay in bed without moving. Unbearable pain wakes me every few hours. Then I hear a fingernail flick against glass, three times, and then the glass snaps. The familiar sounds signal that soon the pain will dissipate, and it does, for a time. Often I focus on the crown as I wait for sleep, for pain relief, for the occasional sterile-paper-clothed visitor. The pattern is like clockwork, and it continues, day to night to day. I think of my daughters, Ava and Julia, six and four. Sometimes I hear their voices calling out to me, but they are imagined. They are nine time zones away. They are waiting for me to "get better" and return home to Los Angeles.

But better I am not. Nor do I get. My body is failing me or so I hear in hushed whispers at my door. Tests are administered daily to determine which organ is now at risk. My appendix. My liver. The list grows, but I am too drowsy to comprehend the danger. My lungs fill with fluid. It is difficult to breathe. When it is decided that the IVs in my arms are not getting enough medicine and liquid nutrition into my withering body, a day nurse turns and holds my head down on my bed while a doctor cuts my neck and sews an additional tube into my jugular vein. "*Doucement*," she tells me.

Scared, and so very tired of needles and tubes, the questions in French, the tests and evolving diagnosis, and drifting in and out of sleep, only partly conscious of the world around me. Trapped in a body that resembles little more than a motionless marionette in a quarantined room, my mind and heart remain the same. Inside I feel like the same woman I have always been: full of thoughts and ideas and a passion for life and those in it.

MY MARRIAGE ended in 2005, but truthfully, and unbeknownst to me, it was over much earlier. While my husband was falling in love with someone else, our daughters advanced to the lively ages of two and four, and I miscarried a third child. By October, our separation was official. Yet, the year reached an all-time low when two-year-old Julia asked Santa Claus to bring her father back home for Christmas. 2005 was a shit year.

Determined to make the best of my changed circumstances, I set out to face the new calendar year with vigor. No longer married, I could return to the things that I loved but had put aside in the name of marital compromise. Travel was at the top of the list, and I began researching places to go with small children. Paris, my favorite place, seemed tough. Alice, my long-time friend and Ava's godmother, suggested we come to Saint-Jean-Cap-Ferrat, between Monaco and Nice in the south of France. Formerly a fishing community, Saint-Jean is now a small port village where boats of various sizes are docked and a few fortunate homeowners open the shutters of their second (or third) homes for the summer. Alice and her three children were planning to visit her parents who live outside Nice. We could all vacation together. I had never been to the south of France, and the thought of the girls and me vacationing with friends who resembled family sounded perfect. So off we went.

We stayed at a sixteen-room Italian villa turned hotel, built in 1878 and positioned on a slight hill just across the one-way road from the water, with modest rooms and a breathtaking view. The hotel had been run by the same family for generations, and in fact, three generations appeared to live on the premises. As we checked in, an elderly woman gently reminded the three young boys, about the same age as my girls, to stop running inside. My girls stood close to me, observing the boys' antics and on guard for cooties.

Our second day in Saint-Jean, Alice and I took the five little ones to Paloma Beach, a private beach walking distance from our hotel, where three rows of *matelas* with optional umbrellas lay between the clear, pale blue water and an open restaurant (although waiters will bring your lunch to your mattress should you be disinclined to move). Because Paloma fills quickly, the *matelas* must be reserved well in advance. Alice made our reservations, and I immediately became aware that this was a good thing because the owner and staff recognized her and gave us *matelas* close to the water, which I doubt I would have received as an unknown American.

Fascinated with a beach carpeted by small pebbles rather than sand, the children spent hours searching for heart-shaped pebbles and "sea glass," small pieces of green glass that have been honed by time and water. After lunch, exhausted by their beach-combing activities, all five children fell asleep on the umbrella-shaded mattresses, sand sticking to their tanned bodies from the sunscreen and wayward ice cream. Alice and I left them with the sitter and waded out in the water. Despite the idyllic setting, my spirit was down. Alice asked what was on my mind, and I told her that the very day the girls and I left Los Angeles, I discovered that their father also left to vacation in Hawaii with his girlfriend. He *should* have been with us, I thought, vacationing with his family.

"Please!" Alice said. "Look at this place! Who cares what he is doing. Hawaii? *Bah!* You have everything you need here, and you have your girls and they have you. You are far better off, Lisa. I promise you. Your perspective is all wrong. I want you to look at where you are and be grateful for this and the life you are going to have. It does not get better than this," she said. "Plus, you don't even like Hawaii."

She was right. About everything. My worries were a broken heart and an altered future. It is not the family I envisioned, but in time the girls and I would adapt to our new circumstances. We have a roof over our heads, food on the table, our health, the love of friends and family, and we are in the south of France, beginning new traditions and surrounded by unparalleled beauty. That day the salt water eased my heartache and replaced the disquiet with gratitude. While location does not permit an escape from one's thoughts, those surroundings changed my perspective, and there in that water, I looked back toward the beach and my sleeping children, and I vowed not to let the experience change me or them, even though I knew there would be some scars.

The following summer, we repeated our visit to Saint-Jean-Cap-Ferrat. One day while Alice and the kids were in the mountains with her parents, the girls and I, with the sitter, passed the sunny day at Paloma. The girls abandoned their Polly Pocket dolls, many of which were now missing limbs and/or heads, to stick their toes in the water with the sitter. As I lay on my stomach and watched them splash about, my reverie was interrupted by a smooth, purposeful voice that addressed me from above:

"*Excusez-moi, Mademoiselle.*"

"*Oui?*"

I peered out from beneath my large, black sun hat. The voice belonged to a handsome, Mediterranean-looking man with a neatly pressed white button-down shirt and navy blue shorts who was casting his shadow over me. Paloma Beach just got even better as a good-looking Italian man seemingly just fell from the sky.

He introduced himself and told me that he lived in Monaco. He asked if I would like to share a drink with him.

"*Peut-être,*" I responded and proceeded to tell him that the drink would have to wait for a few days until I returned from Portofino, where the girls and I were headed for a little Italian adventure.

"*AH, Por - toe - FEE - no!*" he exclaimed, and if I had not guessed that he was Italian before, I knew it then.

And, as all Italians like to do, he immediately volunteered recommendations for the "best places" to eat in "*Por - toe - FEE - no,*" where I could find a shrimp dish that is "one step from paradise," and he gave me names of people for whom to ask. I thanked him. We exchanged telephone numbers, and he walked to the restaurant behind.

When the girls returned to the *matelas* and their dolls, I told the sitter about the Italian from the sky. She nodded and told me she saw him and his friends arrive from an anchored boat, and she pointed it out. Not small, but not a yacht. Last summer when the girls and I were here, I'd met an Englishman who owned a company that built yachts (for sale or rent). Not having much to add to the conversation of brokered yachts, I remarked how nice it must be for families to pass their summer on these large boats. He politely chuckled and informed me that, while there were *some* families on the brokered yachts, the majority were filled with wealthy men and their equally brokered young women. Then I observed what he described: older men in the company of extremely thin girls with designer bags larger than the circumference of their bodies struggling to walk from the Paloma dock to the restaurant for lunch in their high-heeled, red-bottomed shoes. I was pleased that "Mr. Monaco's" boat had no such visible accoutrements. Thinking more about our interaction, I was touched that he'd approached me when my girls had not been present, a sign of respect for my children often unobserved by men.

Mr. Monaco's Portofino tips proved golden. As soon as we crossed the Italian border into Menton, my French phone kicked in revealing a text from Mr. Monaco welcoming us back to French soil and confirming our deferred drink.

The Sea Lounge in Monaco was both a restaurant and lounge, which sat directly on the sand while sultry music played in the background. I ordered a *coupe de champagne*, which the waiter accidentally knocked off his tray, spilling it all over me and the scarf I had tied around my upper half as a shirt, rendering it virtually see-through. I sat, mortified, while several pairs of hands offered me napkins to minimize the transparency. Notwithstanding the mishap, or perhaps because of it, a courtship began that took place after the girls fell asleep. His real name was Stephen D'Angelo, but to me, he would always be Mr. Monaco. We took long walks at night, exchanging our histories and personal stories. He told me about his family and about his brother's untimely death from cancer. He asked me about the girls and my prior life as a litigator and the disappointing end to my marriage. He seemed interested in everything I had to say. He had never been married but was empathetic with the difficulty of divorce with children, especially when a third party was involved. The acknowledgement and compassion made me feel seen and heard. We sat on the docks in the Saint-Jean port where we ate ice cream out of cones and talked into the early morning. He taught me some Italian expressions, and I taught him some American ones. He had a particular fondness for "yummy," and his repetition of it made me laugh.

He loved that I read food magazines on the beach but admonished me, "French cooking, it will kill you, Lisa." And, to prove his point about the superiority and purity of Italian food, one night Mr. Monaco cooked for me. It was indeed the best pasta I'd ever eaten, using the most simple ingredients — fresh garlic and tomatoes, olive oil, and torn pieces of mozzarella. It was how he tossed the *al dente* pasta in the pan, gently marrying its contents. He promised to teach me how.

When the girls and I returned to Los Angeles, Mr. Monaco came to visit weeks later. I showed him around the city and introduced him to my closest friends. Despite his fancy-pants exterior and exotic car, he was down-to-earth, a kind man with a soft touch that calmed my soul and made me smile spontaneously like a young girl. He voiced his admiration for my ability to be in Malibu all day with the girls in tow and then drive to Hollywood to prepare and host a dinner party for eight. He complimented me on inviting the girls' father's girlfriend to Ava's birthday party. He said I reminded him of his mother, and for an Italian man who spoke with his parents daily, there could be no higher compliment. We continued our long-distance romance and made plans for the girls' Winter Break.

CHRISTMAS 2007. I celebrated Christmas morning with the girls in Los Angeles. When they left at noon on Christmas day to pass the second week of their Winter Break with their father, I boarded a plane to Paris where I met Mr. Monaco. We stayed in Paris for two nights, celebrating the holidays with friends; then we left for Nice. The plan was to spend two nights in Monaco and then fly to Milan where we would meet up with his friends to celebrate New Year's Eve. I knew nothing more of the plans. Mr. Monaco told me only to bring clothes for the opera house and to be prepared for *"beaucoup de surprises."*

On the plane, I wrote in a small blue leather travel journal, a birthday gift from a girlfriend, Jasmine, to document my vacation. Mr. Monaco asked me for the journal and wrote:

"Una stella è caduta dal cielo...e'accanta a me."

His cursive writing in black ink looked elegant against the crisp white paper. I looked at him; everything about Mr. Monaco was elegant.

"What does it mean?" I ask.

A star is fallen from the sky; she is sitting by me," he said.

I smiled and I glanced at my wrist bearing his Christmas gift, a watch with two time zones. "*2 Lisa With Love S,*" engraved on the back.

Our first night in Monaco we drove over the border into Italy, a mere twenty minutes away to meet another couple and dine *al fresco*. I ate scallops and drank Champagne. After dinner, our car flew with purpose on the A10 back to Monaco. It was a dream, that contentment and adventure, and I felt special and cared for, because that was how Mr. Monaco treated me. I turned my head toward him as he drove. He had the profile of Julius Caesar, and I pictured him with a bay laurel wreath around his head. Catching my stare, he asked *en français* what I was smiling about. I told him that he has the demeanor of *un roi* and his regal profile should be on a coin. He smiled at me and extended his right hand to my left.

A few hours later I woke up with a sharp pain in my lower abdomen. Mr. Monaco gave me some stomach medicine to ease the discomfort. Not yet light, I tried to return to sleep. But the medicine did not help, and the pain worsened. Damn scallops. Now curled in a fetal position, I clutched my lower stomach. Mr. Monaco called a doctor to come to the apartment, and while we waited, he telephoned his father, a former surgeon, for advice. I stared up at Mr. Monaco from the bed while he paced the floor and spoke rapidly in Italian with his father. The pain was paralyzing. My eyes were wet.

"We cannot wait any longer," he said.

He scooped me up from the bed and carried me to his car, placing me in the passenger seat. We sat in the multi-colored plastic chairs in the waiting room of *les Urgences à Princesse Grâce*. I was doubled over with my head to my ankles to keep as much pressure on my abdomen as possible. It was the only way to ease the pain.

Nurses whisked me to a small exam room. I clutched my Black-Berry in my hand. The pain was no longer isolated; it was all over my core. As I waited for the doctor, I emailed my brother and my close friend, Alison, in Los Angeles. I asked if they could take the girls to school in a few days because I did not think I was going to be able to return as planned. Alison called me immediately. When she heard my voice, she knew better than I:

"Lisa, you are *not* okay. I am sending someone from your family for you. Who do you want there?"

"My brother," I told her.

Jeff and I have been close since our parents' divorce when I was twelve; he was nine. Jeff is an artist. A painter. A photographer. A poet. He lives in Los Angeles with his wife and two young children. An exemplary father and husband, he is kind, patient, funny, and sees the good in everyone and everything. Although the most stubborn person I know, he is also the most thoughtful, and I always wished I were more like him.

We hung up. I struggled to breathe. My yoga clothes, the easiest and most comfortable things I thought to wear to the ER, were too constricting. The pressure on my chest was unbearable. I demanded the scissors that an attendant was holding, and I cut the sports top down the center of my sternum to rid my chest of the constricting material. Within minutes, I began vomiting thick black liquid. It resembled tar, and it was everywhere. The sight of it scared me, and I envisioned that I had somehow been poisoned. People rushed around me. Needles were drawn. A tube was inserted down my throat and more up my nose. Tar on me. Tar rushed through the big tube like a locomotive steaming over the edge of the bed and falling on itself into a glass jar next to the bed. IVs were inserted in the veins in my arms. My heart raced because I did not understand what was happening to me or what they were doing. My throat hurt and my arms were entangled in clear tiny tubes. My eyes scanned the room looking for Mr. Monaco, and I reached for the comfort of his hand, but there were too many people around me, and they pushed him aside.

A doctor introduced himself and extended his hand to Mr. Monaco.

"Docteur Ferrari," he said, and I watched him take Mr. Monaco toward the door, and I heard him say in a hushed tone, *"C'est très, très, très, très grave ... "*

I did not hear the rest. I did not need to; I saw it in Mr. Monaco's face. The regal, olive-colored and happy face I was admiring only hours ago was a sullen ashy gray. There was terror in his eyes. Dr. Ferrari left, and Mr. Monaco sat down in the chair next to my bed. Tears dripped down his cheeks, and the way he looked at me, I knew what he was thinking. And, instinctively, I tried to console him.

"Non, s'il te plaît," I said to him.

My IV-clad hand reached out to him. Holding my hand with both of his, careful to mind the tubes, he kissed it and placed it gently on my bed. He tried to speak, but his words were inaudible. He rose silently from his chair and left the room, wiping tears from his face. Two men clothed in white laid me on a gurney and wheeled me down the brightly lit hallway to an unknown destination. When the gurney wheels passed over the tiny cracks in between the floor tiles, it felt like an earthquake tremor and jolted my body with pain.

"Plus lentement, s'il vous plaît," I muttered to the man by my head.

Our destination was a cold, empty room, and the dye that soon coursed through my veins caused me to shiver visibly. Someone commanded me to remain still. Trying not to move, I felt my body pulse with pain as a large white tube swallowed me whole.

I AWAKE in my ICU room. Alone. With the paper crown.

A team of doctors attend to me, shuffling together in a clump and armed with notepads and pens. They gather around my bed and discuss the medical curiosity that I have become. When Dr. Ferrari speaks, his disciples draw their pens and take notes. The doctors are Italian. The nurses are French. There is a night team and a day team, and I have my favorites on both. Mr. Monaco speaks in Italian to the doctors while I am forced to communicate in French. It is amazing the French vocabulary I recall because I have to. Only one doctor speaks English, and I do not see her often.

Jeff and Mr. Monaco visit me every day. Sometimes I talk to them. Sometimes I am sleeping. They are not permitted to stay long. They are covered head to toe in protective paper clothing and required to wear masks, which I find disheartening because I don't know if the masks are for their protection or mine. I still do not understand what is wrong with me and why I am here. There are a lot of questions and tests. Today they are worried about my appendix, and there is talk of blood transfusions.

My BlackBerry is hidden under my sheet. It is my only way to reach beyond these four walls. The day nurses who change my bed sheets and sponge bathe me know of my contraband, but they do not mind. Using the device to email instructions untangling my immediate responsibilities in Los Angeles (saying that I am "detained" in Europe) proves difficult. It requires all my energy to focus my eyes and mind and steady my hand. Several drafts must be saved before a final is sent. One email seems to take an eternity.

Above all, my thoughts are consumed with my daughters. At times the yearning to fold them under my arms with their blonde heads leaning on my ribs overwhelms me, and I cry alone with only the echo of my sob. Nine time zones apart, but the barrier is a blessing because no child should see her mother in a dizzy, sleepy existence, high on pain medication and restrained by plastic strings. Four and six. No, they should not see me like this. My pointer finger punches out a cryptic email to my sister-in-law with instructions: how to reach the housekeeper, where to find Ava's school uniforms, and what Julia prefers as a snack and how to manage her separation anxiety. The preschool has been informed that I am sick but will come home soon, just a little later than planned. After all, this ICU thing must be some food-related reaction. I am a healthy woman. I run marathons as a hobby. Despite the pain, disbelief is my mind-set as I drift in and out of medicine-induced sleep.

Then one morning, as I anticipated, I feel better. So much better that I can actually slightly raise the bed behind my back to talk to the doctors rather than lie inert horizontally with blurry eyes. I ask the female doctor if I may have some ice cream (believing that is a reasonable hospital dietary request). She denies my request without hesitation, and when I ask her when I can go home, her eyes stare at me in disbelief. She puts down her notepad and says in perfect English, with an intonation of indignation, "You are *not* understanding your situation; you are very, very ill. It is impossible for you to go anywhere."

Her stern words infuse me with a combined clarity of my stupidity and my reality. Jeff told me that I have been in ICU for over two weeks. The very next day her sobering comments prove correct. My condition worsens.

With a realistic understanding of my situation, I lie alone with my thoughts. Practical thoughts. Questioning thoughts. Spiritual and esoteric thoughts. For the second time in my life, the first being my divorce, there is no answer to the *why* and no escaping the circumstances out of my control. I try to envision my daughters' faces on Christmas morning when they opened their gifts and when I hugged them goodbye as they left to celebrate Christmas with their father. It was the last time I saw them and may be the last time ever. I wonder if I taught them everything I could in the time I was given. Will they remember the bedtime stories I read to them? Will they remember the meals I cooked for them? Will they remember *me?* I contemplate whether or not hope and acceptance can co-exist, and I decide that they cannot. Hoping for a particular outcome is inextricably tied to control, and that is not acceptance. Yet, acceptance is not resignation, I tell myself. It is coming to peace with circumstances as they exist. Languishing in an ICU bubble for over two weeks with the pain worsening despite the medication and the attentive care, my hope to return to Los Angeles and see my daughters transitions to a peaceful acceptance that this is as much life as I was meant to have. My mind drifts to thoughts of all the things I did not have a chance to teach them and all the places I wanted to take them. I think of all the advice I wanted to impart and the self-confidence and self-appreciation I wanted to instill in them. I wanted to teach them to be respectful, loving, independent women with opinions, and to show them that they are not defined by whom, or if, they marry, their jean size, or what they do for a living, and that "success" is theirs to define. But I accept that my daughters will be raised by family other than myself, and that they will be fine. They will receive different lessons. All the same, my chest aches thinking of all the love I have for them that I will be unable to bestow upon them, but I rationalize that the loss will be physical only, and if I die here perhaps my spirit can watch over them all of the time (even if in a guardian angel-type way) rather than only a share of the time, and that is something.

Dr. Ferrari again pushes the surgery that I have steadfastly refused. Hospitals are full of germs and super-germs, and surgery is a sure acceleration to the end in my opinion. But such fears for my refusal, however valid, no longer matter. I am headed there anyway. I punch out another email to my sister-in-law and give her the combination to my safe where she can find a few crucial documents of my little life, including my will. My body, limp and numb, is wheeled out of my solitary room on a gurney. I stare up at the white ceiling while a triangular mask closes in on my face. Instinctively, I push the anesthesiologist's hands and the mask away because I feel like I am being smothered. When my hands are held, I move my head from side to side until all of the physical struggle I can muster is taken away. I see the faces of my daughters and hear the pure-toned tenderness of their voices. Then everything goes dark.

I AWAKEN in a new room with five scars on my abdomen. The sun floods the space, and I turn my head toward the sliding glass doors to my right, offering me a view of the Mediterranean. The beauteous view that has helped heal my wounds before feels like an embrace. The paper crown has followed me and hangs above my bed on a traction bar that protrudes from the wall behind my head. The drowsy hush that weighed on my eyelids and extremities for two and a half weeks in the ICU is gone. My mind is alert, and I attempt to sit up, which I accomplish somewhat successfully, although the entirety of my abdomen is still quite painful. Despite this discomfort, I have never felt so alive. Filled with an overwhelming sense of peace and contentment from my sheer existence, I question if it is really the sun filling the room or if it is the light emanating from within me.

Sliding off of the bed, inches at a time, my toes touch the cold floor, followed by my heels. My legs wobble as I unfold them at the knees. Hunched over, I hold onto the bed covers until the black dizziness passes. I move my hands from the covers and steady myself on my IV stand. Gripping the cold metal, I shuffle my feet and move with the wheeled stand slowly toward the sliding glass door, bent over in the middle like someone who has been dealt a serious blow in the stomach. The hospital gown is drafty in the open back. The IV tubes waltz around the metal bar as I inch toward the sun. The slightly ajar door permits me enough space to slip my reduced frame through to the balcony. A dizzy blackness confuses my head, and I reach out to the balcony railing to steady myself while the dizziness dissipates and the view of the glistening water is clear. The yachts sway. A new vantage point of a familiar view.

Peering down beyond the railing, there is an asphalt driveway below which runs parallel to the front of the hospital. A blanket of white slowly creeps across the asphalt drive into the green away from the building. A stream of people follow the white blanket; then the entirety of the creeping brigade disappears into a headstone field. My heart races when I realize what I am watching: mourners following a casket draped with white flowers. Is that me? Am I watching my own burial? I shuffle with my IV cart back to the bedside as quickly as my circumstances allow and press the call button for the nurse. She arrives immediately. Her face announces her shock to see me out of bed, and she ushers me back under my covers and pours some water into a plastic cup resting on the wooden table next to my bed. The physical interaction dispels my panic and confirms that it is not I in the casket below. Not yet. She tucks the blanket over my frame, and I rest my arms in the comfort of pink cotton folds. The efficiency of a cemetery in front of a hospital just seems cruel.

Mr. Monaco visits me after work and sits with me into the evening. He tells me that I am brave. He says that the only time he saw me cry during the last two and a half weeks was when I spoke of Ava and Julia. But he is wrong. He did not see the tears stream down my face while I was hunched over exposing my back as a nurse held my arms and a doctor inserted an epidural-sized needle between my ribs to drain my lungs of fluid. He did not see the tears the pillow caught routinely while I was alone in ICU. He did not hear me wail in pain when the nurse tried to change my bed sheets or brush my knotty hair or rub salve on my lips blistered from my high fevers. I am not brave.

Consommé de bœuf, my first meal, which anywhere else would be mere beef broth, but here in Monaco, at the Princess Grace Hospital on the French Riviera, named after my beautiful fellow *américaine*, with my gold crown hanging over my bed and a surgeon named Ferrari, it is *consommé de bœuf*, and it tastes like a second chance at life. It is served with buttery *pomme purée*, both of which taste as if they have come straight from the famed Le Louis XV, a mere skip down the street, and prepared with the talented hands of chef Alain Ducasse himself. It is the best meal I have ever had. The mashed potatoes glide across my tongue like velvet lava and my mouth leisurely savors the broth with its luxurious meaty depth. The phone rings, bringing me dessert:

"Hi, Mommy!" chirps a four-year-old voice that fills the phone receiver and, indeed, my soul with instant joy.

Distant, but it is still Julia. She played dress-up at preschool yesterday and, with a high-pitched and detailed exuberance, tells me about the puffy black dress with a protruding tulle skirt and three-quarter-length sleeves she'd worn. The phone is passed to Ava who is buzzing at a hummingbird's pace. Her voice resoundingly pure and purposeful, she announces, with pride, that she has been chosen to play the lion in her kindergarten production of *Aesop's Fables*. It is no small role. Not small at all, I am told. She asks how I am feeling and if I will be back home in time to watch her roar. The play is on January 24, less than a week.

"I wouldn't miss it," I say.

Jeff brings me some pens and paper per my request. The displacement and helplessness he has felt since his arrival is evident on his face. ICU rules permitted few visits and only for a limited time and, speaking neither French nor Italian, he could not meaningfully communicate with the medical staff. Away from his own family, he has tried to occupy his days and nights in this foreign country while sending daily reports of my health to our parents. Jeff tells me stories of his adventures and trying to get around. He shows me pictures of a circus he saw in the Monaco streets; the elephants in the tunnel were fantastically odd to see. A man climbing out of a large rubber ball one leg at a time was even more strange. Mr. Monaco has been kind to put my brother up in a nearby hotel and show him around. He even took him to Saint-Jean and Paloma. My brother photographed every-thing—the hospital and the Paloma dock—and as he shows me the images, it is clear they convey the perception of his own frustration and sorrow. An artist, indeed.

The writing materials that Jeff brought me are put to constant use. Mentally I feel strong, clear, and capable of anything. Yet still physically captive in my bed, my active mind is unburdened and lib-erated on paper and I write recipes, poetry, and musings, and I draw. Mr. Monaco comes in the room and sits in a chair near my bed. My tongue is a menace to my speech; it cannot keep up with my thoughts, and I stumble over my own words as I speak with him. He extends his hands in the air and he flutters his fingers, describing my energy as "electric" and makes a buzzing noise for dramatic effect.

When he leaves, restless with my thoughts and stored energy, I sit up writing until the sun joins me because there is nothing to do but commit my thoughts to paper. I close my eyes and try to recollect the feeling of the wind on my face and the embrace of my girls. The proverbial bucket list I made when the girls' father and I separated takes on a new urgency and it is transformed into a "to-do" list, driven by the desire to impart to my daughters as many experiences and as much knowledge as I can with the remaining time I have here. I panic thinking of all the girls' favorite recipes that are not yet written down and only exist in my head. How can they duplicate those when I am gone? I have an urgent need to do all of the things I always wanted to experience, those things placed on the back shelf because they were not "necessary" but indulgent wishes I would get to when I was done doing everything I was supposed to do: really learn how to cook, run the Boston marathon, maybe an international one, travel. Above all, live in Paris and give the girls a global education and perspective. The view of the eternal blue outside my window symbolizes limitless possibilities, and as I look at the vastness of the water, beyond that graveyard below, I realize that death no longer scares me but failing to live does.

While the city lights shine in the port, California is awake, and I begin to tackle my to-do list. I call my divorce attorney; it is time to get everything signed and final and I want to be free of the entire matter. The girls and I don't need that large house in Hollywood; I can sell it and use the money for Paris, but I know that in order to get the best price in a sale, the kitchen needs to be remodeled and other work must be done. To that end, I create endless charts and outlines of what needs to be done to accomplish this and email my contractor, setting up meetings for my return to Los Angeles. While music videos of Vanessa Paradis and Laura Pausini play on the television hanging on the wall, I redesign the kitchen and research and source materials on the internet. The nurses want to give me sleeping pills, but I refuse; I have had enough of sleeping.

With most of the tubes out of me, the days of bedridden sponge baths are behind me. I shuffle over to the *en suite* restroom and open the bathroom door; the full-length mirror hanging on its inside startles me. Not having seen my reflection for over three weeks, I do not recognize the person in the mirror but for the blue in my eyes. This is what forty-two kilograms (ninety-two pounds) looks like on my tallish frame, and I begin to cry. A nurse passing my door sees my tears.

"Ne t'en fais pas ... tu as l'air d'un mannequin de Milan," she says.

Her equanimity and assurance that I look like a model from Milan does not comfort because the tears are not due to my dismal appearance but the realization of how fortunate I am to be standing on these two long sticks that in time will once again resemble legs. Today, I finally see what everyone else saw; I look like a freshly buried corpse pulled from the cemetery below, and it is no wonder the female doctor thought I was delusional. The warm water cascades over my covered bones that sit on the tiled shower floor. *I am still here*, and like the paper crown hanging over my bed, I *know* that I am stronger than I appear.

Dr. Ferrari visits me in the morning and then again around dinnertime. Our conversations proceed in the same manner: "How are you feeling? How is the pain? Did you get up today?" To which I respond, *"Mieux, mieux, et oui."* Better, better, and yes, followed by asking when I can leave the hospital.

He does not give me an answer but tells me to "eat" which I do because the hospital food is *trop miam*, and I have a particular fondness for the *madeleines* handed out in the afternoon with my tea. The basket of hard candy distributed is not so bad either, and the young nurse encourages me to take a second piece, which I do without further convincing. My day revolves around who is bringing me food and when.

MR. MONACO visits me after work. Tonight he lies in my bed with me and feeds me broth. He looks at me like I am a miracle. He tells me that the doctors gave me a fifty-fifty chance of survival, and while I was in ICU, a fifteen-year-old boy in Italy died of the same thing: *Streptococcus pneumoniae peritonitis,* a bacterial infection of the peritoneum, the lining of the abdomen.

We talk for hours at night in my tiny bed. Even though visiting hours have long passed, the nurses look the other way. He tells me about his time in the (then) mandatory Italian army. He tells me about his schooling in Milan. While we talk, I receive an email from the girls' father. It begins with a disclaimer. He knows it isn't the time and place to tell me, but he has gotten engaged and the girls are very happy about it.

The memory of the late nights in the basement-turned-family room floods my mind. My nightly ritual: trying to make sense of my upside-down world in the silence of the basement while the girls, only two and four, slept upstairs, unaware of the changes in their lives. Wanting an explanation, I called him. I was obsessed with the *why. Why,* after ten years together, he left. There was no answer. I changed the question. Nothing rang true.

"*Don't you miss me?*" I asked, my voice cracked on the *me*. I waited for an answer. Carefully chosen words followed:

"I miss the house. I miss the kids."

What the hell did he say? The house? Ten years of my life and he misses the house?

"*No!*" I cried. "Don't you miss anything about *me?*" More voice cracking and earnest vulnerability revealed. The *"me"* pathetic and sad. Literally. Figuratively. My intuition knew the answer that I would never hear and the gut feeling was too painful for my heart to accept. While my heart audibly thumped, I held my breath, hoping for something, anything, kind or explanatory and then, the seemingly eternal silence was broken:

"I miss your cooking…"

The email takes me off guard and my befuddled expression only thinly masks my hurt and surprise. I read the email to Mr. Monaco. He says nothing. He does not have to. The look of disgust on his face is unmistakable. That night Mr. Monaco teaches me some more Italian with the admonition, "Lisa, don't say these things to people."

"Je sais."

And there in room 4609, with my paper crown hanging above us, Mr. Monaco teaches me Italian curse words, which I write in my little blue book with their phonetic spellings:

"Vaffanculo!" ("Go fuck yourself!")

"Fanculo!" ("Fuck!")

"Troia!" ("Slut!")

"Che cazzo fai?" ("What the fuck are you doing?")

"Molto stupido!" ("Very stupid!")

"Stronzo!" ("Dumb asshole!")

For purposes of authenticity and to ease my hurt, I practice the arm and hand gestures to match. Then Mr. Monaco teaches me a kinder phrase:

"L'amor che move il sole e l'altre stelle." ("The love that moves the sun and the stars.")

This one is my favorite, and it renders the curse words obsolete.

I DECIDE THAT in order to see Ava's play, I need to demonstrate to Dr. Ferrari that I am well enough to go home. I sleuth and find out when and where he holds office hours and devise a plan of demonstrative competency and health. Out of Dr. Ferrari's view, I do my hunched-over shuffle, clinging to the plastic chair-rail in the hallway, as I slowly make my way toward his office. Just before I approach his door, I release my grip on the rail and try to stand as straight as I possibly can, forcing a toothy smile.

"*Bonjour, Docteur! Comment ça va?*"

His desk faces the door. He is on the phone as I pass but gives me a head nod. As soon as I clear the door and his view, I resume my rail-crawl and shuffle back to bed. Repeat tomorrow.

I do not know if Dr. Ferrari is onto my scheme (he probably is), but after a couple days of my rail-crawl, he signs my discharge papers. I will be home the day before Ava's play. Thanking the nurses and doctors who have cared for me, I leave the Princess Grace Hospital, my paper crown tucked safely in my bag.

Mr. Monaco drives my brother and me to the Nice airport. While my brother gets a cart, Mr. Monaco hugs me with tender intensity; I feel like a tiny bird in his arms. My abdomen aches preventing me from standing upright. There are tears in his eyes, and he whispers in my ear, "I am so happy to see you return to your girls. I'll come to L.A. when you are settled."

On the plane, I try half-heartedly to sleep, but I cannot because I worry that I will have a relapse over the Atlantic. The remembered physical pain haunts me. I look at my brother and do not know what I would have done without him, even if he could not communicate with most of the doctors and saw me for only minutes a day. Knowing he was there was comfort enough. There is sorrow in his eyes, which is rarely the case, and he admits that he began writing my eulogy when

I was in ICU. The moment is too heavy, so I stick my tongue out at him for some levity and tell him to keep his eulogy for another time.

Jeff and his wife drop me off at my Hollywood home. Family and the very few friends who knew about my hospitalization have filled the house with food, flowers, and signs. Four little arms, outstretched for me as far as they can extend, eagerly welcome me home. The three of us crawl into my bed that night, one little daughter tucked under each arm, their heads resting against my chest, carefully avoiding my abdomen. It is much better than spiritually watching them from a distance. This, this moment, this is everything. And it is far more than just something.

LA GALETTE DES ROIS

Makes one 9 inch cake

Shell
2 sheets puff pastry
1 dried bean (or nut)
1 egg, mixed with 1 teaspoon water

Frangipane
7½ ounces blanched slivered raw almonds
3 ounces granulated sugar
½ teaspoon kosher salt
2 tablespoons powdered sugar, sifted
4 tablespoons unsalted butter, cold and cut into chunks
1 egg, room temperature
1 egg white, room temperature
1 teaspoon vanilla extract
1 teaspoon almond extract
½ teaspoon orange zest

Garnish
A paper crown

To make *frangipane*, place almonds, salt, and sugars in a food processor. Pulse until finely ground. Add butter and continue to pulse to incorporate. Add egg, egg white, extracts, and zest to food processor. Pulse until well-combined. Set aside. *Frangipane* can be made in advance and stored in the refrigerator.

Roll out puff pastry sheets on a floured surface. Use a 9 inch tart or pie pan bottom as a guide. Cut two 9 inch circles in the pastry sheets using kitchen shears or a knife. Lay circles on a baking sheet lined with parchment paper. Place in the refrigerator for 15 minutes to chill.

Remove pastry sheets from the refrigerator. Gently spread the *frangipane* on one circle, about 1 inch in height and 1 inch from the edge of the circle. Place bean or nut in the *frangipane*. Using a pastry brush, brush egg wash on the exposed 1 inch band of pastry surrounding the *frangipane*. Lay the second puff pastry circle on top. Pinch the edges of the two puff pastry sheets together to close. Use a knife to score the top puff pastry layer with a design of your choice without cutting through the dough.

Return the cake to the refrigerator for ten minutes to chill the butter. Remove the cake from the refrigerator. Lightly brush egg wash over the top and sides of the cake. Place cake on a fresh sheet of parchment paper on a baking sheet. Bake in an oven preheated to 400 degrees Fahrenheit. Bake for 10 minutes. Reduce heat to 350 degrees Fahrenheit. Continue to bake for 15 minutes until the cake is golden brown and all layers have puffed.

Remove cake from the oven and let it cool on a wire rack. Garnish with a paper crown.

CHAPTER TWO

Small-Town Roots; City of Light

I grew up in a ski town, which was unfortunate for me because I was (and remain) a below-average skier, and the often-voiced assumption that I must be a "fabulous skier," having grown up in the mountains, is false. One stoplight. A two-lane highway. A tourist-dependent economy driven by the depth and length of the winter snow. Small-town Big Bear, in Southern California, offered neither financial nor educational opportunity and was anemic in ambition. Yet, mine was a quaint childhood, at least until I was twelve, when my parents' marriage ended, along with my childhood, although my special bond with my maternal grandparents remained a source of comfort and inspiration.

My entry into the workforce began when I was thirteen years old when a neighbor gave me a job hosting in her Mexican-style cantina. It was the best money I could make in the least amount of time. Work on the weekends; school during the week. Working allowed me to put money away for college and get the braces off my teeth.

In high school, I learned to say *"bonjour."* My language teacher, Ms. DuBois, resembled a French gamine with the frame of Julia Child. With her fair skin, reddish hair, and simple dresses, she was not *à la mode* for the eccentric '80s, where females wore football-sized shoulder pads, neon plastic bracelets, and Material Girl–inspired clothing. Some students nicknamed her "stinky French cheese," which I found rude and puzzling because I was sure that not one of them had ever experienced cheese that was not out of a pressurized can or in an orange rectangular loaf form wrapped in foil, let alone cheese of the redolent French variety. Ms. DuBois continued to be teased, based upon French stereotypes of cheese and lack of deodorant, until one day when she brought a baguette and a wedge of brie to class; everyone ate the interiors of both, avoiding crusts of all kind. She was more popular after that. If I had to pinpoint the beginning of my enthusiasm for France (as I am frequently asked), it would have to be this French class because our handful of family vacations never extended beyond the continental United States, nor did I know anyone who was French or had even been there.

The French language did not come easily for me, but I devoured everything I could read about France—its food, history, art, and the multitude of Americans—politicians, writers, artists, private citizens—who had been drawn to the European country in the past. While I struggled with my French *rrrrrrrr* roll, Mitterrand was president and Paris was bursting with ingenuity. We discussed the controversy which surrounded the construction of the very modern-looking Centre Pompidou, wearing its seams of function —HVAC and water pipes painted in bright colors—on the outside of the building rather than inside. Then there was the opening of the Musée d'Orsay, a train station turned museum, uniquely housing only artistic expression from the period 1848-1914. I admired the controversial projects and the fact that people cared enough to voice an opinion of them. This French attention to detail and appreciation of human expression in its varied forms fed my curious and romantic personality.

Hungry for something more than the complacent simplicity of the little ski town, I moved to Los Angeles, where I had exactly one friend, within days of my high school graduation. The big city was overwhelming with its freeways and neighbors you never meet. Financial aid and scholarships subsidized my college education, and I covered my living expenses by working in various restaurants, including a French café, which served classic *bistro* dishes with a Basque influence, dishes that André, the owner, grew up with in southwestern France. Other than that brie in French class, it was my first real introduction to French food, and I could not get enough of it: the quiches, the confit duck leg salad with its tangy, warm raspberry dressing, the salmon tartare served on toast points with creamy crème fraîche spiked with freshly grated horseradish. The flavors were a revelation, making my employee meal a small, yet happy celebration in my day.

Study-abroad programs eluded me; I did not have the luxury of time or money for the things that many of my contemporaries considered a necessary rite of passage. Between work and school, I had very little free time at all. The first in my family to attend university, I treated school like a job and, as overwhelmed and lost as I often felt, life was going according to my plan of self-improvement, and the employee meals four times a week at the café meant I always ate well. It is a good life when a girl has tangy béarnaise sauce in which to dip her fries while stumbling with enthusiasm through the pages of Joyce's *Ulysses* and day-dreaming about his career-altering alliance with Sylvia Beach in Paris.

For my college graduation, my father gave me a plane ticket. It was the nicest and most extravagant thing I had ever been given. A college friend and I planned our budgeted backpack journey through several countries. The first stop: Paris.

Full of anticipation and armed with a handful of French expressions, at twenty-two-years of age I arrived in the city that had beckoned me from across the Atlantic. It felt instantly familiar. I felt inspired and comfortable amidst the historical reminders on the blue street plaques and the beauty and expressions of humanity surrounding me at all turns: architecture, literature, wine, cuisine, art, fashion, dance, music, and theater. The pleasure was bested with the "sing" of crispy bread and its airy crumb, and pastries with perfectly piped cream centers or tops adorned with gold leaf, the French attention to detail that makes food art. Paris was a love letter to humanity, and life, with its simple joys and harsh realities, was examined and celebrated with honesty and tender devotion. And I loved it. I loved everything about it.

Jean-Marie, a friend of André's and a frequent diner at the café, was also in Paris visiting his family. He invited us to join them for dinner at an upscale *bistro* in the 4th, which had been in existence *depuis* 1912 and was not far from our tiny hotel. The evening was a revelation, but not one limited to a tangy, buttery *meunière* sauce. It was *everything*: the flavors, appreciation and educated discussion of the food, the civility of the meal itself, the wine pairings, the polite and intelligent company, the service, the ambiance. While I absorbed the experience, I mindfully cut my food with precision and kept my fork in my left hand upside-down (a technique I learned in the restaurant from watching the European patrons) as I listened to them discuss Mitterrand's policies and responded to their questions about our imminent adventures. The warm green asparagus served with *mousseline* and bright green things—*les fèves*—with a nutty substantial flavor delighted me, and I drug each and every bean through the cooking *jus* on my plate. I had never eaten, nor even heard of, a fava bean before. A cheese course followed while the wine was finished. Dessert followed that, and I ordered my dessert *en français* with an American accent—*millefeuille*—I had never tasted a dessert made of "a thousand sheets" before, and the dessert, with alternating layers of vanilla-infused rich pastry cream and thin, light sheets of crisp puffed pastry, did not disappoint. The grace and tastefulness of the entire meal set the tone for how I would forever view French food and the French culture. It was exactly what I'd imagined France would be when I dreamt of it from that small town with its layers of snow.

Law school followed college. I did not have a particular drive to be a lawyer, but I enjoyed law school and valued a solid paycheck. As all young eager-to-please litigators do, I worked with unyielding dedication. At twenty-five I began dating and fell in love with another lawyer whom I had met three years prior, while I was visiting my then-boyfriend in Cambridge, Massachusetts. After law school, he took the California bar and moved to Los Angeles. He told me that when he'd first met me, three years prior, he'd known then that I would be his wife. Thus began a several-year courtship. On our first vacation together, we went to Paris. We stayed at a friend's apartment in the Marais. He had never been to Paris, and I was eager to show him the things I had discovered. And after a romantic dinner in a tiny *bistro* with Sarah Vaughan singing in the background, we went to the Ritz Hotel for a nightcap where he asked me to spend the rest of my life with him. The question, as phrased, seemed more significant than the simple "will you marry me." And I responded without hesitation, "yes."

About three years later, I was pregnant with Ava when I litigated my last trial in Malibu. Seven months after her birth, I stopped practicing law; two ambitious litigators in the family was one too many (two, in some people's opinions). Twenty-three months later we were blessed with Julia. Life was full. Full with the everyday demands and joys of a young family and building a home, and the future was full of promises and dreams for our family of four. In the midst of all this joy, Paris lingered in the back of my mind like a lover I could not forget.

BRIE, PEAR, AND HONEY CROSTINI

A modified version of my high school French food experience, this easy recipe is perfect for appetizers or an after-school snack.

Serves 4 to 6

> 1 baguette
> 1 wedge of Brie de Meaux
> 2 ripe pears
> A/N French honey

Preheat the oven to 375 degrees Fahrenheit. Line a baking sheet with parchment paper or aluminum foil.

Use a serrated knife to slice the baguette crosswise into smaller, somewhat circular, pieces. Place the pieces on a baking sheet and put in the oven. Bake until pieces are toasted.

Slice the pears into halves lengthwise. Remove the core, stem, and seeds. Place the four halves face down on a cutting board. Slice the pears crosswise at an angle. Discard the ends.

Slice the cheese (with rind) into slices about the same size as the pear slices.

On each toasted crostini, smear about a teaspoon of honey. Add a slice of cheese and top with a pear slice.

CHAPTER THREE

What the Hell

NOT LONG AFTER returning to Los Angeles from Monaco, reoccurring abdomen pain fills me with panic sending me to Cedars Sinai Hospital for two nights. The thought of reliving my time in ICU scared the hell out of me and the memory was never far from my thoughts. The Cedars stay proved more psychologically driven than medically necessary, but the unanswered questions left me vulnerable. What if it happens again?

Los Angeles doctors perform more tests in and out of the hospital, but the additional poking and prodding provides no answers. Ultimately, not one doctor, on either continent, can tell me definitively how I acquired such a serious infection with no open wound and without being ill. They speculate that I'd inhaled the bacterium before I left for Paris or drank it in my water in Italy. Either scenario — breathing air or drinking water — is unsettling. With no understanding of the *how*, I try to figure out the *why* and what I am supposed to learn from the experience.

"Lisa, you are over-thinking this. Not everything has to have a lesson," Alison says.

Alison and I met as very young associates. Female litigators were then a minority so I promised her that if she came to work for the law firm I would take her under my wing and make sure she felt supported. It was an easy promise to keep. She was smart, beautiful, and we shared a naughty sense of humor. She had no qualms about giving me her honest opinion, which I trusted and respected, even if I disagreed with it at times.

"*Everything* has a lesson," I retort.

And I think of two lessons and a silver-lined circumstance: the acceptance of things out of my control that come without warning or explanation (apparently, this is a do-over); to teach me to live life fully rather than making the best of things as they are; and that perhaps temporarily taking me out of the picture, giving my daughters the opportunity to spend extended time with their father and his wife-to-be, enabled them to accept and adapt to the changes in their lives. The last one alone made the trauma worth it, but I conclude all three have value.

Dr. Ferrari predicted that it would take four months to physically recuperate. The girls' father suggests that he and his now fiancée take the girls for additional time, implying that I am physically unable to adequately care for them myself. The comment hurt. The girls and I had been separated for nearly a month, and while I never expected a get-well card or flowers from him, his suggestion to separate us again seems cold, rendering my heart feeling as ground up and tender as the rest of my internal organs. While I decline the offer, I do respect his concern.

Alison found for me a woman who would provide live-in home care for a few months. Her name is Mary. Mary is a generously developed, grandmotherly woman who hums hymns throughout the day and fills the house with the warmth of her nurturing spirit. She is exactly what the girls and I need. She runs my errands and cooks me soups and broths, enabling me to regain my strength. Although it is odd to have someone in my space, doing the things I routinely do, particularly the cooking, I appreciate the care. My walking is slow and deliberate and even small distances wear me out. I sleep thirteen hours a day and my biggest physical exertions revolve around caring for the girls before and after school.

Dr. Ferrari's prediction was right. By June, I am able to walk without pain, and I can finally adjust the driver's seat in my car to a more upright position. One block at a time, I begin a light jog. Four pounds heavier and with my strength coming back, we say "goodbye" to Mary, who leaves us to help another family. Her work here is done.

When the girls vacation with their father, Mr. Monaco and I vacation together. Before heading to Sardinia, we return to the Monaco hospital and thank the nurses for all they had done for me. Mr. Monaco tells me that the vacation is a "celebration of a life," and it is, but all relationships proceed one of two ways, and this one could not advance and our time together made me cognizant of this fact. I cannot leave Los Angeles with the girls, and if I were to move to France, it would be to Paris, not Monaco. So when Mr. Monaco conveys sentiments of marriage and children, I cannot commit to either, assuming I want to go down that road again. I love him dearly, but I know I cannot reciprocate the devotion and love he so generously gives me, and the reasons for my hesitation—to marriage, to a future together—do not matter. The hesitation *is* my answer, and he deserves more. In September, when I return to Los Angeles, I ask Mr. Monaco to let me go so that he himself can find the things he wants and deserves. I know if I phrase it that way, he would honor my request. It is one of the hardest things I have ever done, but also the most correct. The fact that he had been so good to me, not to mention the fact that he saved my life so I could go home to my girls, did not make it easier. Undoubtedly, I will compare any subsequent man to the high example he set and I will miss him, but my selfish thoughts do not compromise my decision.

THE INFECTION my abdomen left a fire in its wake. Julia's graduation from preschool meant that both girls were attending the same school, and I now have more than one or two hours at a time to do something beyond errands. With my health back, it is time to make the most out of the gift of additional days.

I have loved to cook for as long as I can remember. My grandmother and mother showed me the way around a kitchen, and I picked up additional knowledge and skills working for years in restaurants. But I always wanted to learn the proper techniques. My first choice, Le Cordon Bleu in the 15th of Paris, is not a realistic option, but Le Cordon Bleu licenses a program in Pasadena, California, and as luck would have it, this month it extended the program to a new location, in Hollywood, fifteen minutes from our home.

The school offers three sessions: morning, 6 a.m. to 11 a.m.; afternoon; and evening. None of them are compatible with the girls' school schedule; however, I decide on the morning session and, through references, I find a young woman to drive the girls from the house to the school bus stop in the morning. My housekeeper agrees to a schedule change from one day a week to a few hours each morning to be with the girls until the driver arrives. Had it not been for her flexibility, I would not have been able to attend school.

Weekday mornings proceed in the same fashion. At 4:30 a.m. I make the girls' breakfast, pack their lunches, lay out their clothes for the day, and write them notes. When the housekeeper arrives at 5:30 a.m., I drive to school. Students have already arrived to set up their stations—equipment gathered and arranged, knives organized, recipes laid out, garnishes cut, seasoning well-placed, and the essentials organized for that day. The kitchens are arranged in stations of four, two students per station. Classes begin with a demonstration by the chef instructor(s) - which we then duplicate with the provided recipes and ingredients. When completed, we walk our plated food up to the front of the classroom to be graded by the instructor(s), one of whom has no qualms about tossing a student's plated food into the trashcan if she finds its appearance or aroma displeasing. She is rumored to be married to a French chef and, as a result of this union, she reportedly acquired a particularly discerning palate. Or, at least a French attitude.

Although I get along well with my co-students, I am an outlier. I am old enough to be the mother to more than half of them. While many of them socialize after class or on the weekends, I race from school, stripping off my culinary clothes en route to my car, and speed from Hollywood to the girls' school across town. There is always an urgency: my turn to bring cupcakes, serve hot lunch, or attend a class performance. The extra food from class I share with teachers and neighbors. In addition to carrying extra food, I smell like food. One day another mother actually plucks fish scales from my hair. Apparently, I wear food, too.

While the girls sleep, I stay up until the early hours of the morning practicing *tournée* cuts on potatoes, variations of *beurre blanc* and other emulsions, or studying for Friday exams. Coco, our sixteen-year-old Yorkshire Terrier, waits at my feet for something to come her way. When I drop a stick of butter, she snaps it up and, holding it tightly in her jowls, she runs throughout the house, the butter melting and dripping on the hardwood floors, which I slip on as I chase after her. The frantic schedule and the sleep deprivation do not dampen my enthusiasm, but culinary school is only part of the equation.

In the past two years, I have mulled over the thought of moving to Paris with the girls, envisioning a two-country time-share arrangement with the girls' father, similar to the one a friend has with her former husband in Italy. Her daughter maintains a strong relationship with both parents and has received a multicultural education and experiences to last a lifetime. With the girls older now, six and eight, but not old enough to have serious ties in school, and at the perfect language-absorbing age, and with a firm relationship with their father, I strategize that the following school year would be the perfect time to make such a move. While Los Angeles is not the small town I was raised in, I still wanted more for them and I decide it is time to use that Paris Hope File, the file of papers I have been collecting over the years containing my notes, tid-bits of information on arrondissements, apartment prices, practical "how-tos," and what to avoid when purchasing Parisian real estate (like street-level apartments or looking at property during misleadingly quiet periods such as *les grandes vacances*).

A FEW MONTHS after I begin culinary school (a year after my hospital stay), I seek the court's permission to relocate to France with the girls. The costly decision was filled with moments of doubt, and I wondered if I was acting selfishly. Some friends warned me that the girls' father would ruin me financially and emotionally. A divorced man I met on a blind coffee date (and in a custody dispute himself) had no qualms about calling me a bitch and said he hoped that I would never meet his ex-wife. However, others applauded the decision as perfect for me and a tremendous opportunity for the girls. Yet, the opinions of others seemed a reflection of their own personal circumstances and perspectives and had no bearing on my decision. Through all of these opinions and my own reservations, I had hope. It came as no surprise when the girls' father countersued for fifty-fifty custody.

So, I am in culinary school and litigating a move-away case at the same time. During class, I keep my phone in my pocket in case the school calls. However, it is never the school. It is always my attorney. The issues vary as does the urgency. Litigating a case as a lawyer is one thing, but the stress and emotional toll of being the client, particularly when the subject matter is your children, is entirely different. Although I remind myself that I was the one who opened this can of worms and I keep my focus on the goal, there are a few occasions that cause me to linger in the walk-in refrigerator to regain my composure before returning to my station and my culinary tasks. One morning, my phone reveals more emails from my attorney and none of them are good news. I enter the walk-in, sit on a covered white tub of chopped vegetables, and stare at the shelves of *mise en place*.

As I sit there in the cold, I reflect on the moment when my perception changed. That night in the basement when I decided that those four words — *I miss your cooking* — were diminutive only if I allowed them to be, and I refused. After all, I am a good cook. That night I decided to view the "compliment" as encouragement. It was the open window for the closed door my grandmother foretold. The cold air steadies me, and I return to my work station. The topic, Bordelaise sauce. The instructor is comparing traditional methods with newer ones using reduction. Reaching for my saucepan, I spontaneously smile; my cooking is far better now.

I graduate from culinary school and begin teaching classes, as well as serving as a private chef, both of which allow me more control over my schedule than cooking in a restaurant. The girls and I move to a smaller home ten minutes from their grammar school, and I rent out the Hollywood home. The reduction in car time and the tighter living quarters increase our quality of life ten-fold. Meanwhile, the move-away case proceeds.

IN THE SPRING of 2010, the court reaches a verdict. I sit at the counsel table with my two attorneys, awaiting the judge's decision. The male attorney on my legal team leans over to me and whispers something which I think he intends as a compliment, but because it is at the expense of the girls' now-stepmother, it does not feel like one. I do not respond. I anxiously fold my hands and lay them in my lap for the appearance of calm. The court reporter's fingers click away on the steno phone. The judge begins:

> The court does find that [the mother] is a Franco-file [sic] and has a genuine interest in French culture, language, and culinary traditions [...] [T]he distance of the move places far less of a burden on mother than on father. [...] The court can create a custody order that maintains joint physical custody for mother even if the mother moves to France by allowing extensive visitations between mother and children in Los Ange-les - mother will have a 40% time share.

The judge says unflattering things about both the girls' father and me. He classifies me, or at least my desire to move to Paris, as "whimsical," and he does *not* mean it as a compliment. The judge continues. If I do not move to Paris, I maintain majority physical custody of the girls. He then dictates a custody arrangement if I remain in Los Angeles, with a "fifth" weekend (who knew that existed?) and which Thanksgivings are "mine" and which ones are my "ex's" and on which years I can select my vacation dates "first." He orders that the girls' birthday parties be planned in alternative years by myself and their father. Did he just tell me that I can only plan my daughters' birthday parties every other year? It is the most ridiculous thing I have ever heard. As for the relocation request itself, I cannot say that the judge's decision is legally wrong or that it is an easy decision for any court, but for a third time in just a four-and-a-half-year period, I feel like I have no control over my life. This sunny southern California paradise represents a jail sentence for me, stretching into the foreseeable future. Twelve years. I will be released sometime in my fifties. I am divorced, with two small children living in a place I am not from and where I never wanted to raise children, particularly girls. And now, I could only plan their birthday parties every other year and Thanksgivings would alternate between an empty house and a full one, depending upon the year.

The court, however, leaves the decision to me. I *could* move to Paris and pursue a life there. One week per month I would be with the girls in Los Angeles during the school year, and they would be with me in Paris for the entire summer, as well as spring and winter breaks. Living the majority of the time in Paris would give me the opportunity to find meaningful employment while I am still young enough to gain experience in the French culinary scene and begin a second career before my opportunities diminish with my energy. Summers together could provide the girls some of the world experience I want them to have and the opportunity to learn the language, even if they do not attend school there. However, Paris and I are not above them. For me, there is really only one choice.

The girls and I eat breakfast at the kitchen table before school. The space is consumed by an unusual silence that Ava cautiously breaks. Julia sits in her chair, folding the pleats in her plaid uniform skirt, looking to her big sister to find her words.

"You are not going move to France without us, are you?" Ava asks me. Her big blue eyes meet mine. Julia stops folding her skirt and waits for my answer. A wave of guilt washes over me for the worry I have caused them and I usher my reassurance.

"No. I would *never* move anywhere without the two of you. I promise."

A smile spreads over Ava's face. Julia joins in. Unspoken worry dissipates, and the air becomes instantly lighter. Conventional breakfast conversation and laughter ensue. When your original recipe does not turn out the way you intend, you modify it. Sometimes the modification is better than your original plan.

MY AMERICAN SANDWICH COOKIE

When I was young, my mother did not allow us to eat any pre-packaged food. Cookies, and even bread, were homemade. When I had children of my own, I continued this tradition (although I could never duplicate my mother's bread). I created this recipe for my daughters while I was in culinary school. It instantly became a favorite. You can find the black oynx cocoa powder online.

Makes 3 dozen cookies

Shells
1½ cups all purpose flour
¾ cup black oynx cocoa powder
¼ teaspoon kosher salt
1 stick unsalted butter, room temperature
¾ cup granulated sugar
1 large egg, room temperature
2 teaspoons vanilla extract

Filling
½ cup non-hydrogenated vegetable shortening
1½ cups powdered sugar
1 teaspoon fresh lemon juice.

Sift all dry ingredients (salt, flour, and cocoa powder) into a bowl. Whisk together. Set aside.

Using a standalone mixer fit with a paddle attachment, turn the mixer on low speed and cream the sugar and butter. Once thoroughly mixed, add the egg and extract. Mix.

Slowly add the dry ingredients into the butter-sugar-egg mixture. Mix until incorporated.

Remove the dough from the mixer bowl and pat into a disk. Wrap in plastic wrap and place the dough in refrigerator for 30 minutes.

Preheat oven to 375 degrees Fahrenheit.

Remove dough from refrigerator. Use a rolling pin to roll dough until it is about $1/8$ inch thick. Sprinkle flour on the dough as needed to keep it from sticking to the rolling pin. (Usually, I roll the dough out in between two sheets of parchment paper and skip adding the flour because the dough is more dry than wet.)

Using a 2 inch round biscuit cutter, cut out the shells from the dough. Place the shells on a baking sheet lined with parchment paper.

Bake for 6 to 7 minutes (until the shells are crisp). Remove from oven. Use a spatula to remove shells from the baking pan and place on a wire rack to cool.

In a bowl, combine shortening, lemon juice, and sugar.

Using your clean hands, roll a pinch (about a teaspoon) of the filling into a ball. Place the rolled filling on one shell. Place a second shell on top of the filling and gently press down. (Make sure to use the tops of the shells —the side facing up when baked— as the outsides of the cookie.) Repeat process until all shells have been filled. Cookies can be stored in an air-tight container for one week or frozen.

PART II

CHAPTER FOUR

Paris Is My Hometown, Too

"LISA, HAVE YOU heard of an Australian woman who loved France so much she purchased a château in Normandy and moved her family there? Her name is Jane, I think."

"No. I am not familiar with her. Lucky woman," I reply.

Tracy, Julia's classmate's mother, who knows my affinity for France and French cooking, continues, "She renovated this château and now tourists stay there for a week in the summer. I hear that she offers cooking classes in the château. You should contact her."

That evening, I research Jane and her château. Her story inspires me and hoping to glean some French cooking experience, and perhaps learn from her example of following her dream, I email her offering my services as a chef instructor in August while the girls vacation with their father. Her response is not immediate so after some time, I follow up. She replies and requests sample menus and recipe ideas for proposed classes. After I send her the information, Jane responds by offering me the opportunity to teach for a week in August on the condition that I provide her with the recipes for the classes I will teach and prepare a sample dinner (demonstrating my cooking ability) for her and her family when I first arrive. *Bien sûr, avec plaisir!*

In Los Angeles, I study traditional Norman recipes and the cheese, produce, and seafood indigenousness to the region. With great repetition, I prepare classic dishes such as *marmite dieppoise* to the point that my daughters beg me for mac-and-cheese instead of "Norman food." When the girls vacation with their father, I make the transatlantic flight during which I memorize French cooking terms, cuts of meat, and temperature and measure conversions. The hour-and-twenty-minute train ride from Paris to the unfamiliar region of Normandy is used for additional study of distinctions—the difference between French versus American dairy products and between *sucre en poudre* and *sucre glace*—which I routinely mix up (the former is granulated sugar, not powdered sugar).

It is a ten-minute drive in my zippy, compact rental car from Rouen to Château Bosgouet, where a full frontal view of the majestic four-plus-storied château greets me as I enter the drive. The château stands grandly amidst acres of abundantly round trees, secured for three hundred years in the emerald green earth scattered with eruptions of mushroom clusters. When I emerge from my car, a little black dog stops running circles around a stationary tractor to see what I am doing and an equally curious duck waddles toward me. A friend once told me about her summers in Normandy where the weather was warm, but not unpleasantly hot, and she would lie in the thick grass among the apple trees and look up at the sky and feel the earth's energy pulse through her body.

"Normandy is a powerful place," she told me. I never knew what to make of that statement. But now, traversing the expansive green with my curious duck escort, I feel the powerful energy of which she spoke.

When I enter the large door, Jane is descending the internal staircase. We both chuckle when we catch a glimpse of each other, as we are dressed identically: white polo shirts with jeans and our hair in ponytails. The communal bond of food, motherhood, and love of

France makes conversation and the introduction effortless. Jane gives me a tour of the château while delineating its history and recounts the massive undertaking of restoring the old building with its challenges and mishaps. My room, impressive down to the sheets (Jane's taste is impeccable), has a view of the expansive green I recently crossed, but it is the kitchen that is my favorite.

EARLY EVENING. Tonight is my sample dinner for Jane and her family. I go to the kitchen, which is partially set in the ground, allowing the windows to provide an eye-level view of the acres of earth surrounding the château. Through the back windows I see wild blackberry vines in the distance, and I decide to improvise and add fresh blackberries to my planned chocolate *soufflé* dessert. Dressed in shorts, flats, and my cooking apron, my high steps are deliberately placed as I try unsuccessfully to avoid the stinging nettles. Once I reach the patch of berry vines, and with the dinner hour approaching, I deem that the most efficient way to gather the berries is to pull on a vine. So, I do. It does not budge. Instead, it slips through my hands leaving them red and irritated with imbedded small, soft thorn-like fibers. Undeterred, I wrap another vine around my hand to secure it and tug again, but the vine is more stubborn than I; it does not give way, and in fact the force of my pull causes me to fall backwards into the patch of vines, rendering the entirety of my legs as red and afflicted as my hands. There is no speeding up this process, and I pluck the berries one by one, and when my basket is full, I walk back to the château reflecting on the lunacy of my plan, hoping there are no witnesses. That evening, despite my discreet itching of my legs throughout the meal, dinner gets the thumbs up.

With my enthusiasm at a high, I have difficulty sleeping and sometimes I go down to the kitchen in the middle of the night to prepare for classes or practice a recipe I thought of while lying in bed trying to sleep. Each morning feels like a discovery of uncharted territory, and I begin my days with an early run along unknown country roads that sometimes land me at the water, which I presume is the Seine. Preparing for classes means frequent trips to the markets in Rouen. Jane tells me where to source the best fish and the freshest produce and which days I will be working. Scouring the local markets for my ingredients, I soon discover that some of my recipes, written in Los Angeles, need tweaking. Although I know leek season is *technically* October through May, this staple kitchen item is available year round in Paris or Los Angeles and with this assumption, I included leeks in the recipe. However, it is August and not leek season. There is not one leek in Rouen.

The students range in experience. Some have advanced cooking skills; others do not make toast. Adapting the lessons so each person feels challenged provides resounding satisfaction when I feel I've taught each one of them something they will be able to duplicate at home. On my non-class days I make the most of my free time. I explore Rouen and even manage to visit some museums. I drive to Honfleur and the beach in Deauville (where Parisians used to visit with such frequency it was dubbed "the Parisian Riviera"). Jane invites me to go with the group to Le Bec-Hellouin to listen to the monks chant at the Bec Abbey. Before our visit to the abbey we stop at a local antique shop where I discover a beautiful eight-pound antique copper pot and a large copper jam spoon. And, after a little negotiating, I acquire these beauties for my own kitchen.

At the conclusion of the week, I say goodbye to Jane and her family and pack the car with my small roller suitcase and three beach bags brimming with my sourced treasures, including cookbooks, bottles of Calvados, Norman cider, and of course, my antique copper finds. With only eight hours until my 8:10 p.m. train, I make use of every minute and drive westward. In Caen I lunch on chicken from nearby Auge Valley, served with slices of blood sausage and sautéed apple wedges with a note of cinnamon, while befriending some *rouennais* over my meal. Continuing westward through Bayeaux (known for its two hundred and thirty feet of tapestries), a two-lane country road surrounded by wildflowers and the flags of various countries leads me to the American Cemetery in Colleville-sur-Mer with its dramatic plunging coastline and its once-bloodied beaches below. After paying my respects to those who served, I call my father to share the moment, but he is not home, so I drive back to Rouen, reflecting on the history this region has witnessed and the lingering presence of cruelty, devotion, and gratitude.

It is 8:09 p.m. when my rushing feet cross the threshold of the train car. Three male train employees standing just inside the door stop their conversation to observe my entrance. Visibly exhausted and sweating, I clumsily struggle with my awkwardly shaped bags and the three help me place them in the baggage containers. One laughs and tells me that I should not have rushed; they would not have left without me, but I have never seen a French train wait for anyone. My body collapses in my seat as the train pulls away from the station. Acquaintances made. Cooking inspired. An offer to return in the future. Normandy was a good trip.

IT IS NEARLY 10 p.m. when I arrive in Paris. I wobble through Gare Saint-Lazare with my bags while the handle of the jam spoon sticks out of one bag and clanks on everything I pass. Witnessing this, a Frenchman carries my bags down the stairs to the street where he secures me a taxi, unhooking the jam spoon handle from his jacket pocket.

My taxi cab driver takes the longer route to Jasmine's apartment in the 16th (which she has loaned me for a few days), but I am too tired to protest.

"*Arrêtez-vous; c'est là,*" I say when we arrive.

The driver charges me an additional fee for my luggage (which he is entitled to do, but I have never had anyone actually do it) and then proceeds to offer his assistance with my bags for "*deux euros de plus*" per bag. Two euros more for each bag to take them out of the trunk? Offended at his price gouging, I pull my bags from the taxi trunk myself and no sooner do I set the last one on the sidewalk does the driver shout at me, in English, on quiet Avenue Georges Mandel: "Why don't you go home, tourist!"

His surprising statement evokes a visceral reaction: "*je suis chez moi, connard!*" ("I am home, you asshole!")

An elderly couple walking their Scottie on the sidewalk stops and all three heads turn to see the disturbance on the peaceful, elegant, tree-lined Haussmanian street. Yet, despite the vulgarity of the statement, and its gauche deliverance, it is how I feel: I live in Los Angeles, but Paris is my hometown, too.

SEAFOOD CASSEROLE À LA NORMANDY
(Marmite à ma façon)

This is one of the recipes I developed for my time in Normandy. The recipe tastes best with a milder white fish. (Do not use halibut or swordfish.) It is perfect for a chilly evening.

Serves 6

> 16 ounces of 3 types of white fish fillets (i.e., sole, turbot, cod, plaice, daurade, or brill), trimmed, skins removed
> A/N kosher salt
> A/N freshly ground pepper
> ½ cup white wine
> ½ pound clams
> ½ pound mussels
> 1 stick unsalted butter, divided
> 2 large apples, peeled, cored, and sliced
> 2 cups fish stock
> 1 cup non-alcoholic apple cider
> 2 garlic cloves, thinly sliced
> 2 shallots, thinly sliced
> 1 leek (white portion only), sliced
> 1 fennel bulb, thinly sliced
> 1 cup sliced mushrooms
> 1 cup reduced *cuisson*
> 12 shrimp
> ¾ cup heavy cream

Season both sides of fish fillets with salt and pepper. Set aside.

Remove heads, legs, and shells from shrimp, leaving tails on. Devein and rinse well. Rinse clams and mussels with cold water (do not soak). Remove beard from mussels and use back of a spoon or knife to clean shells. Set aside. (Do not clean clams and mussels more than one hour before cooking.)

Melt 2 tablespoons butter in an ovenproof sauté pan placed over a medium flame. Place apple slices on top of butter (as a bed for the fish). Place fillets on top of apples. Add stock and cider (fish should not be submerged). Bring to a simmer on the stovetop.

Once you have reached a simmer, remove the pan from the stovetop and cover with a buttered cartouche (circle of parchment paper cut to fit the pan). Place pan in an oven preheated to 400 degrees Fahrenheit. Fish is done after about 5 to 7 minutes (when it is just beginning to flake). Carefully remove the pan from the oven. Discard the cartouche.

Use a slotted spoon to place the fish on a plate. Cover with aluminum foil to keep warm. Use the slotted spoon to remove apples and reserve in a separate bowl. Cover with foil.

Pour the *cuisson* (liquid in which you poached the fish) into a clean saucepan and reduce to 1 cup. Set aside.

Place a large sauté pan over high heat. Add 3 tablespoons butter. Once butter is melted, add garlic. When garlic is fragrant, add shallots, leeks, mushrooms, and fennel. Cook until tender. Add white wine and *cuisson*. Add cooked apples. Add shrimp, mussels, and clams. Cover for about 3 minutes. Remove shellfish and shrimp once the shells have opened (do not over-cook). Add seafood to the fish and cover with foil.

Place cream in a bowl. Whisk some of the cooking liquid from the sauté pan into the cream to bring up the temperature of the cream. Add all of the warmed cream to the sauté pan. Reduce to *à la nappe* stage (the liquid coats the back of a spoon).

Remove from heat and swirl in butter. (The addition of the cold butter is optional.) Season to taste. Add fish and shellfish into the liquid and gently toss to coat. Garnish with parsley. Serve warm.

CHAPTER FIVE

Marathon Weekend

I RECEIVE an inside tip on a Paris apartment, and although I am not actively looking to buy at the moment, the tip is too good to pass up. The apartment, in slight disrepair and its price adjusted accordingly, is in the 16th in a beautiful building on Avenue Georges Mandel. Jasmine's mother sits on the *syndic* board and, knowing of my desire to purchase a Parisian apartment, she told Jasmine that I could preview it before it officially goes on the market. The timing of the tip could not be better as next weekend (when the girls are with their father), I have a stop-over in Paris before proceeding to Venice, Italy, to run the Venice marathon. I deem the timing and geographical coincidence as a positive sign and arrange to view the apartment Friday afternoon before heading to Venice. The marathon is Sunday morning, and I will be back in Los Angeles Monday afternoon. Three countries. Four days. *Pas de problème*. It is October 2010.

PARIS, FRIDAY AFTERNOON. It is the beginning of La Toussaint, the two-week break in the French school system covering the holidays of All Saints' Day and All Souls' Day. As a result, the taxi ride from CDG to the 16th takes twice as long, rendering me fifteen minutes late for my *rendez-vous*. The *gardienne* buzzes me in, and as she greets me in the lobby, my French cell phone screams: *cocorico!* My hand flies into my purse to silence it. The *gardienne* looks at me inquisitively, and I offer the *"Je suis chef de cuisine"* explanation. She nods in understanding because *c'est logique* that a cook would have a rooster ringtone. Especially in France.

The *gardienne* escorts me through the hallway where I meet Colette, the *syndic* member who will show me the apartment. Colette wears modest heels with a well-tailored navy blue dress. Her coiffed hair is neatly tucked behind her ears. Colette speaks only French, and very quickly. She tells me that if I do not need an apartment immediately, she is moving in four months and she can show me her apartment as well. My head is still nine time zones away, and I struggle to respond to her questions, but I manage a *"oui, s'il vous plaît,"* because viewing two apartments is even better than viewing one

JEF AND I AGREED to meet at Café Trocadéro, which is ideally situated around the corner from the subject apartment building and next to a taxi stop for my return to CDG. Alison introduced me to JeF (short for Jean-François). The two met as teenagers in Saint-Tropez and re-connected through social media. When he was in Los Angeles last spring, she put the two of us in contact, believing that we would hit it off due to our mutual affection for France and food (which is an integral part of JeF's culture, as well as his job filming and producing cooking shows). Alison's instincts proved correct, and although JeF and I tried dating for the length of a sneeze, we decided that we were much better friends.

JeF is seated on the *terrasse*. He stands when he sees me and greets me with a double-cheek kiss and an exuberant hug. Generously dimpled, his beautiful smile could warm me on the coldest day. We last saw one another after my Normandy adventure two months ago.

"So, how was the apartment. Sorry, I could not join you," he says.

"It's fine. I actually was able to see two."

"Cool!"

"Yes, but neither works. The ground-floor apartment (the one I was supposed to see) was small and dark and the whole thing has to be redone, not just the kitchen and bathroom. The brown shag carpet holding on for dear life to the '70s was something to see. You should be sorry you missed that."

"Oh, no!" he says, laughing.

"Pretty garden view though, " I say, and pause as the waiter sets our *cafés* on the table. "The second one was gorgeous. Multi-leveled with lots of windows and closets but way too expensive. I cannot even afford the couture clothes in the closets," I say, my disappointment negated by the obvious impracticality of either choice, not to mention that any purchase would be contingent on the sale of our Hollywood home.

JeF laughs and drops a sugar cube in his *café*.

"*Un sucre ou pas du tout,*" he says and proceeds to tell me about his grandmother who repeated that phrase — one sugar or not at all — throughout his youth. I enjoy JeF's stories and love that our conversations are smattered with an exchange of new vocabulary: French for me and English for him. The beautiful weather makes me momentarily contemplate staying in Paris for the weekend, but I dismiss the thought because an international marathon has been on my to-do list. Thirty minutes later, JeF gives me a *gros baiser* and wishes me *bon courage*, and I take a second taxi to return to CDG.

THE GUN SOUNDS sending thousands running into the countryside and away from the Baroque-style Villa Pisani with its grandiose column facade and caryatids. Hans Zimmer's "Now We Are Free" plays on my iPod, perfectly echoing my emotion as my feet trail my spirit running in this beautiful setting and the crisp Italian air with thousands of others. By some miracle, I do not feel the least bit tired. My memory recalls my eagerness to leave the confines of that hospital bed and the months it took to walk and then run. Now, my feet barely touch the road, yet they propel me forward. Golden leaves fall from the trees around my head and lie in the road, a slippery yet beautiful hazard, while children row in the Giudecca Canal to our right. Families brave the chilly weather, umbrellas in hand, to cheer us on and a large blue sign hangs on a wrought-iron gate, *saluta mara-toneti* spray painted in red. Too early for endorphins, this high at mile one is pure joy.

We pound through fields of radicchio and treviso, prompting recipes and food combinations in my head. I think about the markets I visited yesterday, with their autumn abundance and the numerous fish stands on small metal tables piled high with fresh razor clams (a rarity in the States) and imagine the pasta dishes to complement them. I relive yesterday's lunch of seafood steamed *en papillote* that released a whoosh of steam that warmed my face when the waiter cut it open, suffusing the air with the heady scent of fresh dill and other herbs. Last night's dinner at La Caravella replays in my head too, and I imagine various uses for *saor*, the traditional Venetian dish I discovered. My thoughts bounce to Paris apartments, the ground-floor disaster and the fifth-floor palace I viewed on Friday and all of those I have yet to see. Dreaming of a Parisian kitchen of my own, my speed picks up. Unlike American marathons, where spectators line the course handing out gummy bears and orange wedges, here designated food stations display carefully arranged baskets of fruit, raisins, and Italian butter and honey biscuits —the very ones Mr. Monaco used to dip in his morning cappuccino. I grab a handful of biscuits and eat them while running and think of him.

As we cross the Ponte della Libertà, the Venice Liberty Bridge, we have run more than thirty kilometers (about nineteen miles), and the bridge, just shy of four kilometers, feels endless. Mile nineteen. The hardest part of the race for me. The drizzly, damp weather is chilling me despite my pace and my overindulgence in those damn Italian biscuits has given me a terrible stomachache. I place my right hand on my stomach and keep running because I know that good miles always follow the difficult ones and that the feeling of accomplishment will far outweigh my present complaints.

We cross the Grand Canal via a pontoon bridge specifically built for the marathon and arrive in the borough of San Marco to a slight rain. Fourteen more little bridges to cross until the finish. My stomach no longer hurts, but the rain picks up significantly and my feet slosh in an inch of water. I count down the bridges as I cross them and when I reach Piazza San Marco, my rain-soaked shoes have little traction. Approaching the finish line, a fellow runner encourages me to go faster and without warning, he grabs my hand and we cross the finish line together. 3:31:05.

The finish area is congested with runners stripped down to their undergarments, anxiously changing into some clean, dry clothes. Under normal circumstances, Italian men in their underwear would definitely be something I would slow down for, but I am cold and drenched and eager to treat myself to a very hot bath, a plate of spaghetti Bolognese, and a call to JeF to give him my race report. All of which I do, in that order.

ON MONDAY MORNING the water taxi pulls me away from Venice before the retreat of the night. In Paris I have only enough time to board my connecting flight to Los Angeles. Taking a break from revising my outline and recipes for tomorrow's fish class, I amble to the self-serve beverage station where I befriend a man who introduces himself as Russ. Russ is returning to Los Angeles after a cycling tour in the south of France and shows me photos of his cycling route. I recognize the venue immediately.

"You rode through Cap Roux?" I ask nostalgically, reflecting on the times I have driven through that distinctive seaside tunnel between Monaco and Saint-Jean-Cap-Ferrat.

"You know it?"

"Yes. My daughters and I have vacationed not far from there. It's a beautiful part of the world."

We talk about France, food, children, and athletic endeavors. The conversation makes the flight pass quickly and we make plans to connect back in Los Angeles. Within hours I am reunited with my girls. Their music lessons proceed as they do every Monday after school and by 6:30 p.m. homework is completed and dinner is served. It feels like a typical Monday night and difficult to believe I was in Venice this morning but for the two pairs of tiny Venetian red velvet slippers adorning the girls' feet, the medal lying on the kitchen counter, and my sense of accomplishment as a result of my marathon weekend.

SAOR

Saor is a sweet and sour garnish that pairs well with firm white fish, scallops, shrimp, polenta, and puréed sweet potatoes. One of my favorite ways to serve *saor* is to place a dollop of it on a large steamed shrimp and serve it as a passed appetizer.

Makes one-half pint

   1 tablespoon olive oil
   2 red onions, thinly sliced
   ¼ cup red wine
   ¼ cup currants
   A/N kosher salt
   ½ cup packed light brown sugar
   ¾ cup balsamic vinegar
   1 tablespoon Xérès or sherry vinegar

Place a large sauté pan over high heat. Add olive oil. When oil is hot, add onions. Add a few pinches of salt. Turn down heat and cook onions until they are very tender. When the onions begin to stick to pan, add the red wine and currants. Toss to coat. Turn off heat. The wine will almost completely be absorbed by the onions. Set aside.

Place a saucepan over a medium-high heat. Add balsamic vinegar and sugar. Cook the vinegar-sugar combination until it is bubbling and you achieve a syrup consistency. Pour the hot syrup over the cooked onions. Toss to coat. Add sherry vinegar and combine. If the *saor* is thin, you can thicken it by cooking it a little longer over a medium flame (but remember that it will thicken when cooled so be careful not to overcook it).

Refrigerate the *saor* for at least 6 to 8 hours.

SOLE À LA MEUNIÈRE

This is the classic way to prepare *sole à la meunière*. I reduced the butter for this recipe but if you want more sauce, add more cold butter (clarified butter does not brown). Dover sole has a meaty, but delicate, taste. If you cannot find Dover sole you can substitute other types of sole or even trout.

Serves 2

> 4 fillets from 1 beautiful Dover sole (skin on or off)
> A/N all-purpose flour
> A/N kosher salt
> A/N freshly ground black pepper
> 1½ tablespoons clarified unsalted butter
> 3 tablespoons unsalted butter, cold
> 1 to 2 teaspoons fresh lemon juice
> 1 tablespoon finely minced fresh Italian parsley

To clarify butter, place a stick of unsalted butter in a saucepan over a low heat and let it melt. Do not let the butter brown. Remove from stove and set aside to cool. The milk solids and water will separate from the butter fat. You can easily ladle off the butter once cooled or use a fat separator. This can be done in advance and stored in the refrigerator.

Rinse fish fillets well. Pat dry. Season the fillets with salt and pepper. Preheat oven to 350 degrees Fahrenheit.

Place an ovenproof skillet or sauté pan over a high flame. Once the pan is hot, add the clarified butter. Dredge fillets in flour. Tap off the excess flour. This should be done immediately before cooking. Once butter is hot, place fish in the pan flesh side down. Fish should sizzle. Cook for 2 to 3 minutes just until the fish is slightly brown and crispy. Use a fish spatula to turn fish over and cook the bottom side for 2 minutes.

Add *cold* butter to pan. Use a large spoon to baste the fish with the butter by scooping the melted butter out of the pan and pouring it over the fish a few times. Place pan with the fish in the oven. Fish is done when the flesh appears opaque. (Fillets only need to be in the oven about 3 minutes.)

Carefully, and with an oven mitt or dry kitchen towel, remove the pan from oven and place it back on the stove. Add lemon juice to the pan. Season with salt and pepper. Continue to baste fish with butter sauce which should brown and begin to smell nutty. Add parsley.

Plate fillets flesh side up. Pour sauce over the fish. Add more parsley if desired.

CHAPTER SIX

Joie de Vivre

THE LOSS OF time with my daughters was the toxic coating on the divorce pill I was forced to swallow. It is hard to accept that suddenly your children will only be with you part of the time, and when they are not with you, you have no say or control over what they do or whom they are with. When their father and I separated, I found a therapist who encouraged me to handle this life alteration by taking advantage of the alone time. It was a kind of mind trickery, in truth, proclaiming these doses of unanticipated early empty nest-dom to be a healthy and enjoyable opportunity for me.

"Focus on things in your control and do what makes *you* happy," she told me.

So, I made a list of those things I wanted to do and the things that brought me joy. France was at the top.

SPRING BREAK 2011. The girls' two-week vacation is apportioned evenly between their father and me. The first week they are with me and the three of us rent an R.V. (a/k/a the "house on wheels"), pack it with all the creature comforts it can carry, and drive ten hours through the desserts of California and Arizona to the Grand Canyon with Coco. Although the girls are not tall enough for the mule rides in the canyon, it is a week of untold beauty and discovery and often we wake to a family of deer eating outside our window. When we return to Los Angeles, the girls leave with their father, and consistent with my post-divorce "happy" plan, I head straight to LAX Paris-bound for culinary inspiration, to spend time with friends, and to run the Paris marathon.

THE PLANE TOUCHES down at CDG. I turn on my phone and find a multitude of emails from my real estate agent in Los Angeles. The tenants in our Hollywood home declined their buy option and, three potential buyers later, the house is finally in escrow. I am hoping this potential sale does not go south as well (because I plan to use the proceeds for Paris) and in anticipation, I continue to scour explorimo.com almost daily just to see what apartments are on the market and for how much.

Escrow matters aside, it is springtime in Paris, and the entire city smiles with flowers; the recently bare trees boast popcorn-like blossoms on their branches. Bulbs have erupted from the ground into a fraternity of tulips, pink, yellow, and purple, all worshiping the sun. Parisians swarm to the green metal chairs in the *jardins* and neighborhood squares with their lunches and books. Vegetables in the *marchés* and the neighborhood produce markets are predominantly white and bright green, signifying the rebirth that only comes with spring, and the displays of the season's first, sweet strawberries render me hungry in anticipation of enjoying some myself.

I stay at a small, recently remodeled boutique hotel with modestly sized rooms and a charming library on ground zero. It is well-situated for me as it is near the heart of Saint-Germain-des-Prés, and walking distance of Pierre Hermé and Jardin du Luxembourg (where I can run after the Hermé *macarons*). The clerk hands me my faxes of escrow addendum and revised menu proposals for a private group cooking class I am teaching the day after my return to Los Angeles.

Deeming that a street run to survey this year's Easter creations (and to stretch my airplane legs) is just what I need, I don my running clothes and leave the faxes in my room. Second to Christmas, *Pâques* is the biggest holiday in France and, like all *fêtes*, it is celebrated with food, particularly *chocolat— oeufs au chocolat*, bunnies in every shape and size, and indeed, all animals are represented. I run past *chocolatiers* both unknown and familiar, and delight in the creations artfully displayed. At Christian Constant's Salon du Chocolat I find elaborate chocolate eggs the size of small children decorated with gold medallions and wrapped in gold foil. An even larger chocolate egg with the Sagittarius archer painted on it in gold is fifty euros (roughly seventy U.S. dollars), and I cannot help but wonder if the fifty euros actually covers the labor cost.

JeF and I meet for dinner at Sensing, Guy Martin's new place in the 6th. JeF orders lamb. Feeling confident after my recent R.V. driving challenge in the windy conditions and on dark winding mountain roads, I order the scallops—*coquilles Saint-Jacques*—on spinach with an airy foam, preceded by a creamy lentil and seared *foie gras entrée*. I have not had scallops since my hospital episode, and the *foie gras* is not marathon-conforming, but I think it is time to overcome the irrational fear of the bivalve mollusk. And, as for the *foie gras*, I accept that it will be impossible to keep to my pre-marathon dietary rituals while in Paris.

Our conversation proceeds with the familiar comfortable rhythm as if we speak every day. He updates me on daily life and we exchange some mutual language lessons in the process. Dessert arrives. As I study the precision of the tiny white dots of pastry cream covering my plate as a functional decoration, JeF asks me if I would like to attend a taping of *Carinne & Vous*, a cooking show he produces for French television. They are filming the day after tomorrow and

Carinne's guest will be *chocolatier* Patrick Roger. I look up from my plate. Patrick Roger is a MOF, a *Meilleur Ouvrier de France* (Best Crafts-man of France), an accolade he won in his early thirties. He sculpts life-sized chocolate forest scenes, roosters, and *Pères Noël* that domi-nate the interior space of his Parisian boutiques. His *pralinés* melt on your tongue. A *chocolatier* of deity-like proportions, if there is such a thing, and while I have no aspirations to become a *chocolatier*, I am giddy with anticipation of being in the presence of genius and hoping that I will learn something usable for my blog or my classes.

"*Oui, s'il te plaît!*" I say, thanking him for the thoughtful offer.

WHILE SWIRLING MY teaspoon in my cappuccino froth at Bread & Roses, Bostonian accents catch my attention. They are coming from the couple sitting next to me who are chatting with my waiter about his upcoming first-time marathon experience on Sunday. When the waiter brings me my *fromage frais*, delightfully blanketed with nuts, muesli, and acacia honey, I wish him "*bon courage*" for the race and tell him I am running it as well. From there, the waiter, the Bostonian couple, and I strike up a conversation. Mike and Trudy. They are antique dealers and come to France to buy antiques that they export to the States, where they live the majority of the time. They also have an apartment here, a stone's throw from the park. When I tell them that I am hoping to buy an apartment in Paris but have not found anything yet, Mike commiserates with me about the daunting task of Parisian real estate.

"Finding an apartment in Paris takes time," he says.

He invites me to their apartment for a *café* and to continue our conversation. Delighted with the offer, I accept without hesitation.

I leave the café in search of inspiration for upcoming cook-ing classes and catering jobs and it does not take me long to find it. At Pâtisserie Aoki Sadaharu, the traditional French desserts are made with Japanese flavors such as green tea and yuzu and serve as a creative springboard for me in my planning of a dessert table for a Japanese-themed birthday party. Wandering the Paris streets, I discover dish stores and antique shops and find myself stumbling upon pathways I have never seen. After hours of wandering, note-taking, and photographing the beauty in which I am immersed, I have very little time to clean up and meet Maryam for an *apéro* at La Quincave.

WHEN MARYAM and I met in 2009, we immediately hit it off. A successful Parisian business owner and parent of two children (a few years older than my own), Maryam took me under her wing when I was looking at schools for the girls. She understood what it is like to move to Paris with children, especially as a single parent. She gave me immeasurable amounts of practical, sound advice on apartments, schools, and life in Paris and even visited schools with me in the 16th and introduced me to the headmaster of her children's former grammar school. When I told her about the court's decision, she understood my disappointment and what began as an act of generosity—she bestowing upon me much nonreturnable counsel—developed into a friendship and I admire her in countless ways.

Maryam arrives five minutes after I do. She is *très chic* with her black hair, brown eyes, and minimal makeup. She is always dressed in something I would want to borrow. Tonight, it is a simple black dress with a light jacket appropriate for the tricky spring weather. And, yes, I want to borrow this too. We cheek-kiss twice and sit at one of the high tables outside the tiny wine bar and shop. The owner selects a *vin rouge* for us from his floor-to-ceiling inventory. He is generous in his pours, which we enjoy with the thin slices of salami he serves us on a little paddle cutting board. When we have run out of salami and wine, we meet Maryam's boyfriend at a nearby *bistro*, quaint with its small wooden chairs and crocheted half-curtains in the window. Dinner is beef braised in *cocottes* served with sides of creamy *pomme purée* drizzled with *jus*. We close the tiny place, ending our meal with ample slices of walnut and vanilla *gâteau*, which is so delicious, I shamelessly ask for the recipe and they, flattered to be asked, give it to me.

After dinner, unable to sleep, I stay up reviewing escrow documents and writing recipes. At 7 a.m. I use a cold washcloth to de-puff my eyes from the lack of sleep, but it is not working and I am forced to wear sunglasses in overcast weather to cover my puffy eyes, sure to signal to everyone that I am American (as four stereotypes, all of which I represent today, invariably reveal one's Yankee status: smiling too much, talking too loudly, painted fingernails, and wearing sunglasses). With no time for the *métro*, I take a taxi to the northeast suburbs of Paris to a little house where JeF and his crew are filming.

I am on my third espresso when "Chocolate God" arrives on his motorcycle. His scruffy thin brown hair is held back from his face in a loose ponytail. He wears faded gray jeans and a chef's jacket with the distinctive red, white, and blue MOF collar over his slight frame. Timid, but approachable. When I am introduced to him, I forget all my French and my *bonjour*, is barely audible. JeF looks at me and mouths, "*Ça va?*"

The *chocolatier* shows Carinne his *Pâques* theme this year: speckled chocolate eggs that resemble chicks with beaks, eyes, and little wings; chocolate hedgehogs with little black noses; and fried eggs made of chocolate, which remind me of Dalí's melting clocks. He demonstrates how to make the French staple *œufs au chocolat*, emptied and cleaned eggshells filled with a chocolate lining and *praline* center and sold in cardboard egg cartons tied with raffia. They are gorgeous. And *trop miam*, which I discover after our *sauté de veau* lunch because the demonstration chocolate is our dessert. I leave the taping before another session begins, having already written several recipes and with the inspiration for a blog or two as well as Easter ideas for my own table.

MIKE AND TRUDY'S apartment in the heart of the 6th is bright with ornate, high ceilings and sculptured walls. As expected, every room is filled with beautiful antiques and while it is indeed far grander than anything I am in the market for, it is a pleasure to behold. Trudy offers me a seat in a Louis XVI chair while Mike brings me a *café*. They tell me that foreigners do in fact purchase Parisian apartments without ever seeing them first. Mike says that I must be fully prepared to make an immediate offer on any apartment I am seriously interested in or it will be gone.

"You must *act fast*," he says ruefully.

My visit with Mike and Trudy fills me with optimism. Selling our Hollywood home will give me the ability to "act fast," and I recognize that it has been for the best that my apartment searches on explorimo.com have come up empty thus far.

I FIND IT ironic that it was a woman, Eugénie Brazier, who was the first person to attain *trois étoiles* at two restaurants and is credited for training Paul Bocuse, but the professional kitchen in Paris is essentially a man's world. Very few female chefs own their own restaurant. Hélène Darroze is part of this elite minority. She and Anne-Sophie Pic are the only two female chefs, in my opinion, truly celebrated in Paris for their culinary talent. I have a list of restaurants I hope to experience this week and Hélène Darroze's restaurant, with its Basque influence and bearing her name, is tonight's destination.

I pass on the more formal *salle à manger* and opt for the casual room with the smaller potions where I can sample a variety of flavors and dishes. I am not disappointed: tuna tartare served atop whipped guacamole (Parisian chefs are obsessing over avocados, which, as a Californian, I find amusing); crispy-skinned fish with potatoes; and lamb chops with beet balls (created by using a melon baller) and glazed vegetables. My (second) dessert of dehydrated thin pear slices set in vanilla ice cream on top of a chocolate sauce moat is the most beautiful interpretation of the classic *poire belle Hélène* I have ever seen. The attentive young sommelier, in his dark suit and yellow tie, assists me with a wine pairing for my cheese plate of southwestern specialties. I have had trouble sleeping since I arrived, but tonight I expect a self-induced food coma will take care of that.

LAST SUMMER, after my Normandy adventure, JeF took me to dinner at Drouant and introduced me to chef Antony Clemot, its director. Owned by Antoine Westermann, the Art-Deco setting is home to the Goncourt Academy (the French literary association that bestows the prestigious annual Prix Goncourt for fiction). Drouant is also the place to find many chefs — Parisian and international — dining. That evening we were joined on the *terrasse* by American writer Bill Buford and chef Michel Richard (whom I have long admired and had it not been for the Champagne-induced courage, I would have forgotten how to speak French to him, too). It somehow came up in conversation that Antony knows Éric Kayser, the *artisan boulanger* who owns bakeries around the world and dozens in Paris alone. Upon learning my admiration for Kayser's work, Antony offered to introduce JeF and me to him, and today is the day.

However, our planned foursome becomes three because en route to Drouant, JeF calls me to say that he is tied up at work and cannot join us. *Zut!* The change in plans makes me nervous; I'm not prepared to hold my own in French with someone as impressive as Kayser with my still-evolving command of the language. Despite my nerves, I continue to the restaurant and take a seat on the *terrasse*. Kayser arrives with his business manager. He looks like a red-headed country boy but with the sophistication and charm of a Parisian. Our conversation goes smoothly because we primarily discuss food, baking techniques, and ingredients, all of which I can do in French. Antony spoils us with Champagne and flawless *foie gras* among other delectables. Before leaving, Kayser invites me to visit a kitchen in one of his Parisian bakeries. We exchange information, and I leave Drouant, thrilled with the offer and envision writing a blog post on the experience. JeF is going to be bummed he missed this lunch.

GABRIELLE AND I met in the south of France one summer at Lou Fassum in Grasse. Grasse is known for its perfume-making, and Lou Fassum is known for its *chou farci* (a traditional dish of cabbage stuffed with seasoned meat, rice, and onions and poached in a light stock). Gabrielle, seated nearby, introduced herself when she heard our Californian accents. Also from southern California, Gabrielle married an Italian and moved to Paris. They now reside in Grasse where she designs handbags, and they raise two daughters. She is in Paris for business and, as a person in the fashion industry, she is ever alert for what's trending, which makes her seem legitimately *parisienne*. Gabrielle made the dinner reservation and told me to meet her at a wine bar in the Marais. The venue is unfamiliar to me, but the owner is a friend of hers and she wants to introduce the two of us, should I be interested in catering in Paris. Another contact in the Parisian culinary industry is not something to turn down.

Friday night traffic and central Paris is at a *circulation* stand-still. Gabrielle is fashionably late and sweeps in, awash in sequins. Burlesque, she divulges, is the rage right now, and *"toutes les choses ont des sequins et des plumes."* I will have to take her word for it "that everything is about sequins and feathers" and hope that this fashion phase passes quickly. I greet her with a double-cheek kiss feeling *très* underdressed in my linen dress and ballet slippers.

Gabrielle introduces me to her friend and, after a brief chat over a Kir, a taxi takes us across the city to the swanky Matignon restaurant (another discovery for me), humming with models scantily clad in black and lots of sequins. The restaurant tables are close enough to one another to be positively communal. Above the DJ, two tables away from where we are sitting, is a woman who appears to be lying in a cage, and the music is so loud that there are ripples in my Bordeaux. Gabrielle talks about her Paris days and tells me that a friend of hers is selling his place; she will inquire on my behalf. The apartment talk is brief, however, and over dinner we primarily discuss (and laugh) about men and the lifestyle difference between France and California. Paris *chic* from head to toe and speaking flawless French, I cannot imagine Gabrielle ever living in reserved Orange County, California.

It is just before midnight when we finish our meal. We contemplate going to the club downstairs, but Gabrielle deems it "too early" and the crowd *"vulgaire"* (a word commonly used in Paris). She proposes a change in plans and I hesitantly agree, as that 26.2-mile run in less than two days weighs in the back of my mind, and I have hardly slept the entire week. We go to the 6th and stop by a private club tucked behind Café de Flore, but it is still "too early." We have a tea at Flore, which I am pleased about because I am not far from my hotel and I am planning my graceful exit in my head. However, there is no exit. Gabrielle grabs my hand and pulls me across the street to the taxi stand where a waiting taxi whisks us to a former movie theater in the 8th. We descend the stairs of the signless venue that empties into a large basement room with a bar and thumping music. On the stairs we pass a glass tank with two live chickens under a red light. Chickens? Will they fight? It is a *terroir* statement? What kind of club is this? The chickens, with their *plumes*, are more *en vogue* than I in my linen. Gabrielle and I are the same age, but everyone in the club to whom she introduces me seems at least ten years younger and the thumping underground scene is not really for me, at least not tonight. Now early morning, I excuse myself, bidding Gabrielle and the chickens a *bonne nuit*. And, that was my taste of Gabrielle's Paris.

THE MORNING of the marathon I meet Kathy and other New Yorkers in her running group and together we walk from their hotel in the 8th to the Étoile where the race will start. Jasmine introduced us, and the last time I saw Kathy was in Paris, days before my Monaco hospitalization. She lives in New York but is in Paris this week to run the marathon and visit her sister and her newborn baby who live in the 11th. Although we do not know one another well, I am pleased I have a familiar face to run with.

It is late by the time we reach the Étoile and we cannot access our corrals due to the crowds. Strangers help us climb over the metal barriers into the sea of the non-seeded group. Excited to run the Paris streets, we snap a photograph of ourselves on the Champs-Élysées just before the gun sounds and after it does, I survey my surroundings, apartments included. Some Parisians come to their windows to watch, while others close their shutters. It is Sunday morning and this race is a sleep disturbance. We run eastward on the cobblestones toward the Bastille. The smells of rising bread and world food are inviting but interrupted by the male elbows that find their way to my ribs with much frequency. Despite the posted "No Parking" signs, there are cars on the side of the road and I run on the sidewalk to avoid other runners, which is not an altogether successful tactic as the French's inventive parking methods mean that there are cars parked on the sidewalks, creating an obstacle course of sorts. As a result of the runner/car chaos, I lose Kathy in the crowd and, even worse, I cannot get over to a water station until mile seven.

We reach the Bois de Vincennes in southeast Paris and turn back toward the center of the city. Mile sixteen and the running pack has thinned considerably. Crowds stand along the Seine, which is on our left, and a bystander, reading my bib, shouts "*Allez! Allez Morgan!* Her words boost my dissolving energy, and I enter the Tunnel des Tuileries, the three-kilometer underground expressway, with confidence. The rhythmic drum of runners' feet hitting the pavement echoes in the tunnel and endorphin-fueled shouts sound like thunder, but the air in the tunnel is hot and stagnant. Half-way through, the heat becomes unbearable. Claustrophobic and dizzy, I run on the side of the tunnel next to the wall with mounted fans, but the fans are few and far between and seem to be circulating only the hot air. It is a record-breaking seventy-seven degrees Fahrenheit, but with the humidity, it feels like it is in the high 80s.

When I reach mile twenty in the 16th, I escape the ever-thinning running pack and run into a Chinese restaurant, the only open restaurant I can find, where a singular hunched-over elderly man is setting up the tables for lunch. I ask him for "*sel*" and he looks at me as if I were *très folle*, but I know I am low on sodium and, with no bystanders handing out salty pretzels, salt out of a shaker is my only hope. I pour some in my sweaty hand and thank him as I run out the door.

The roads in the expansive and woody Bois de Boulogne are more narrow than usual due to the cars parked on both sides. Ambulances and emergency workers weave their way through the runners to pick up the flaccid bodies lying or sitting in the road who have succumbed to the heat. The salt came too late and I give in to walking, but it is more painful than a slow, steady pace to which I return. We are approaching Avenue Foch, which leads to the finish. One mile to go. A man sits on the side of the road with a sign offering runners *un verre de vin rouge*. The thought of a glass of red wine in the heat makes me want to throw up. And, I do.

After I collect my medal, I climb over the metal barricades, one leg at a time, and walk south in an attempt to get away from the crowds. A taxi at Place Victor Hugo takes me to the hotel where the staff observes that I am not looking so well and sends bottles of cool water to my room, which I drink in measured doses. Lying inert on the bathroom floor, the cold tiles feel good on my over-heated skin. Movement hurts my head and there is no point being far away from the bathroom anyway. When the nausea seems to have passed, I pull myself to the bed and wrap myself in a cold sheet. The rooster ring wakes me. It is Kathy. I did not see her the majority of the race. Unlike me, she had a great race and feels fine. She wants to know if we are still on for dinner. I hesitate but say *"oui"* because I was looking forward to our dinner, and lying in my hotel room is not how I want to pass my last night in Paris.

In a couple of hours I've sufficiently recovered from my dehydration to join her at Les Deux Magots. I ease my marathon disappointment with Champagne, a steak and *pommes frites*, and lively conversation. The square is buzzing with smartly dressed locals and tourist groups with their cameras slung around their necks and open maps. A male quartet plays their instruments by the *métro* entrance, providing live entertainment for all to enjoy. Paris can be many things; boring is not one of them, and I think about the stories of my week I plan to tell the girls tomorrow—the things I have done, the people I have met, the food I have eaten, and even the chickens in the nameless, underground club. While it seems I am juggling a thousand things at once—from escrow and raising children on one continent to cultivating contacts and researching food and apartments on another—I know things will come together. Weeks like this are my *mise en place* for the future, and even better, I'm experiencing the joy in the process itself. *Joie de vivre.*

CHAPTER SEVEN

The Desire to Cook a Coyote

ASK ANY PARENT, April and May are routinely busy months. For me, the combination of winding up spring cooking classes in Los Angeles, juggling catering jobs, and the end-of-the-year activities and events at the girls' school eliminate any established routine and challenge my organizational skills. I try to savor the moments, knowing they are fleeting, but I am rushing to everything, often five minutes late, and I am ready to declare email bankruptcy.

Mother's Career Day. While I look forward to the day that parents and their careers are celebrated without regard to gender, until then, mothers have their own special day at the girls' school. Tables are set on the grass under tents in the middle of campus and each participating mother is assigned a table where she may demonstrate what her work entails. While the girls stayed the night at their father's, I cooked to prepare for my presentation. Thinking of something child-friendly but interesting, I make various chocolate truffles and put them on popsicle sticks for handling ease. For a savory treat, I braise pork with caramelized diced apples, which I will serve in sample serving cups.

Up at 5 a.m. to strain and reduce the braising liquid and caramelize the diced apples, I first take Coco to the front-yard for her morning ritual. She waddles out to the grass and just as she steadies herself, a coyote bounds from the street over our rose bushes and our fence into the yard. He grabs Coco in his mouth and, without any pause, leaps back over the fence and runs up the road with my dog in his jowls.

Did that just happen?!

I dash out the gate and up the street after the dog-napping coyote, but he is too fast. I race back into the house, grab my keys hanging by the door, and jump in my car. Charging up the street I scream, "Coco!" out my open window. Out of my peripheral vision, I spy the mangy coyote in a neighbor's yard to my left. Coco is still in its mouth. Turning my steering wheel a hard left, my car jumps the curb and lands in the neighbor's yard, trapping the creature in between my car, the house behind, and a tall hedge on the right. Enraged, I fly from out of my car and charge at the thin, homely looking thing with clenched fists.

"GIVE ME MY FUCKING DOG!" I scream.

The coyote is motionless. His desperate eyes stare at me with puzzlement and apprehension, then he drops Coco from his jaws and flees the yard. Coco lies motionless on her back, all fours in the air and a wild look in her eyes. Scooping her up from the wet grass, I search her furry body for puncture wounds but find none. The wild stare has not left her eyes, and I am not sure if she is in shock or suffered a heart attack or a stroke. Coco lies motionless in my lap as I drive to the vet's office with no regard for speed limits.

The vet tells me they need to examine her. I wait in the lobby and after twenty minutes I drive to the corner Starbucks, forced to use the handful of change I've scrounged up in the ashtray and the folds in the seats of my car. As I wait in line, the morning's events replay in my mind. The man behind me fidgets uncomfortably and soon I feel the weight of stares from others in the line and become conscious of my own appearance: I am barefoot, wearing only a white cotton nightgown, my hair is unbrushed, and I am holding a hand full of change. Ducking out of the line, I leave the Starbucks as discreetly and quickly as possible and return to the vet's office. Coco has been shaved and resembles a New York City rat with large eyes. They cannot find anything wrong with her but want to keep her today for observation; they have never seen a dog escape a coyote attack unharmed.

Back at home, I clean up and finish the food and take my presentation to school. As I set up my table, the headmaster approaches. I greet him and begin to offer him a sample, but he does not want my food. In fact, not at all, and he informs me that no food can be served at the event. Now, this is understandable for those who might have brought gratuitous sugary treats that have nothing to do with their profession, but eliminating the food portion of a chef's job? Without having given me a heads up? Annoyed and frustrated, I contribute the food to the teachers' lounge, and return to the grassy presentation area where I am limited to showing the students pictures of my food and classes on my iPad. However, the sight of my girls cheers me and my morning becomes instantly better.

"Hi, Mom!"

THAT NIGHT AT the dinner table, I recount the tale of Coco and the coyote. After much laughter and wide-eyed curiosity, we talk about the other news: the sale of our Hollywood home. The papers are signed, making it official that the large house that held so many memories, as well as the girls' handprints in cement, now belongs to someone else. The next day we say our good-byes with the remaining cookie dough I left in the freezer for emotional emergencies. When we have walked the halls one last time and they bid their playhouse goodbye, I close the iron gates behind us. While I may miss the large, beautiful kitchen I designed from my hospital bed, I do not look back. And, that very afternoon, I go to the closest international bank and open an account in Los Angeles and another one in its Paris branch while Mike's advice rings in my ears: "When you find it, *you must act fast.*"

Fast as a coyote with a stolen dog in its jowls.

CHOCOLATE CHIP COOKIE DOUGH

To avoid a danger of Salmonella poisoning, you *must* use fresh eggs from a source you know and trust. We use the eggs from our chickens. If you have any doubt about the eggs, or prefer the warm cookies, bake the cookie dough.

Makes 1 dozen cookies

> 1 stick unsalted, quality butter, room temperature
> ½ cup granulated sugar
> ½ cup light brown sugar
> 1 fresh egg, room temperature
> 1 teaspoon vanilla bean paste
> ~1½ cups all-purpose flour
> 1 teaspoon *fleur de sel*
> ½ teaspoon baking powder
> ¼ teaspoon baking soda
> 1 handful of quality milk chocolate chips
> 1 handful of quality 60% cacao bittersweet chocolate chips

If you plan to bake the dough, preheat oven to 375 degrees Fahrenheit.

In a bowl, mix together the flour, salt, baking powder, and baking soda. Set aside.

In a standalone mixer fit with a paddle attachment, on low speed, mix the butter and sugars together until well-combined.

Add the egg and the vanilla bean paste to the bowl and continue to mix until combined.

Slowly add the dry ingredients to the bowl. Continue to mix on low speed. Once combined, add the chocolate chips. Mix. Place dough in an air-tight container and keep in the refrigerator for up to a week or freeze.

For cookies, line a baking sheet with parchment paper. Roll dough into twelve balls of equal size and place them on the baking sheet. Bake for about 7 minutes (you will smell the cookies and they will be slightly browned). Remove from the oven and let the cookies continue to bake on the sheet for another few minutes. Place on a cookie rack. The chocolate chips should be melty and the cookies soft.

CHAPTER EIGHT

All That Green

WHEN THE GIRLS leave for their summer vacation with their father, I leave for Paris. I had planned to return to Normandy to teach, but it did not work out this year for various reasons. Jane and I agreed to look to the following summer, and I viewed the change in plans as a gift of extra time to continue my Paris apartment search. However, the Parisian apartment in which I am staying is not available immediately, giving me a few days for a culinary expedition, which I decide to do in Alsace, east of Paris, bordering Germany. The Alsace region is far different than any other region in France that I have visited and has produced fine chefs such as Antoine Westermann and *chocolatier-pâtissier* Thierry Mulhaupt, both of whom I admire. A new region means a new style of cooking, new flavors, and new ingredients. The anticipation of such discoveries thrills me.

On the plane I lean my head against the window's edge, my iPad replays videos from yesterday's music recital at our home. Ava on violin. Julia on the piano. They even played many pieces together thanks to the coordination of their teachers. The recital was attended only by our closest family due to the state of the bathroom remodel, a project weeks behind schedule with wooden planks acting as temporary flooring over the dirt. We have one functioning shower and one toilet but, as we can only access these necessities from outside the house, it seems like camping inside. The girls think it is fun and pretend they are "walking the plank" as they enter the facilities. However, I am mortified to expose others to the conditions, especially my grandmother who is finding it increasingly difficult to get around these days. In her usual manner, she quiets my concern and says no one minds "making do," a phrase I have heard her utter in a variety of circumstances throughout my life. Making do. I also replay a video of Julia's birthday party, which we had the day before the recital. Despite going to my happy place, the videos tug at my heart and I watch them again, acknowledging the familiar ache.

Once at CDG, I spend no less than forty minutes wandering the downstairs train area searching for the correct platform. Yet my frustration and fatigue dissolve to contentment once I am in my seat because I am soon transported through the green countryside scattered with rolled hay bundles, which match the tiny country houses in color. The rolling hills lounge in the background and puffs of cotton clouds dot the powder blue. Generously full emerald trees mark property boundaries, but the speed of the train turns the view into a combined smattering of honey, blue, green and white. I am sailing through an impressionist painting, mottled and colorful.

WHEN I ARRIVE in Colmar, the platform is full of travelers and their luggage. Three young boys run slalom-style around both while their backpacks bounce from side to side, just missing other passengers. A round train official paces the platform and smiles from beneath his blue, red-banded cap at their boyish shenanigans. I weave around it all and cling to a red handrail for support as I descend the stairs, easing my luggage down step by step. At the bottom, a gray and white tiled subterranean area leads me to the *gare* itself, where I confirm immediately that the rumors are true: neither French nor German is spoken in Alsace but "*alsacien*," a mixture of the two. "*Oui*" sounds like "*ah -wee*," a stark contrast to the efficient Parisian "*oui*" and the lazy "*waee*" heard in Provence. My nose leads me to a stand with fresh *bretzels* (known in the States as soft pretzels). I am starving and indulge in one standing up while the new linguistic sounds swirl around me.

Château d'Isenbourg lies just minutes outside Colmar. The château, which once served as a post for the Roman military road (which runs behind it), a fortress for the town below, and even a home to bishops, will be my peaceful refuge for four nights. My taxi drives up the pea gravel driveway circling a large fountain; three men jump from the entrance to collect my bags. The reception area is comprised of a humble wooden desk and pleasant staff, and I am led without delay to my room.

My room is on the top floor of the château with three steps leading up to French doors that open to a private patio, lined with geraniums of various colors, enveloped in a view of vineyard rows as far as I can see. I listen to the porter but half expect someone to arrive at any moment to tell him that he brought me to the wrong room and that my room is the tiny one in back with no view. However, he finishes his tour without interruption, and I decide not to look this gift horse in the mouth and simply say "*merci, Monsieur.*"

Eager to remove my travel clothes, I put on a fluffy white robe hanging from the antique armoire and lie in a reclining chair on the patio with my computer to edit my weekly blog post. Rows and rows of uniform vines, a shade paler than grass, peek through the three-foot high Tuscan order stone column railing. Never in my life have I seen so much uninterrupted green and certainly not in this unique shade. It is hypnotizing. As I lie between the blue sky and the sea of green on this patio fit for royalty, an empty feeling touches me because I think that it would be nice to have someone here to experience this beauty and space with me. But the thought passes as quickly as it arrived. I have a full agenda of things to see and taste and a lot to learn. Another person would slow me down because I would be more concerned with making sure my companion is having an enjoyable time. Not wanting to bother them, I would forgo stopping the car to take a picture of something that caught my eye. At dinner, I would focus on our conversation, rather than the compatibility of the ingredients or ingenuity of the dish and whether I want to do something similar. And, there is the practical matter that no one I have met walks as fast as I do, and my present mindset is one of movement and personal growth.

Apéro time and *j'ai très faim.* I change out of my robe and go downstairs where I am seated at a *terrasse* table overlooking Rouffach, which resembles a cluster of habitation dropped in the middle of this pale green sea. A few more habitation clusters appear in the distance. The pink sun, the same color as the potted geraniums hanging off the metal green railing, recedes slowly. The waiter serves me a Muscat in a tiny wine glass with a tall, dark green stem. It resembles my grandparents' cordial glasses, the ones I used to beg to drink my milk out of when I was much younger and desirous of the fancy. The rose-colored wine is sweet, but crisp, and lighter than a Sauternes. The *gougères* are still warm and when I bite into them my mouth is welcomed by the fresh tang of the whole fennel seeds and melted Munster cheese. The delicious combination disappears quickly from my plate.

Foie gras is a regional specialty, so I begin my dining experience with a pressed *terrine de foie gras.* It is beautifully smooth, without blemish, bearing three thin layers of finely puréed berry jam interspersed in the velvety terrine and flanked by six delicate drops of a balsamic glaze with a gratuitous dab of a microgreen salad. I have had jam layered in brie or Camembert, and I have had jam served as an accompaniment to *foie gras*, but I have never had it layered in the terrine itself and the delightful discovery appeals to several sides of my tongue. As I dab bites of sweetened *pâté* in the glaze, I think of directions to take this layered idea, as well as new uses for fennel seeds inspired by my savory *gougères*. I take copious notes only to set down my pen to focus fully on my next course. Jean-Anthelme Brillat-Savarin's declaration that the discovery of a new dish is better than discovering a star was not merely a matter of opinion; for me, it is fact.

THE SUN'S MORNING rays climb over the vines, fall through the French window and warm my cheek, stirring me from my lazy slumber. Eager to explore my surroundings, I dress in running clothes and my feet fly over the turning, small road to Rouffach below, which remains asleep despite the sun's appearance. I skip on the *pavés* of cobblestone and run around the pale green painted lamp posts, their arms heavy with hanging potted geraniums. Humble stone houses with worn shutters hold up thatched roofs, some of which are penetrated by a rebellious vine. Even those in an objective disrepair exude charm. The well-tended patches of earth in each villager's backyard bear vines of currants, raspberries, or in some, grapes, all of which delight me.

The village center is not dissimilar to other small French villages: a small church, a few restaurants, and *pâtisseries*, except here there are signs for *tartes flambées à volonté* (all you can eat) everywhere. Boulangerie Kempf is closed but the *pâtisserie* across the street opened its door, releasing the smell of butter and sweet raisins into the cobblestone street and revealing the tall baker's rack filled with *kouglof* (also called *kougelhopf*). They look like fluted Bundt cakes with an almond crowning each curve, and the sweet aroma makes me so hungry I return to the château for *petit déjeuner.*

Colmar, a wonderland of bright color and abundant in charm, is similar to Rouen in that it is filled with half-timbered homes built right against one another, which vary in size, height, and color scheme: an orange home with brown beams and blue shutters is next to a yellow home with beige shutters and brown beams. Colorful flowers dangle from window boxes and balconies. Yet, in contrast to Rouen, which is large with the Seine dividing it, Colmar is quaint and homey.

My culinary curiosity takes me to the *marché couvert*, which is located next to the Quai de la Poissonnerie. A middle-aged accordion player wearing a bright purple shirt greets market goers with his music and radiant smile. Inside, two stationary aisles run the length of the covered market where produce is carefully arranged but still in its wooden crates displayed on their sides. *Alsacien* specialties include pork products, especially *charcuterie maison* (homemade charcuterie) and every variety of *chou*, including *le chou pointu* (the cone-heads cabbage variety). *Berawecka*, a sweet honey bread, and *pain d'épices pur miel*, spiced honey bread, are tied with red and white checkered ribbon and marked *"fabrication artisanale."* Stacks of boxed *kougelhopf* are ready to go and *bretzels* fill entire display cases, segregated by sweet and savory varieties, and range from chocolate frosted with sprinkles to those stuffed with *lardons et oignons.*

Petite Venise, near the *marché*, is a small section of Colmar where visitors cruise the canals in small motorized boats guided by a French gondolier while lunch-goers on the *terrasses* of the *brasseries* and *winstubs* look on. No boat ride for me. I am on a mission for *choucroute garnie* (a serving of sauerkraut with pork sausages and braised pork shoulder) and at Maison Rouge I find it. Inside the timbered four-level red building, the rooms buzz with patrons and *choucroute* is on almost every table. My starter, a salad, arrives covered with *croûtons* (which in France is any toasted bread of any shape) topped generously with melted Munster cheese and fennel seeds. This is followed by my *choucroute* served on a platter bearing enough food for three people. The waiter places the platter on the square enamel hot plate sitting on my table and serves me a portion. Tangy and rich, the freshness of juniper berries and mildly acidic bite of sauerkraut flood my mouth. The slowly cooked meat, tender and not short on fat, dissolves on my tongue. It was worth the wait.

I separate *déjeuner* and *dîner* by exploring Colmar's *fromageries*, dominated by Munster cheese (certainly not the square orange-tipped cheese of my youth), its *pâtisseries* with *citron* and sugared loaf cakes, and admiring the window displays of *en croûte* creations in all shapes and sizes, enveloping *pâtés* and *farcement*. My late evening dinner is at taxi driver-recommended and château-approved Jy's, in the heart of Petite Venise. The large covered *terrasse* sits next to a canal, and I begin my culinary undertaking with a glass of regional Pinot Gris and my *amuse-bouche*, which is a bite-sized sandwich on a stick and a mousse in a miniature cone. As my teeth crunch into the delicate cone, my lips fall on the light mousse interior, there is audible groaning, followed by a licking sound, and it is not coming from me. I look discreetly around me. To my left, a woman dines alone but under her table lies a large, floppy-eared black dog.

"*Ça lui plaît, mais à moi, pas beaucoup*," she says to me and laughs as the pampered canine continues to lick the *foie gras* from her fingers.

Although not traditional *cuisine alsacienne*, my meal is a delicious indulgence: thinly sliced duck breast with an Asian-inspired dipping sauce, followed by a blue lobster stuffed with summer vegetables with an herb salad, and happily, the portions are Parisian, not Alsacian.

The next morning begins with a run among the grapevines followed by a visit to the weekly open *marché* in Colmar. The sellers appear to be the growers, and the average age seems to be about sixty. The women dress in dirndl-inspired aprons and cotton clothing with stitching, reminding me that we are closer to Germany than to Paris. After I stock up on *quatre épices* for my anticipated holiday baking, the sunlit day invites me to take a *terrasse* seat at Winstub La Krutenau. The tables are filled with patrons, most of whom are enjoying pints of *bière* with their *tartes flambées*, a regional specialty that resembles an individual pizza. *Tarte flambée* is on my list. The restaurant offers two types: the *tarte nature* and *tarte gratinée* which adds grated cheese. I choose the latter and pass on the beer.

A young, plastic-gloved Frenchman dressed in all white works fastidiously at his *tarte* station not far from my table. He spoons a generous heap of the creamy white mixture of *fromage blanc* and *crème* over the round thin dough, adds onions, bacon, and grated cheese, then places the creation in the oven. The production in rapid succession is mesmerizing; then the waiter brings me mine. The crust, cracker-thin but not as crisp, offers the perfect contrast to the velvety, creamy-cheesey indulgence on top, which, despite its high fat content, is not greasy at all. Thirty minutes later, I have a page of notes, a draft recipe, and an empty plate.

LA ROUTE DES VINS runs one hundred and seventy kilometers through Alsace, roughly from Strasbourg in the north to Thann in the south, passing through one hundred and three vineyards. The tourism guides break down the route into four regions to make the journey more manageable. One suggested route is devoted to the fifty-one grands crus. Another route boasts the most medieval castles. I have no agenda with respect to the wineries except for one and it is north, near Kaysersberg, known for its devoted celebration of *Noël*.

The jumping windshield wipers smear rain droplets across my field of vision, but the June gloom does not cloud my enthusiasm. Where one vineyard ends, the next begins, and the entire landscape has the appearance of a woven quilt with varying patterns and shades of green. The successive discovery of each winery is as exciting as a first kiss, and I realize that I am driving too quickly for the weather as I make my way through this regional quilt, made with historical fabric, bound together with the influence of neighbors past and present. Every so often I pass large letters set amidst the green, spelling the name of the village. They mimic the Hollywood sign in size and appearance and the unfamiliar names I attempt to pronounce — "Kaefferkopf," "Ammerschwihr" — appreciative there is no one listening.

When I reach the Kaysersberg sign, I park my car and walk up the street toward the village, advancing no further than two hundred yards where I find a huddled group stopped in the road, their attention focused on the sky. Fingers point toward a distant chimney high above a building. My gaze follows the pointing fingers expecting to see a giant *Père Noël*; it is not Santa Claus but a large nest set atop a steepled chimney and inside is a mother *cigogne*. The beautiful white stork with her substantial, black-tipped wings is feeding three small, eager beaks protruding out from the giant round nest. The display of maternal love and life overwhelms me. It is far better than an over-stuffed man in a red suit with material gifts. My eyes scan the skyline, and I see that it is dotted with more nesting storks on chimneys with their young, and I now understand why this vision is the symbol of Alsace.

Kaysersberg looks like a church Christmas bazaar and the smells of ground ginger, nutmeg, cloves, and black pepper with a hint of citrus fill my nose, reminding me of my grandmother who shares my affection for spiced cake. *Pain d'épices* (spice bread topped with candied fruit and/or nuts) and *bredle*—butter cookies made with small, special cookie cutters in the shapes of stars, moons, Christmas trees or hearts—are in abundant supply and wrapped in red and green.

MY WINE DESTINATION—Domaine Weinbach (a/k/a Domaine Weinbach, Colette Faller et ses filles)—lies just south of Kaysersberg. Established in 1612 by Capuchin monks. Like so much of the property owned by the church, it was sold as national property during the French Revolution. Théo Faller, an advocate of the region's A.O.C. recognition, inherited the property from his uncle and father. The fact that all wines from Alsace are given A.O.C. status is thanks, in part, to him. When he passed, his wife Colette and their two daughters carried on the tradition. I read an article about the Faller women running the vineyard, and it is the story of this strong woman and her two capable daughters that brings me here.

The château is at the end of a long drive surrounded by thriving rose bushes. Pink geraniums garnish the top of the double front door, and I ring *la sonnette* as directed. A tastefully dressed woman with blonde, graying bobbed hair and a flawless complexion greets me. She wears little makeup, but for a smidgen of pale blue eye shadow. Her white embroidered blouse is cinched at the waist with a wide black belt and her necklace and earrings are blue and violet glass, matching the colors of the stitch-work in her cotton blouse. Madame Faller. She welcomes me in and leads me to a wood-paneled room, where she offers me a seat at a round wooden table upon which sits a vase spilling with pink and red roses from the garden. This isn't just a winery; this is her home.

Etherial-like in her white, she traverses the room carrying a small gold and blue enameled tray filled with empty wine glasses with lips that flare out like parrot tulips. With her reserved manner and soft-spoken, deliberate French she seems like one of the most effortlessly elegant women I have ever met. She sits with me as she offers me samples of a variety of Alascian wines, uniquely named for their grape variety (not their *terroir*). The Alsacian wine bottles, too, are unique from those used in the rest of France as they are poured from "*flûtes*," the tall, slender, and green bottles used in Germany. I sample the Sylvaner, Riesling, Pinot Blanc, Pinot Gris, Muscat, Gewürztraminer, and Eldelwicker (a blend). I am not fond of buttery Californian whites, and I am pleasantly surprised by the dryness of these. The Muscat is predictably sweet. Ultimately, I choose the Gewürztraminer Furstentum Vendanges Tardives and a Pinot Gris. The labels bear the names "Colette, Catherine and Laurence Faller," and I gaze at the family photos hanging in abundance on the walls. My thoughts wander to my own two daughters and how satisfying it would be to someday have our names on something that we care for.

La sonnette interrupts my speculation. The door opens and a man's booming voice with its American accent incises and drains the stillness from the room. Tall and lanky, outfitted in jeans, running shoes, and an oversized, sloppy T-shirt, he rambles on about how many cases he intends to buy from her this time, which I believe he intends as flattery, but it comes off as arrogant. Madame Faller writes up his order and solicits help from her assistant as he continues to discuss his travel escapades. Madame Faller smiles, saying little, and from my vantage point the large purchase appears transactionally cold and within minutes my fellow countryman departs with the stormy bravado with which he arrived. Madame Faller re-enters the room. We smile at one another and the non-verbal communication says a mouthful. She sits down with me at the table, and we talk about our daughters and food, while her assistant packages my modest purchase. To my delight, she offers to give me a tour of the property, including the cellar, and does not mind that I snap photographs. When we part, I ask if I may take her photo as well. She obliges and when I leave, it is with far more than three bottles of wine; I leave with the gift of her time and knowledge, and gratitude for the experience.

SUNLIGHT OVER the green wakes me. The drizzle of yester-day has turned into the blue of today and while I contemplate lying on my royal patio in a gluttonous, lackadaisical fashion, I take only a cup of coffee. My last day in Alsace and I am eager to begin my day exploring the wine route, this time south of Rouffach.

With all four windows down and my hair whipping about my head, I try to sing *en français* to Zaz, the young female French singer, playing loudly on the radio. The road stretches out far into the distance. My car is surrounded by fields and more fields of corn. The French do not eat corn and I momentarily contemplate the purpose of the fields, but the answer is unimportant because the tall stalks are uniformly drifting in the breeze. Gracefully and hypnotically, they invite me to join them. And, I do.

I park the car on the side of the road and walk on a dirt path that runs alongside the cornfields. There is no one around, and I relish in the swirling corn and the sun smiling on my skin. My walk is now brisk, and I take off my shoes. Soft dirt comes in between my toes and before long, I am running because my body intuitively wants to catch up with my spirit that is soaring with the dancing corn which my fingertips comb as I run. Only when my car is far out of my sight for some time do I decide to turn back before I run all the way to Thann, the southern end of the *route du vin*.

MY LAST MEAL in Alsace is an eight-course tasting menu at Maison des Têtes in Colmar, after which, I return to the château and I sit on my royal balcony and watch the sun dissolve behind the vines. My grandparents and I used to sit on the porch and watch the sun set. I call my grandmother. It is lunchtime in California. She greets me with the familiar bounce in her voice.

"Well, hello, my girl! Where you at?"

"Hi, Grandma. I'm in France."

"Oh?""In Alsace; it is next to Germany."

"Oh. Is it pretty? What's it like?"

And so I try to describe the land of *"ah-wee"* to my grandmother who has traveled little and is losing her eyesight. I begin by depicting the green, how the entire horizon, as far as one can see, is alternate rows of a pure pale light green, broken up only by clusters of small villages and medieval castles. I tell her that the people warmly greet one another in the streets like reunited loved ones and that the food portions are as generous as the Alsacian people are welcoming. The spice cakes are sweet with honey, and the moist fruit cakes jump from their loaf pans. The juicy overstuffed sausages have a sweet hint of rendered duck and goose fat, the sauerkraut offers the perfect amount of tang, and dishes boast the fresh notes of fennel seeds and juniper berries, and the spice of cumin. I tell her that there is a soft *bretzel* for any and all occasions and cravings, and that the biscuits and breads are generously baked with creamy blonde Normandy butter, nuts, and fruit that has been dehydrated just enough to sweeten it but not rob it of all moisture.

"Sauerkraut! It all sounds wonderful!" she exclaims, and the inflection in her voice proves the truth in her words.

"It is, Grandma. It is wonderful. I wish you could see it."

"I just did, my girl. I just did."

TARTE FLAMBLÉE

Inspired by my visit to Alsace, I recreated this *tarte*. I added fennel seeds to the crust and a touch of *quatre épices* to the topping, because, to me, these flavors capture this special region.

Makes 1 *tarte*

> *Dough*
> 1 teaspoon instant yeast
> ½ cup water, warm
> 1¼ to 1½ cups all-purpose flour
> 2 tablespoons olive oil
> 1 teaspoon kosher salt
> 1 teaspoon fennel seeds
> A/N olive oil

> *Topping*
> ½ cup crème fraîche
> 3 tablespoons grated quality Munster cheese
> Pinch of *quatre épices*
> 2 tablespoons Riesling (or similar white wine)
> 1 cup thinly sliced white onions
> 4 ounces lardons
> ½ teaspoon kosher salt
> 2 turns on black pepper mill

Place a pizza stone (or an upside-down baking sheet) in the oven and pre-heat oven to 425 degrees Fahrenheit.

Dissolve instant yeast in the warm water. Place flour, salt, and fennel seeds in a bowl on a flat surface. Make a well in the middle of the flour mixture. Add olive oil to the well. Then add the water mixture. Place two fingers in the liquid, and using a clockwise, swirling motion, incorporate the dry ingredients into the liquid. (Alternatively, use quality prepared pizza dough, incorporate the fennel seeds into the dough and follow manufacturer's instructions.)

Remove the dough from the bowl and knead dough lightly into a ball. The dough should still be moist but not too sticky. If it is too sticky, add a little more flour. (If the weather is damp, you will use more flour.) Lightly grease a large bowl with olive oil. Place the dough ball in the oiled bowl and cover with plastic wrap. Let dough rise until it doubles in size.

After dough has doubled, lightly press on the dough to expel gas. Knead dough a few times with your hands. On a lightly floured surface, use a rolling pin to roll the dough out until very thin circle, about one centimeter thick.

Place a skillet over medium-high flame. Add the lardons and partially cook. Remove lardons from the skillet and place them on paper towels. In a bowl, mix together the crème fraîche, cheese, wine, salt, pepper, and *quatre épices*. Let the mixture rest for about five minutes.

Spread the cheese mixture all over the rolled out dough, about ½ inch from the edge. Scatter the onions and the lardons on top of the cheese mixture. Let rest for five minutes.

Using a pizza peel, place the *tarte* directly on the baking stone or baking sheet. (If you do not have a peel, you can place the *tarte* on a piece of parchment paper and carefully place it directly on the stone.) Bake *tarte* until the crust is golden brown. If onions and lardons are not browned, place the *tarte* under the broiler. Serve immediately.

PAIN D'ÉPICES

This spiced quick bread is my embellishment on the classic *pain d'épices* which is typically sweetened with honey alone. The addition of the molasses and the muscovado sugar adds a depth to this easy bread, but it also adds weight. As such, it is best baked in smaller loaf pans.

Makes three 3¼ inch x 5¾ inch loaves

    2 cups all-purpose flour
    1 cup bread flour
    ½ teaspoon kosher salt
    1½ teaspoons baking powder
    2 eggs, room temperature
    1 yolk, room temperature
    ½ cup muscovado sugar
    ½ cup light brown sugar
    ¼ cup unsulphured molasses (second molasses or blackstrap
    molasses), room temperature
    ½ cup quality honey, room temperature
    1 stick unsalted butter, room temperature
    2 teaspoons *quatre épices*
    1 teaspoon fresh orange zest
    1 teaspoon vanilla extract

Preheat oven to 350 degrees Fahrenheit. Spray the loaf pans with non-stick spray. Set aside.

In a bowl, combine the flours, salt, and baking powder. Set aside.

In the bowl of a standalone mixer, combine the eggs, sugars, honey, molasses, zest, butter, extract, and spices. Mix on low speed until combined. Add the dry ingredients to wet ingredients in the mixer bowl. Mix until combined.

Pour the batter into the prepared pans. Place the pans on a baking sheet and place it in the oven. Bake for about 3o minutes. Let cool in the loaf pans for a few minutes and then lift out of the pans and let loaves finish cooling on a wire rack.

Normandy

Venice

Alsace

Alsace

CHAPTER NINE

The Leads, the Dead Ends, the Cat Lady, and a Date

I LEAVE THE humble green of waving strangers and swaying cornfields for the elegant city with its serious inhabitants. Eight years ago today the lungs of my youngest announced her arrival with vigor. The thought of her makes me smile and a little sad. I watch the landscape stream by, thinking of my daughters, and allow the ever-present hand of divorce to touch my thoughts but remind myself that three years ago, I almost never saw them again.

A taxi takes me to the apartment in the 7th where I will stay for the week. The apartment is owned by Michael, an American lawyer I met through a mutual friend. Michael loves food and France as much as I do and has given me advice on purchasing French property. Knowing that he occasionally rents out his Paris place, I inquired as to the price and he responded with a trade: a free stay in exchange for culinary services of the same monetary value. It did not take me long to respond, "*Oui!*"

Xavier from the management company meets me at the property. Thin and reeking of cigarette smoke, he locates the key on his large key ring and leads me up to the very top floor. The apartment is a converted space once used for servant quarters and is the shape of an American attic and, although the room is accessible by full-sized doors, the ceiling is sloped and cuts into the wall. The windows jut out from the walls and extend over the descending roof, rather than laying flush as they do on the floors below. Newly remodeled with modern conveniences, the kitchen window provides a view of the very active Boulevard Saint-Germain below.

No one in my family has ever really understood my affinity for France, but in truth none of them had ever been. Notwithstanding this lack of first-hand knowledge, my father is not shy about denouncing my affection for the "socialist country," and he happily boycotted French fries when the opportunity arose. He rationalized that I might be drawn to France because my uncles fought in WWII and my great-uncle had died fighting in the Battle of the Bulge. Some friends' theories trended to more metaphysical explanations, that I must have had a past life in France. But for me the root of my passion did not need to be understood or explained; its existence is enough because when you love something or someone, you just know.

My dream of living in Paris prompted practical questions. How *does* one buy an apartment in Paris? How much would it cost? Can a foreigner purchase property in France? Obtain a French mortgage? How? My curiosity caused me to collect real-estate price sheets and "how to" articles from magazines I read over the years. I took notes from my conversations with Parisians, born or turned, and documented their "how-to" tips as well as what to avoid. The coalesced information was put into a file, and I added to my file each time I visited France. While I had no current *need* for the information, I likened the file to the accumulation of baby clothes and sentimental family treasures that my mother put away for me in a cedar chest long before I was married. She called it a "hope chest." I dubbed my French property research my "Paris Hope File." Now, I can use it.

The phrase, *"vous n'êtes pas encore arrivés, mais vous êtes plus proche qu'hier"* (you have not yet arrived but you are closer than yesterday) accurately describes my situation. I have five brokers, on two continents, looking for Parisian apartments. The French brokers are more promising than the American ones because they have an intimate knowledge of Paris and its arrondissements. In contrast, I have found that some of the American brokers (or agencies) are essentially middlemen going through French brokers and know very little of the apartments or the neighborhoods themselves.

In my research I learned that the keys to navigating *la Ville Lumière*, the City of Light, are a boat and a snail. The organization of the arrondissements (of which there are twenty) can be understood to be organized in a pattern that resembles an escargot shell. As Paris grew, the arrondissements spiraled up and outward, clockwise from the center of the city (the Louvre and the Jardins des Tuileries). The continuation of this escargot layout was, funnily, the result of "Plan B" when Napoleon III and Haussmann redesigned Paris in the mid-19th century, demolishing buildings and relocating hordes of Parisians in order to eliminate the unsanitary and haphazard medieval neighborhoods to create the well-laid-out municipality we see now. Their original plan placed the 13th to the west—where the 16th is now—rather than to the east, its current location. However, it is said that this proposed plan did not set well with the bourgeois on the west side due to the expression *se marier à la Mairie du 13e*, or "to be married in the 13th district" which referred to people living together out of wedlock. They refused to live in the "13th district" and to avoid this social calamity, the arrondissements were redrawn, thus creating the escargot shell which is flanked on either side by large parks: The Bois de Vincennes on the east side of Paris (the escargot's tail), and the Bois de Boulogne on the west by the 16th (the head).

Cutting through the escargot's shell is the Seine which meanders east to west like a frown. The Seine gives Paris its symbol, the *Fluctuat nec mergitur*—a floating, unsinkable boat in the center of a coat of arms—signifying Paris as a commercial center due to its central position on the Seine (which runs northwesterly from northeast Burgundy through Paris and then to Le Havre and into the English Channel). The Seine divides Paris into two riverbanks: basically, north of the Seine is *rive droite*, or Right Bank; south of the Seine, is *rive gauche*, or Left Bank. The implication that one bank is preferable to the other is without merit. In Paris, it is all about the arrondissement.

People are surprised when I tell them I am looking in the 16th, but I like the wide streets and Haussmanian buildings and the proximity to the Bois. Ten minutes from the city center, but just far enough to be peaceful, the 16th is predominately residential but with all the conveniences one would want.

"Lisa, the 16th is only old ladies with the shopping carts *partout*," JeF teases me.

JeF knows the area well and he is correct. The 16th is full of sharply dressed women of advanced years pulling their *marché* caddies behind them or walking their tiny dogs. It is referred to as the "Poodles and Pearls" arrondissement, I believe in reference to its former inhabitant, Maria Callas, who had both the poodle and the pearls and lived on Avenue Georges Mandel. However, there are just as many people walking about in sweatpants or jeans today as there are sharply dressed women, so I am not sure the title remains applicable.

Julien, one of my Parisian real estate brokers, specializes in the 16th. However, the place I planned to view was snapped up while I was in Alsace and the other apartment he has will not be available to view until September when the renters vacate. That does that.

Another Parisian real estate broker, Guillaume, is a referral from JeF. Guillaume not only returns my phone calls (unique for Parisian brokers I've found) but has some listings in the 16th to show me. We meet in front of the first building in the 16th. He is polite and gives me the property details. Two male brokers representing the seller join us. Only French is spoken but because it is conversational and not too fast, I understand it all.

We walk through the gate toward the modern building. It reminds me of the apartment complex my father first lived in when my parents divorced: large apartment building with long hallways, a communal feel, and a tennis court in the center. When we arrive at the apartment, the seller, an elderly woman, invites us in. The apartment is bright. The kitchen is tiny, painted in yellow, with a plank of wood attached to the kitchen wall that comes down to serve as a table or a cutting board. Next to the kitchen is *le salon* (the living room) with a park view, and next to that is *la chambre* (the bedroom). *La salle de bain* (the bathroom or "*sdb*") doubles as the laundry facilities and the compact space makes it necessary to keep the bath salts next to the laundry soap. The owner is sweet and I thank her, but the apartment is not for me. As we approach the sidewalk, the three brokers light up their cigarettes. I give them a polite "*non, merci*" and leave hoping the next showing is more promising.

The second showing Guillaume has arranged is in the north 16th, which I prefer to the south 16th. It is on Victor Hugo and boasts a view of the Étoile. I meet Guillaume on the sidewalk in front of the address and an entourage of men in nicely tailored suits soon join us. Today, a total of four men surround me in cigarette smoke. They give Guillaume instructions in French about locking and unlocking the door and hand him the key. The three of them remain on the sidewalk, smoking and chatting, while Guillaume and I enter the run-down building and climb the stairs to the seventh floor.

We reach the apartment, but the climb was only worth the exercise. The apartment is essentially a large room with a kitchen in the left corner. The bathroom is a little off-shoot of the room and very small. The apartment is dark because the windows are few and small. And, as for that "view" of the Étoile, it exists only if you stick your head through a twenty-by-twenty-inch square space and crane your neck to the left. The bedroom is a loft if you consider a plank of wood added on top of the living room with a staircase that resembles a ladder to be a loft. Truthfully, the apartment reminds me of the playhouse my father reworked from a laundry shed for my brother and me when we were small. I cannot wait to tell my brother that in the city of my dreams, I found an apartment with the set-up of our beloved playhouse. The three male brokers, still smoking on the sidewalk, await my assessment. I want to say: *"C'est une blague?"* I had to climb eight flights of stairs for that jail cell?" Instead I thank them for their time and explain that I need an apartment with more light.

Coming up empty in the 16th, I decide to expand my Paris search to include the Marais, the 6th, and the 7th and this results in an immediate viewing in the Marais. It was arranged through an American agency that has a relationship with a Parisian agency, known for its luxury listings, and I am hoping that there is no mistake as to the price. A young *parisienne* from the agency meets me at the building and introduces herself as Marianne and states in perfect English, "There is no elevator. The building also needs some work and needs to be painted."

There has been no price mistake. The work to which she referred is the large circular common stairway in the center of the building. We have a difference of opinion on what "some" constitutes, because the entire staircase is so severely sagging in the middle that it forces you to walk along the inside rail as you climb.

"Are you sure it is safe to walk on?" I ask.

"Yes. It's fine."

I do not find her words reassuring, and if her tone is to be believed, I think she questions the safety of the stairs, too. We knock at the door, which an unkempt woman slowly opens. Although polite, she is not eager to meet us and lets us into her space with hesitation. The woman has an affinity for cats and magazines and is well-stocked with both. Cats run from the drape rods to the stacks of literature lining the walls; allergic to cats, my eyes begin watering and itching. When a cat jumps from a cabinet top and brushes my head en route to its landing spot, it is time to go. My allergies are in a frenzy; my throat feels as if it is closing. The broker and I move quickly down the sagging stairs. She appears embarrassed by the conditions, and I tell her to call me if something with less work comes up and that I do need an elevator. After my pharmacy stop for an antihistamine, I return to the 7th where I lie down with a cold washcloth over my eyes as discouragement sets in.

Tight quarters, I anticipated. I also knew that the euro (especially, converted from the U.S. dollar) would buy a modest amount of *mètres carrés* in the arrondissements in which I am looking. But, putting aside the outlier hoarder, many of the Paris apartments are dark, in disrepair, have sagging floors or moisture problems. A closet converted into a bathroom. Lofts considered rooms. No elevators. Kitchens with hot plates. In truth, I have encountered these conditions in America when looking for apartments when I was in college, and I have heard that conditions are similar in New York, but here, in Paris, in the land of beauty and romance, where the view around every corner seems an architectural wonder and aesthetically pleasing, I did not expect the utter decay and disorder I have found inside. I can only image what the apartments looked like before Haussmann re-did everything. With the cafés a preferable environment to the dreary apartments, maybe that is how Paris became a café society. It certainly was not for the coffee.

I FIRST SPOKE with John King during my move-away case. He was referred to me by a mutual friend. John and his wife, Mary, are New Yorkers who moved to Paris with their children, put them in a French school, and made a business from their talent of buying and renovating apartments in central Paris and selling them turn-key to eager foreigners who wanted a place in Paris but were overwhelmed by the process. When we first spoke, my search was scattered because I had to be prepared for all situations. If I was allowed to move and put the girls in a French school, we needed a *quatre pièces*, and if not, we only needed a *pied-à-terre*. To make matters more complicated, I was also on rental lists in the event we were permitted to move but I could not find a suitable place to purchase before school started. The court's decision, and my promise to the girls, eliminated my "cover all the bases" approach. Having expanded my search outside the 16th, I reconnect with John to see if by chance they have anything or know someone who does. We make a *rendez-vous* to meet at their office in the 7th.

Their office is a short walk from my temporary home, but I still manage to pass it a few times before finding it. John and Mary sit at their desks, which occupy the center of the office. They greet me warmly and offer me a seat on the couch, which faces John's desk. Two female assistants bustle about in the background with paperwork. John turns his swivel chair to different positions to face various staff members as he poses questions or responds to theirs. Without missing a beat, he swivels his chair to face me on the couch and asks:

"How old are you?"

The question takes me off guard and I pause before I respond, "Um, 41."

"You live in L.A., right?" he continues.

"Yes."

"Can I set you up?"

"Um..."

I am not quite sure what to make of the question nor do the other females in the office, including Mary, who stops what she is doing to look at her husband.

"I have a friend who lives in the Palisades. Three kids. Divorced."

He swivels his chair to survey the females in the office to see if his friend, Mark, is considered "good-looking to women." The consensus is "yes," and with this endorsement, and hearing a little more about him, I agree that he may pass my number on to his friend. *Pourquoi-pas?* Stranger things have happened, and at least now we can move to my greater interest: Parisian property.

Mary and the assistants continue with their work while John provides me with a current view of what I can expect price-wise per *mètre carré* and how much I can reasonably expect to pay each year in taxes. He stops.

"What is your price range?"

I tell him. He is not impressed.

"Have you ever thought of buying a *péniche?* They are more reasonable."

A *péniche* is a boat docked alongside the Seine. People live on them. People who, unlike me, do not get sick on boats. Worse yet, the boats are cold in the winter and hot in the summer, and I only know this because a friend told me about his experience living on one with other students when he was in his early twenties.

"I get motion sickness."

"Oh, well, that does that," he says. Another subject exhausted. More chair swiveling. We move on. They do not have anything available at the moment, but they are renovating something nearby which may be of interest. John also knows an American selling her place down the street, and he will call her to see if we can look at it while Mary takes me to the renovation.

A quick ten-minute walk and Mary and I are at a modern building set amongst Haussmanian buildings. An elevator takes us three floors up to a gutted apartment with a large step-out balcony. I open the sliding glass balcony door, which faces north and offers a stunning panoramic view of central Paris and the Seine. Mary shows me the blueprints for the remodel. The spacious kitchen opens to *le salon,* and I envision hosting cooking classes and dinner parties in the space. But despite the visions of culinary possibilities, the price is too much and even if I could justify the number in my head, I could not have a business in my home where my children would be. An American couple did that, hosted private dinner parties out of their Parisian apartment for years before opening their own restaurant in the 1st, but with children, and living primarily on another continent, it does not seem a realistic option.

We return to the office. John got the *"oui"* to show me the American's apartment down the street on Rue de l'Université, the very street on which Julia Child lived. We walk to the apartment. It is a *quatre pièces* and it is *parfait.* Perfect location. Perfect building. Perfect *cuisine américaine.* Large bedrooms and laundry facilities not in a bathroom or kitchen. Not a thing has to be done to it. John says he will speak with the owner tonight and ask about a reduced price.

That evening I crunch the numbers over and over, before and after the euro conversion and with various mortgages. It would be a stretch with no cushion, and I would have to take out a bigger mort-gage than I want. I decide to sleep on it and when I do, I dream of the apartment on Julia Child's street, but when I wake, the numbers are the same. John tells me that the owner will not take less than asking price, and I tell him I will need to pass.

Of the twenty inquiries I made through explorimo.com this week, only two brokers replied. One broker cannot show the listing to me until after I have left Paris. The second broker, Claire, has a listing in the north 16th. However, I had inquired of so many properties, I cannot remember to which property she is referring until I re-read the property description:

> *3ème. dans un bel immeuble en pierre de taille...Il com-prend une entrée, un salon sur rue, une cuisine, une cham-bre avec salle de bains et espace dressing. Annexe une cave. Grâce à une bonne exposition, cet appartement est très ensoleillé.* (Fourth floor. Beautiful stone building with entry. Living room on the street. Bedroom with bath-room and dressing room. Wine cellar. Good location. The apartment is very bright.)

It is the *très ensoleillé* —very bright—which sets it apart. I reply to her email requesting to view the apartment as soon as possible. She responds that she will arrange to get the key for tomorrow. She asks for my requirements and says that she also has a listing in the 6th on Rue du Cherche-Midi. We make a *rendez-vous* to see it tomorrow after my Rungis visit. The possibility of two showings has restored my hope, and I get ready for dinner with Giovanni.

WE FIRST MET in the fall of 2006 at Fashion Week in Los Angeles. My friend Betsy took me as her guest to fashion designer Kevyn Hall's show. Betsy knew both Kevyn and the show's producer, and, as a result of these acquaintances, we were seated in the front row. When the show concluded, we mingled with other invitees. A tall man with a heavy Italian accent approached me wearing glasses and a dark suit. He introduced himself as Giovanni. He resembled a young Yves Saint Laurent and his low, melodic voice with its inflections at the end of each word sounded like a ballad. He asked for my number. I paused. My dating experience in the nine months since my separation had been trial and error with significant misses and the last thing I needed was a slick, sexy Italian to mess with my head and heart.

"I do not have anything to write with," I say.

"Just tell it to me. I'll remember. I am good with numbers."

I did not think he would remember. He did.

Our first dinner was a tennis match of conversation. We had the same interests, same values, similar hobbies, we were both Catholic, and we both possessed an innate curiosity about the world around us. We closed the restaurant and the night air was quiet as he walked me to my car. When he stopped and kissed me in the middle of the empty street, I felt the stars in the evening sky smile at me.

Six feet two inches tall with creamy pale skin, a chiseled face, and a thin frame that Michael Angelo could paint and Dolce & Gabanna could clothe, Giovanni was born in Pavia outside Milan. He worked for an international company that transferred him to its Los Angeles office. A good-looking nerd, my favorite type of man. He called me the next day.

"*Ciao, bella! Ça va?* Whata are youa doing?" He wove between the three languages once he learned I spoke some French.

"Baking a cake."

"Oooooo. Sounds-a gooda." His accent, even stronger over the telephone, made it difficult to understand him, particularly with the girls vocally demanding to know when the cake will be finished and if they can lick the mixer paddle. I said yes to his request for a second date and then he issued some instructions:

"Bring-a bathing suita, clothesa for dinner, and uh, exer-cizzea clothesa."

Slightly apprehensive at the undisclosed agenda, particularly since it involved a bathing suit, I had Plan B worked out in my head.

Two days later, I met him at his apartment with a bag of clothes in one hand and a piece of cake, boxed and tied with string, in the other. He drove me to the beach where he taught me how to roller-blade, and we watched the sun set over the western pink sky. Dinner was at a small family-owned Italian restaurant with ten tables and fresh homemade pasta. We returned to his apartment and talked in the hot tub until morning and our hands reached a state of prune-dom. After that second date, we spent all of our free time together (free time meaning when he did not work, and I was not with the girls). He called and texted me all the time. He was one of the smartest and most capable people I had ever met. Worldly and interesting. He spoke five languages. He could pack up himself, an apartment, and his exotic cars (a hobby) on a moment's notice and move anywhere in the world. He co-founded and ran a modeling agency in Milan and had his hand in a number of other businesses in Europe. All of this he did while working insane hours at his finance job, and most importantly, he called his parents in Italy daily. I had never met anyone like him.

"Planting the seedsa" was his mantra. While he lived for today, he believed in investing for the future: the investment of money. The investment of time. He was indeed a planner, and I drank in his experience and examples and I listened attentively when he recounted his experiences living in cities throughout the world. When he spoke of living in Paris, I thought of my Paris Hope File:

"I'm going to live there one day," I announced at dinner.

"I can see you therea," he replied. "What do you wanta to do there?"

"Maybe cook. Write a book. Write a book about cooking."

"You cannot make any real money writing booksa," he said. "But, you are a very good cook, *Principessa.*"

His advice did not deter me, but it did help manage my expectations.

In December we met in Paris for the holidays after we celebrated Christmas with our respective families, me in Los Angeles, and he in Milan. Giovanni took care of all the Paris plans and took me to his favorite restaurants and clubs where we danced until 4 a.m. On New Year's Eve, he made an exception to his no-drinking policy and we shared some Champagne. Bundled in heavy coats and scarves, we took to the holiday-festive Paris streets, exchanging wishes of *Bonne Année* with strangers. We took a selfie, years before they were *en vogue*, in Place Vendôme amidst the circle of jewelry stores and the holiday lights. It was the happiest I had been in a very long time.

Two weeks after our Paris vacation, his company unexpectedly transferred him to Sydney, Australia, to fix an ailing communications company. He was told it would be temporary, maybe nine months. We spoke every day and in the interim, he returned to Los Angeles and, while the girls were with their father for Spring Break, I flew to Sydney to visit him. His corporate apartment had an entire wall of glass in the living room overlooking the harbor and Sydney Opera House. It was a view we took advantage of in many ways.

Giovanni was eight years younger than I, but despite this age difference, it was he who taught me so much. About life. About myself. About forgiveness. About patience. I do not think I would have accepted my separation as I did had it not been for his guidance. I fell in love with him long before we went to Paris, but his move to Australia made our expiration date clear to us both. Like most things, I analogize relationships to food; both expire in their own time. Sometimes relationships last a person's lifetime. Most of the time, however, they expire sooner. Ours was seven months. We had no long-term future. The age and geography disparities were too great. The pragmatic separation was painful because neither of us really was ready to let go, but with the respectful passage of time, we were able to maintain a friendship. While I was in culinary school, Giovanni left his job and returned to Milan. He began working for an Italian family, handling their real estate holdings and developments in Paris. He now lives in Passy, in the north 16th.

EVENING, BUT STILL light, Giovanni and I *flânons*, taking the leisurely stroll one can *only* do in Paris, arm in arm, crossing the *ponts* and *rues* we explored four years before. A lifetime ago, it seems, yet he remains familiar to me. He visited me after my release from the Monaco hospital and over the years I have kept him abreast of my Paris apartment search and solicited his advice on several occasions. We catch each other up on the events in our respective lives over a meal. His chiseled cheeks are the same, and I study his green eyes. He is visibly happier and less stressed in Europe than he was in the States or Australia, and I always knew he would return to Europe. He belongs here.

After dinner, we meander back across the Seine. We watch the dinner cruises inch their way along the river, offering the dining passengers a completely different view of the city than ours above. We pass by the carousel across from the Trocadéro where the passengers are both young and old, big and small. As we continue toward Passy, arm in arm, I keep my eyes open for *à vendre* signs.

"*Et voila, Principessa!*" he says stopping in his tracks and out-stretching his arms toward a modern building with traces of orange and gray.

"*C'est moche!*" I exclaim.

It is, in fact, the ugliest building in Paris I have ever seen. He joins in my laughter and, while acknowledging that it is aesthetically challenged, he points out the promise of the ongoing remodeling, then adds:

"Leeezzza, don't judgea a booka by its cover."

We take the gauchely mirrored elevator to his apartment several floors up. He opens the door, and I see what he meant. Inside the disturbingly *moche* exterior, the apartment is large and beautifully arranged. *Le salon* faces northeast with an entire wall of glass and a full view of the City of Light and the Tour Eiffel. When I see the glass wall, I immediately know what he is thinking.

"Remind you of Sydney?" he asks and smiles at me with that beautifully shaped mouth.

"*Oui. Mais c'est mieux. C'est Paris,*" I say and return his smile.

We kiss in the center of that room with the *moche* exterior and, expired or not, we re-live that first spring night in Sydney, smudging the wall of glass and blurring the view of the Tower, which is bright behind my back and casting a dancing glow in the otherwise dark room. I forget about the for sale signs and the fact I am leaving Paris in a few days. I am present in this moment, this old, yet familiar love. Giovanni told me that once you have given a part of your heart to someone, it is always with them. Like so many other things he taught me, he was right about this too.

CHAPTER TEN

Places to Go; Tripe to See

IT IS DARK and cold when I meet my internet-arranged tour guide in front of A4, the fish and seafood pavilion, at Rungis Marché International, the world's largest wholesale market. Seven kilometers south of Paris, Rungis is something to see and has been on my list for some time because it is where everyone in the Parisian food industry—chefs, restaurants, markets, and caterers—buys their food (unless they grow or raise it privately). Previously located in the center of Paris at Les Halles, the lack of space and the congestion caused by the delivery trucks going in and out of Paris prompted the new location. The construction took over twenty years, and it was completed in March 1969, the month I was conceived. Rungis and I are basically the same age. This nugget of worthless trivia amuses me.

Nearly 4,500 acres, Rungis is organized like a city in and of itself. Named roads separate the food pavilions, which resemble large airplane hangars. There are stores, *brasseries*, and even an ice house. The majority of the pavilions are devoted to the sale of fresh fruits and vegetables. Five pavilions are devoted to animal proteins. My guide introduces himself, Michel, and provides me with a white paper gown and a Rungis baseball cap to wear. Sanitary, but by no means *chic*. As we walk toward A4, Michel begins: "One million tons of food arrives here every day by train, truck, and airplane," he reports. "Friday, busiest day."

Product suppliers, called wall-sellers, each have a designated space against the wall on either side of the pavilion to display their product while purchasers traverse the center aisle. Wall-sellers wear white jackets bearing their company logo on their backs. Each seller has a mobile phone in one hand and little receipt book in the other, and their hands are constantly busy, as are their mouths, as they take phone orders and shout them to their colleagues. Behind the seller's wall is an empty hallway with a series of large doors opening to the outside. As the wall-sellers sell, buyers and delivery trucks move products in and out by backing up directly against these doors. Wall-sellers arrive at about 10 p.m. to unload their product. Selling begins at 2 or 3 a.m. and concludes at 7 a.m.

"Here, you find everything. Fish from the north and south coasts (of France), Norway, Sweden, Scotland, Denmark, lobsters from South Africa and Brittany. Even the U.S.," Michel says and he touches a tagged fin demonstrating the accuracy of his comments.

Hundreds of clear-eyed, fresh fish sit in ice in stacked white polystyrene crates. While Michel talks to some familiar sellers, I photograph the large John Dory and the salmon from Norway. We then move from fish to meat.

The tripe pavilion is devoted to offals, animal parts that the French soak in milk overnight and then cook in a generous amount of butter and parsley, the parts most Americans do not eat in times of peace. Butchers work away in the back-rooms, separating the skin from the flesh, butchering feet from legs and tails from bodies. It is an assembly line of gray and pale pink parts. Clean. Detached. Surreal. Rows of cattle heads hang upside down on hooks. Innards and other parts are separated and organized in square, metal bins: tongues, ears, thymus glands, stomachs, brains, intestines, and kidneys. Every part is used. I photograph all of this too.

Next pavilion: beef, veal, and lamb. More parts. Less detached. Dozens of skinned, bloody carcasses hang on large meat hooks. Purchasers can buy the whole carcass, a side, or a quarter. It is not for the squeamish, and I think of my vegetarian, empathic mother who would cry and vomit at the sight. Many people would and, sadly, I feel numb to my surroundings due to a lack of sleep and the fact that culinary school desensitized me. Once you hacksaw through a lamb's backbone at 6 a.m. and then learn how to butcher the rest of the "product," separating the good fat from the bad, the flesh of once-living animals becomes a process and technique. My own numbness to this disturbs me and as I contemplate my lost humanity, a butcher in a white, blood-smeared jacket emerges amidst the now swinging carcasses and asks if I would like to share a *café*. Neither flattered, nor offended, I am taken aback as the circumstances are neither conducive to such a proposal nor inviting in the least. When I decline, he persists and, as a result, I laugh uncomfortably because now I don't know what else to do as I am trapped in between bloody carcasses and a flirty butcher who does not comprehend "*non*." Hearing my awkward laugh, my guide leaves his conversation with another guide and tells the butcher to buzz off in a stern way, apologizing profusely to me for the incident.

After a couple of hours' exploration and much note taking, we make our way to the poultry and game pavilion, which is without a doubt the coldest pavilion due to salmonella dangers. Everything from blue-footed chicken to suckling pig and goat meat is sold here, but the pavilion is so uncomfortably cold that my teeth are chattering and I am visibly shivering in my paper gown cover. Seeing this, my guide suggests a *café*.

As the sun rises, the selling concludes and the *brasseries* and restaurants in this self-contained food city begin to fill. Brasserie Les

Embruns is full of patrons, ninety-nine percent of whom are men, drinking beer, wine, and enjoying *steak frites*. I sit at a table in this underworld of food and have a *café* and a *tartine*, keeping a wary eye out for the flirtatious butcher. When we have finished, my guide walks me to the administration office and introduces me to several people he knows. They are eager to help me when they learn that I cook and provide me with all the paperwork I will need to obtain my own Rungis card so I may access the world's largest wholesale market any time I choose. This small offer of integration into the Rungis world of everything food, combined with my acquired information, makes the morning even more productive, butcher notwithstanding.

IN THE AFTERNOON I meet Claire on Rue du Cherche-Midi to view the apartment. Claire is in her early thirties, at most. She is filling in for her boss who is out of the office this week, and I think that circumstance is good luck for me because this younger associate seems eager to prove herself in her boss's absence. There are two apartments available in the same building. Claire shows me both. They are small, but not shockingly so, and while they are a definite step up from the others I have viewed this week, neither feels right for me. Noisy and lacking in character. It is a double *non*. As we leave, Claire's mobile rings. She tells me we are set for tomorrow morning at 11 a.m. to look at the *très ensoleillé* apartment in the 16th. When she gives me the address, I recognize the location immediately. The very sunny apartment is just around the corner from where I yelled profanities at the taxi driver last summer.

STUFFED AND BRAISED CHICKEN BREASTS

Serves 2

    2 chicken breasts, skinless and boneless
    A/N kosher salt
    A/N freshly ground black pepper
    2 portobello mushrooms
    3 tablespoons unsalted butter, divided
    2 teaspoons minced fresh sage
    $1/8$ cup dry white wine
    2 ounces Gruyère, sliced

Preheat the oven to 350 degrees Fahrenheit.

Prepare the chicken by removing the tenderloin. Set aside. Butterfly each chicken breast by making a slice horizontally in each breast. Do not cut all the way through. Lay the breast on a flat surface and it open like a book. Season with salt and pepper. Set aside.

Remove stems and gills of the mushrooms and discard. Rinse mushrooms with water and pat dry with paper towels. Slice the mushroom caps, about $1/8$ inch thick.

Place an ovenproof pan over a medium flame. Once the pan is hot, add two tablespoons of butter. When butter has melted, add the sage and toss to coat. Add sliced mushrooms and a pinch of salt. Toss in butter (the pan will look a little dry but do not worry because the moisture in the mushrooms will soon be released). Cook the mushrooms until they are brown and begin to stick slightly to the pan. Add wine and toss the mushrooms with a wooden spoon, scraping any mushroom fond off the bottom of the pan. Cook until all of the moisture from the pan has been cooked out. Remove the pan from the stove.

Add the cooked mushrooms to the right interior side of each butterflied chicken breast. Add cheese on top of the mushrooms. Fold the left side of the breast over, enclosing the mushrooms and cheese. Secure closed with a small skewer or a toothpick.

Place the empty pan back on the stove over a medium-high flame. Add 1 tablespoon of butter to pan. Once melted, add both breasts to the pan. Brown each side.

Place the pan in the oven and cook chicken until done (about 16 minutes). Using a large spoon, baste the chicken breasts with the cooking juices in the pan. Carefully remove the pan from the oven by using a dry kitchen towel or oven mitt. Let chicken sit for a few minutes. Remove toothpicks. Cut in half. Serve hot.

CHAPTER ELEVEN

Coup de Foudre

SATURDAY MORNING, June 25. Arriving an hour early, I sit at the corner *brasserie* and enjoy a *café* while observing the comings and goings of the neighborhood and verify the accuracy of the *très ensoleillé* description. A steady stream of Parisians make their way to the Monoprix or the nearby three *boulangeries* for their daily bread. Orders are taken at the *boucherie* for the herbed whole chickens, which are slowly rotating on spits in a large inset rotisserie case; the tantalizing aroma I can smell from here. The neighborhood produce markets have a steady stream of locals; fresh cherries from the Luberon are the dominant theme.

The morning sun shines directly on the Haussmannian building in which I am interested. The architect's name and the date,1929, are carved in the stone facade. Claire arrives and I leave the *brasserie* to join her. The entrance is comprised of two large glass doors covered with wrought iron bars. Claire punches in the door code on the keypad to the right of the doors and we enter a tiled lobby, which leads to a second set of double doors, wood with glass. We pass the *gardienne's* apartment and walk to the left to the three-person wooden elevator (generously sized for Parisian elevators) set in a double iron birdcage casing. A stone staircase spirals around it, and light from a stained-glass window set in the wall behind the elevator illuminates the entirety of the area, the stone walls spotted with a rainbow of colors. Claire and I take the elevator with its small black leather corner seat which the girls would love, and most certainly squabble over who gets to sit in it.

The *troisième étage* consists of three apartments. Claire walks to the center apartment with the large wooden door fit with a brass handle, and sunlight leaps out of the apartment into the hallway as she opens the door. *Très ensoleillé.* The foyer is partially blocked by an American-sized refrigerator, but when I look past the stainless steel appliance, *c'est le coup de foudre.* It is love at first sight.

A front apartment facing the street, the space boasts several large southeast-facing windows offering a view of the Parisian roof-tops. High ceilings, the walls have wooden trim which form large square panels (a detail which I love). *Deux pièces* (one bedroom). Both *le salon* and *la chambre* have floor-to-ceiling French doors which open in to step-out balconies fit with Haussmannian wrought-iron railings. The outdated kitchen, which looks to have been remodeled forty years ago, is very, very small, but *le salon* and *la chambre* are spacious and the latter has two inset bookshelves on either side of a curved inset enclave which is flanked by long mirrored closets with extra storage on top. The bedroom is large enough for two beds or one large one, which I envision to be the obvious choice for the next few years, given that both girls end up in my bed anyway. Next to *la chambre* is the *sdb* and a dressing area. The bathroom is aesthetically challenged with its muted avocado green color and a low plastic tub inches from a compact washing machine. On the opposite end, a wooden closet (eight feet long, two feet deep, and eight feet high) had been added to the dressing area. The large wooden addition over-whelms the space and towers over the small mirrored vanity built into the wall across from it.

Neither turn-key nor a complete fixer: good bones, lots of light, great location, a beautiful building, and in my price range. I liken the apartment to a solid man in an ill-tailored suit or with bad table manners, and I can do wonders with both. Instinctively, I know that this *très charmant* apartment is for us, and I envision the three of us in the space, laughing, eating, and the girls playing. My mind races with possibilities, and I try not to outwardly display my excitement for fear of losing all negotiating credibility (but knowing my lousy poker face, I am probably only fooling myself).

"I will think about it," I say to Claire. "I like how light it is, but the bathroom and kitchen need work."

"I understand," she says. "My mom is a designer. I am sure she could help you. You are the first person to see it. It was just listed. I have another showing today."

"Okay. I will think about it and let you know."

We shake hands, and I thank her for her time. I know that, even if the second group likes the apartment too, we would not get in a bidding war; the seller cannot take over asking price, and I was the first to see it. French law favors the buyer.

When I arrive back in the 7th, an email from Claire outlining the French procedure for purchasing property in France awaits me. The letter is consistent with the contents of my Hope File.

I consult the *notaire* website and email Michael and JeF to see if they have a *notaire* recommendation because the key is to get a good *notaire* or you will pay for it later. I call John and tell him about the property and the amount that I am thinking of offering. He does not know the 16th, but he thinks the discount is fair. He gives me the name of the *notaire* he uses and dictates to me the magic words for a French offer:

"Chère Madame,
Suite à ma visite de l'appartement situé [insert address] *troisième étage*
...., je veux faire une offre de [insert price] *euros, frais d'agence, inclus.*
Cette offre est valable jusqu'à vendredi premier juillet. Mon notaire est
[insert name and address of notaire]. "

We hang up and I begin typing my offer email to Claire, but my nervous, anxious hands quiver, causing me to type the same words repeatedly. My fingers are all thumbs. The automatic spell check is on overload. Even worse, I cannot even see the screen clearly because I am so anxious that I am actually have difficulty focusing. I stand up and pace the length of the apartment a few times to steady myself and re-focus. I re-read the offer and send it to Claire, blind-copying John. With nothing to do but wait, I walk in and out of the kitchen, not knowing what to do with my nervous energy. There is nothing to cook but aged goat cheese and bittersweet chocolate in the refrigerator. Chocolate nibbling commences and is interrupted: *cocorico.* I drop my French phone before I manage to answer. It is John.

"Hi!" I say with nervous enthusiasm. "Funny you should call, I *just* sent the offer. Thank you so much for helping me with this."

"I saw it," he says. "Lisa, you forgot something."

"I did? What?"

"You forgot the offer."

"What? Are you kidding?"

I re-read my email. He is right. *Une offre.... une offre* of what? My shaking hands must have accidentally deleted the offer amount in my revisions, and I am embarrassed by the stupidity of such an error.

"How ridiculous of me. Thank you for letting me know," I say and I immediately fix the omission and email Claire a corrected version.

With the offer out of my hands, twice, I am incapable of being still or confined to the small space. I throw on my running clothes and run from the 7th back to the apartment in the 16th just to observe the sun exposure in the early evening.

The *bistro* tables at the corner *brasserie* where I sat this morning are full of Parisians sipping their *apéros* and *bières*. Patrons, purchasing hosting gifts for Saturday night dinners, keep the florist busy. The two banks and two pharmacies at the Place maintain a steady, normal stream of business. *La boucherie, la boulangerie*, and the produce store on "my" street are patronized by Parisians marketing for their evening meal. The buildings across the street do not block the light; *l'appart* remains *très ensoleillé*.

A man unloads groceries from his car and walks into "my" building. A resident! I decide to ask him for the inside scoop.

"*Bonsoir Monsieur. Pardonnez-moi de vous déranger, mais j'ai regardé l'appartement libre et je voudrais savoir si le parking est difficile ici?*" I ask.

Now, I do not know why I asked him if parking is difficult as I neither have a car in France nor any plans of buying one any time soon. Still, I asked. He tells me that his wife is the *gardienne* and to ask her, pointing to the petite Portuguese woman emerging from the building calling out to a three-year-old running about in the lobby. She introduces herself as Maria. She tells me that street parking is not difficult to find, but the cars must be moved every so often. Thanking her, I excuse myself again for the interruption and I bid her a *bonne soirée*.

Filled with more enthusiasm than I can contain, I take the long way back to the 7th and detour up through the 8th to Parc Monceau, then back down to the 1st past the Bristol and Crillon where the valets tip their hats at me and one blows me a kiss, which I air-catch with my hand. Saturday evening and the Place de la Concorde is alive with movement and noise and I cross the Seine, returning to the 7th. Parisian summer days do not end until 9:30 or 10 p.m., yet, despite the lengthy day, the sun has less energy than I due to my apartment euphoria. Long after the sun has gone to bed, I am strategically packing my suitcase. I email Michael, thanking him for the trade, and I tell him where I will leave him a bottle of wine from Domaine Weinbach. A second email is sent to the rental company, thanking them for their assistance and telling them to please enjoy the cheese and remaining chocolate in the refrigerator. They are appreciative; the French like good food and do not waste it except for maybe a precise *brunoise* or *julienne* cut.

There is no email from Claire when I wake. Sunday morning and the streets are quiet. I run the empty paths along the Seine and across the bridge through the Trocadéro to look at the apartment one last time. The morning sun hits all windows of my potential nest. *Parfait!* With only minutes for a shower, I catch a taxi to CDG, which is its usual chaotic self, as it is every June. The line to board the plane is the length of a football field and I anxiously check my phone every five minutes for news from Claire. No news. Looking up from my phone, I see a familiar face.

"Sophia?" I call to a woman ahead of me in line.

"Lisa! What a surprise. How are you?" she asks.

"Good. What are you doing here? Were you in Paris?" I ask.

"No. I had to attend a funeral in Rome and my connection was in Paris."

Sophia is Alice's sister-in-law. I have not seen her for at least two years. We catch up about work and kids and I tell her about the apartment because I must share the news with someone as my excitement cannot be contained. She shares in my joy, knowing of my fondness for Paris.

I settle into my tiny aisle seat, but before I can even arrange my reading material, the woman to my left taps me on the arm: "I want to warn you that I am sick. I have had diarrhea all day, and I will probably have to get up a lot."

"TMI!" (too much information, as my girls would say) I think to myself, confident my face expresses my displeasure at the unnecessary revelation that my mouth will not acknowledge. She turns to the man to her left and voices her displeasure on a variety of topics. Ear plugs do not shield me from diarrhea-suffering woman in constant complaint mode, indicating this flight will be every bit of eleven hours.

THE MINUTE OUR plane meets the LAX tarmac I turn on my phone and find an email from Claire. The seller countered 10,000. euros. Without hesitation, I email Claire accepting the counter. Sophia, a few seats up, sees my face and gives me a thumbs up. Not even cranky, double-exit diarrhea woman can spoil this moment. Elation tempered with disbelief: after all this time, we are finally going to have that apartment in Paris.

CHAPTER TWELVE

Sauter Dans la Poêle et Prendre un Risque

BY THE TIME the taxi approaches our driveway, I have two offer letters from Claire — *LETTRE – PROPOSITION D'ACHAT* — one in English and the other in French. I also have a telephone message from Mark, my Los Angeles set-up, thanks to John. The offer letter restates my offer and the seller's counter-offer, but it also waives the "benefit of the Scrivener Act." Eliminating the Scrivener Act means I only have seven days from the date of signing the *promesse de vente ("PDV")* to change my mind about the purchase. Beyond that, if for some reason I cannot obtain financing (and cannot proceed with the purchase), I will lose my deposit, which is no small chunk of change. Mike did not say that "act fast" meant "all cash," and I did not agree to the waiver nor was that ever communicated. Risk, particularly after the financial debacle in 2008, is not in any fiber of my being. I call Claire.

"The seller will not sell the property with the condition. She does not want the property tied up for months if you cannot obtain financing. Although you have priority, there is an all-cash offer made by a Brazilian couple who saw it after you," she says.

It could be broker posturing, but based upon the location of the apartment and what is on the market, I doubt it. I tell Claire that my preference is based upon financial strategy rather than need, believing that this rationale will calm the seller's concern.

"The U.S. dollar is not very strong right now," I explain with fabricated confidence. "I am hoping to hedge the euro against the dollar and would prefer to finance a portion of the purchase price rather than make an all-cash purchase."

"Okay. I will tell her and tell you what she says," Claire says.

Summer in Los Angeles is a blend of controlled chaos and domestic bliss. The girls clamor for entertainment and playdates with friends until their day camp begins. In between entertaining children and shuffling them between their father's home and mine, there are my classes and writing that continue. Nothing ever stops and now everything continues with this *grand secret*, which I decide not to tell anyone about (unless necessary) because I don't want to jinx it and because, if the girls know, so, too, will their father, and I do not want him to know until it is done. I have had enough of his control over my circumstances.

While the girls sleep, France is awake. Sitting at my desk I consult my Hope File and outline the steps for the process ahead:

1. Make an offer √
2. Counters √
3. *Notaire* gathers info for *PDV*.
4. *Notaire* prepares power of attorney (if I cannot be present).
5. Wire 10% of purchase price to *notaire*.
6. *Notaire* prepares/finalizes *PDV*.
7. Sign *PDV*.
8. Set date for *la vente*. (Continue?)
9. Obtain financing from bank.
10. Obtain life insurance for mortgage.

11. Fund the balance. (*Notaire* holds money.)
12. Sign *la vente*. Get key from *notaire*.
13. Deed is prepared, recorded, and mailed to me
(months later).

My present goals are two: obtain financing approval as soon as possible, and get the seller to change her mind about the condition precedent (or at least delay the signing of the offer letter until I can get a bank commitment). The business day ends in France at 8 a.m. California time. The work week in France is thirty-five hours and overtime is not only discouraged, but is limited by the government should there be a desire to work harder. As such, all of my secret French business must be done before the girls wake and our morning routine begins.

I make inquiries with a few banks, including the Paris bank with whom I already have a relationship. The bank offers mortgages to non-residents and will finance a maximum of eighty percent of the property value for a maximum of twenty years. Once I've completed the necessary forms, I inquire about a bridge loan as well. I email John and thank him for both "the apartment guidance [and] the set up." I ask him if he has spoken with the *notaire* and what is the inside scoop regarding the condition precedent in France.

"I spoke with the *notaire*, and he is going to call you," he says. "You need to consider going forward without the 'clause suspensive.' French sellers do not like them."

The news is sobering.

The *notaire* requests the documents that he needs to begin preparation of the *PDV* including my passport, birth certificate, marriage certificate, divorce information, address and personal information, and my parents' names. He then unexpectedly requests similar information for my ex-husband, which thankfully I have. I don't know if, as a practical matter, the *notaire* has any influence over the seller through her *notaire*, but I convey the same U.S. dollar-euro concern to him that I relayed to Claire, thinking he may pass it on to her *notaire* and maybe he can talk her out of her present mindset if Claire cannot.

The next morning I awake to a flurry of transcontinental emails about the condition precedent. They are all bad news. The *notaire* makes no headway with the seller's *notaire*, assuming he tried. The seller remains "nervous" and insists on the waiver. In order to alleviate the seller's "nervousness," I change my approach and tell Claire that I can obtain a letter from my bank assuring her of my financial means for the purchase, or alternatively, that the seller's *notaire* can contact my bank to verify the sums. Claire believes both options are reasonable and promises to convey the information to the seller. Meanwhile, I turn my attention to a subject over which I have some control: transferring some funds from Los Angeles to my Paris account for the deposit. However, this, too, does not go smoothly as I cannot find the various pass codes I apparently need for online access. *Zut.*

After I drop the girls off at camp, I drive to the FedEx office to overnight the requested documents to the *notaire* and then proceed to the local branch of my bank so they can transfer money to Paris. My transfer request is met with a fee and a twist; I cannot do a straight transfer. I must first convert the U.S. dollars to euros because the Paris bank only set up a euro account, not a U.S. dollar account, and there cannot be more than one type of currency in an account. I need two separate Paris accounts, with separate account numbers, and double the access codes (which I have yet to receive). The entire scenario seems like lunacy and what I envisioned as a ten-minute process, takes hours.

The next day while I am making the girls breakfast before camp—chocolate chip pancakes—their favorite, Claire tells me that the seller is not interested in my options. Changing my approach again, I tell Claire to tell the seller that I am only requesting a mortgage of thirty percent of the purchase price and that I will agree to limit the contingency to an abbreviated period of time, such as three weeks from the date the *PDV* is signed. This way, the property is not tied up beyond that three-week period. Sounds rational to me. The girls clamor with their forks for more pancakes. I ladle pancake batter onto the griddle in between typing an email to the *notaire*. The business day in France is now over and we are late for camp. The kitchen floor is dotted with beige drops of batter, which are now hardened, hallow circles on the floor because Coco has lapped up the batter. I leave the mess for later. I pack up the kids and the dog and another package of documents to drop at the FedEx office to overnight to the *notaire*.

THE FIRST DAY of July interjects a noticeable breath of fresh air of competence and attention into my mortgage search. Her name is Sachi. Transferred from the Tokyo branch to the Paris branch, she is watching a colleague's files while he is on holiday. My file apparently went to him (where it sat). When I wake, there is an email from Sachi about my mortgage request. I call her immediately.

Sachi and I discuss the property details and the status of negotiations and within thirty minutes she emails me a quote with the pertinent information. Some of the terms are foreign to me, in the most literal sense, but I figure it out and tell her that the quote is acceptable. Sachi then requests a list of documents and the signed *PDV*. The documents are not a problem but a signed *PDV* poses the ultimate catch twenty-two. I do not want to sign even the offer *until* I get a bank commitment and the bank wants a signed *PDV* in order to move forward. I tell Sachi that the *PDV* is being worked on, but not finished yet. She agrees to work with the information she has.

Waking at 4 a.m. is out of character but becoming habitual. While the girls sleep, I make my cappuccino and go down the check-list of people and issues I must address via email before I take the girls to camp: bank, *notaire*, broker, the mortgage approval, the *PDV*, and the contingency. The seller rejected my latest creative solution and Claire re-sends me the *LETTRE – PROPOSITION D'ACHAT* and reminds me of the all-cash Brazilians. I used the Fourth of July holiday to buy time because if there is one thing the French respect, it is a holiday. With the holiday now over, both the seller and the *notaire* want me to sign off on the contingency. There is no more stalling. *La vente* has been set for September 30.

I telephone Sachi. She says that the approval itself does not appear to be a problem, but there is a concern whether the Paris bank can do all it needs to do to approve and fund the loan by September 30 due to *les grandes vacances*, the month of August, when all of France vacations. Sachi tells me that the mortgage approval and funding usually take six to eight weeks and that is about the time frame here. After much delay and worry, I go with my gut and put my faith in Sachi's non-French sensibilities to complete the paperwork in a timely manner and I sign the offer letter waiving the contingency. This will either be the bravest thing I have ever done or the dumbest, and I drive from camp straight to the FedEx office to over-night the original offer letter to Claire. *Les carottes sont cuites*. (What is done is done.)

IT HAS BEEN TWO weeks since I signed the offer waiving the condition precedent and still no mortgage approval from the bank. The *notaire* sends me a formal request for the deposit, and I make arrangements to have the funds transferred from my Paris euro account to the *notaire's* account. The *PDV* is scheduled to be signed in two days. Jessica, the *notaire's* assistant, prepares a power of attorney enabling the *notaire* to sign the *PDV* on my behalf. Her fluency in English streamlines the process, but between the gathering and sending to her the requested information, and reviewing both the English and French versions of the power of attorney, I spend an extraordinary amount of time reviewing and revising the documents. All of it done on very little sleep.

Then my inbox goes silent.

There is no corrected version of the power of attorney. There are no answers to my questions posed concerning the *notaire* fees or answer to my request to push *la vente* to October. There is no complete copy of the *PDV* or the *diagnostics* so I can review them. The combined silence from the bank and my *notaire* is unnerving. I email John asking for guidance.

"Ah, Summer in Paris! Everyone is out and out of it!" he replies. "Call me."

John offers to call the *notaire*. Which he does. My revisions to the power of attorney have been made and I sign it, have it notarized, and scan and send the documents to Jessica. I fax wire instructions to the Paris bank for the deposit to my *notaire*. After I drop the girls off at camp, I go to the FedEx office to overnight the original power of attorney to the *notaire*. It is just after 9 a.m. That night, I go to bed, exhausted by the fullness of my day. At 1 a.m. the phones wakes me; it is the Paris bank. They need verbal authorization to transfer funds to the *notaire*.

On July 21, I awake to the proposed *"Promesse Synallagmatique de Vente"*—the *PDV*—twenty-seven pages of legal French, replete with expressions and words I have never seen—*faculté de rétraction? le sat-urnisme?* The *PDV* is *the* critical document in the purchase of property in France, and it is included in and recorded with the deed. I call Samy, my French instructor, and ask if he can help me cull through the lengthy document. He agrees.

I began taking French lessons from Samy after the girls' father and I separated. He has since become a friend and helped translate all my medical records from the Monaco hospital for my insurance. Samy and I sit at the table in the backyard with espressos and the *PDV*. The *PDV* outlines the building's history and the apartment's chain of custody. It makes sure that the seller really owns it and the buyer can really buy it and there will be no other family member coming out of the woodwork claiming to own the property or trying to undo the sale.

It begins:

1. The seller was born in the 12th in 1922. She was widowed by her only husband and never re-married and there is no civil pact. The property belongs to the seller only.
2. The seller is not responsible for *vices cachés* (hidden defects).
3. The property is sold "as is." There is no guarantee of good condition of the *réseaux* (the networking of the water, electricity, gas, telephone and other things).
4. The seller must get inspections for asbestos, lead, elec-tricity, plumbing. The reports will become part of the *PDV*. These disclosures mean that the buyer takes it or leaves it. It is not customary to ask for a credit to repair items disclosed.
5. The seller confirms that her *syndic* charges are up to

date and paid for and if they are not the *syndic* can
stop the sale.

6. Seller confirms that there are no *procédures en cours*
(lawsuits pending).

After hours of going through the document and taking notes,
I am exhausted. Samy, too. I email the *notaire*, requesting the referenced and missing reports and the minutes of the last three *assemblée générale des copropriétaires* so I can gauge the *appel de fonds*. Then I
send a copy of the proposed *PDV* to Sachi. She replies immediately:

"This is good news...P.S. I checked your website and your
beautiful food. Amazing work...!"

As I stare at the stack of French documents and fees, all of
which make my head spin, the unexpected compliment could not
have come at a nicer time.

CÉLINE SITS AT my kitchen counter. I open a bottle of Bordeaux and pour us each *un verre de vin rouge*. One of my oldest and
dearest friends, Céline is staying with me for a few days while the girls
are with their father. Born and raised in France, she has lived in Paris,
New York City, Los Angeles, and now San Francisco. She has stories
of triumph and tragedy that no one can top, including surviving meningitis as a child and a viper bite in the south of France. She is one of
the most capable and talented people I have ever met and can expect
to meet in this lifetime. I ask her for her help reviewing the stack of
French documents from Jessica. The fact that she is a lawyer does not
hurt. I promise *foie gras* in return.

While I de-vein the *foie gras*, Céline begins with the electrical report, which reveals that the electrical is "out of code," but the
revelation is not very enlightening because we do not know what the

code requires. The *appels de fonds* from the last year are almost twice what I had been told. The minutes refer to unspecific emergency plumbing issues and planned roof work in which I will be expected to financially share. When I have finished adding the Armagnac to the liver, I cover it to let it marinate overnight and email Claire, requesting more information about the electrical, plumbing, and roof issues. Céline and I turn our attention to non-apartment conversation and our earthy Bordeaux.

TODAY IS SIGNIFICANT in two respects: the *PDV* is signed in Paris, and it is Ava's 10th birthday. As for the former, I do not know whether to celebrate or feel sick because, after three weeks, I still do not have loan approval. However, I refuse to think about the former in favor of the latter. Obtaining the "double digits," is a true childhood right of passage. At dinner, Julia and I give Ava her birthday gift. Julia is grinning from ear to ear in anticipation of her older sibling opening the small box, and when Ava cannot open it quickly enough, Julia offers her assistance. Ava declines. Inside the box is a white plastic travel wallet bearing the British flag and inside are three tickets to attend Shakespeare's *All's Well That Ends Well.* Ava pulls the tickets from the wallet, looking a bit perplexed.

"In seven days we will be watching it live at the Globe Theater. In London," I tell her. "We will fly to London first, then take the Chunnel to Paris to meet Uncle Jeff, Aunt Christine, and the cousins."

Ava, a Shakespeare enthusiast, has wide eyes filled with gratitude.

LES GRANDES VACANCES begins in five days. I lie supine in bed and watch the clock click to 3:00 a.m. Still no loan approval and France is on the slippery slope to a functional shut-down. The bank has all of the information they need, and I meet all the requirements. I mull over the terms of the loan itself, contemplating possible reasons for the delay beyond French slowness. Someone is uncomfortable with something and I recall a comment Sachi made earlier in the month when I was filling out the loan documents. She encouraged me to identify my work experience as a lawyer as well as a private chef. Maybe it is the modest chef income that is causing concern. I leave my bed to sit at my desk to review the mortgage paperwork.

Sachi set it up as a twenty-year mortgage, but I would prefer it to be shorter. I calculate the increase in monthly payments for a ten-year mortgage opposed to twenty years. Euros to U.S. dollars. The higher payments do not offend the French debt/income ratio. I could also reduce the requested mortgage amount and I calculate the payments for a smaller mortgage and confirm that I still meet the debt/income ratio. I email Sachi my thoughts and ask if I can modify my mortgage request. Two hours later, I awake to her reply:

"I have had the final credit committee with the manager regarding your mortgage application and we are happy to offer you [the requested mortgage]. Here is the new quote issued today, would you take a look and tell me if you could accept it?"

My anxious fingers are clumsy on a keyboard for a second time this summer, "I accept the quote."

One email unburdens thirty days of anxiety and sleepless nights. We make a *rendez-vous* for August 4 at her Champs-Élysées office to sign paperwork, and when I close my laptop, I sit down at the kitchen table in slight disbelief that this—Paris—is finally happening.

TERRINE DE FOIE GRAS
(*Foie gras* cooked in a terrine)

Makes 1 terrine

~3 pounds *foie gras* lobes (grade A-B), duck or goose
3 tablespoons port
1 tablespoon Armagnac
1 teaspoon nutmeg
1½ teaspoons kosher salt
½ teaspoon freshly ground white pepper

Rinse the *foie gras* with warm water and soak the liver in warm water for about one hour. This bath will bring the liver to room temperature, making it easier to work with and clean. Remove and drain on paper towels.

Once the liver has reached room temperature, separate the liver into two lobes and identify the central veins, one running on each lobe. Make an incision along the central vein and carefully remove the vein and the attached vein network by lifting it up with one hand, and disconnecting the veins from the liver with the other. The less you handle the liver, the better. Discard the veins.

In a bowl, combine the nutmeg, salt, pepper, Armagnac, and port. Add the seasoned alcohol to the liver. Wrap liver with plastic wrap and place in refrigerator overnight.

Preheat oven to 190 degrees Fahrenheit.

Remove liver from refrigerator. Let it come to room temperature (about 1 to 2 hours). Cut the liver into large pieces that will fit nicely into the terrine mold. The smooth sides of the liver exterior should be placed to form the exterior of the terrine. Press down *carefully* to expel air pockets.

Fold a kitchen towel and place it in a roasting pan. Place the mold on top of the towel. Add warm water (100 to 110 degrees Fahrenheit) to the roasting pan. (The water should come halfway up the side of the terrine.) Bake for about 90 minutes until the terrine reaches an internal temperature of 115 degrees Fahrenheit and there is a thin layer of melted fat on top. Remove from the oven.

Remove the mold from the roasting pan. Let rest at room temperature for two hours. Once cool, pour off the fat.

Cover the terrine with a press plate. Alternatively, cut a piece of cardboard to fit the terrine shape and wrap with aluminum foil. Place it on top of the cooked liver and place a slight weight (1 to 2 pounds) on top of the aluminum foil. Wrap in plastic wrap and place in the refrigerator for 24 hours.

Remove from the refrigerator. Remove the plastic wrap and plate (or weight). Use a knife warmed with hot water to release the liver from the sides of the mold. Remove from the mold. Remove the congealed fat. Tightly rewrap the terrine in clean plastic wrap. Refrigerate for one to two days before serving.

CHAPTER THIRTEEN

Pip Pip Cheerio and *Oh Là Là*

OUR TIME in London is filled with adventure, discovery, and frequent explosions of "pip pip cheerio" and old words made new with our recently acquired English accents. The girls fight jet lag and intently watch brightly clothed actors at the Globe while "my eyes smelled onions" as I watch them absorb the experience. We conquer the regal, obligatory sites, confirm that Ben is indeed big, and waltz through the Victoria and Albert museum where the girls are taken with the museum's collection of dresses spanning four centuries. They "oo" and "ah" at the dinosaur skeletons in the same-named gallery at the Natural History Museum and are delighted and intrigued by the mummies of all shapes and sizes, in gold and hand-painted coffins at the British Museum. As we leave, the girls stand on the stairs in front of the museum in the same place my grandfather was photographed. A second family photo, separated by fifty years and two generations, to hang next to his, maybe, in *l'appart*.

The "so cool underwater train" from London St. Pancras to Paris takes only about two hours and a quarter. The girls' enthusiasm wanes, however, because after twenty minutes of looking at grazing English cows the view turns to black, and their electronic devices are more interesting. The Chunnel is not all that.

Much to my father's dismay, my sister-in-law is also a Francophile and as a gift for her 40th birthday, my brother brings her and their two children to Paris. It is early evening when we meet them as planned at the fountain in Place Saint-Sulpice. The four kids enthusiastically greet one another and climb upon the large stone blocks in the Place, one thin-framed child per block, each dancing and making silly poses while Jeff snaps photographs. Christine and I chat about tomorrow's appointments. She is excited to be in on the secret and happy to help.

AFTER THE GIRLS have excavated the chocolate center out of their *pain au chocolat* with ceremonious dedication, we catch a taxi to *l'appart*. I tell them that we are looking at the apartment for a friend who wants my help with some renovations. The girls have seen me remodel two homes, so the fib is plausible but does not prevent Ava's inquiry: "What friend?"

"Jasmine," I respond.

"How are you going to cook in L.A. and fix up a place in Paris?" she continues.

"Your mother can do anything," I jest, secretly wondering how many years I have before she sees me for my weaknesses as well as my strengths.

She is not satisfied and, politely, yet rationally, presses further, "Yes, but Jasmine already has a place here."

"This one is an investment."

Ava eyes me suspiciously and lets the subject go for the moment, but I know she knows something is up and I have the sense that this kind of dialogue is a mere foreshadowing of upcoming years.

We ring for the *gardienne*. Maria is in the lobby watering the plants and when she sees us, she opens the door.

"*Bonjour Madame*," I say. "*On dit quoi?*" I ask the girls.

"*Bonjour Madame*," they say in unison, nervously tipping their heads downward in shy anticipation of French questions. We follow

Maria to the elevator. Julia is first to run through the doors and place her tiny bottom on the black leather-covered seat.

"This is so cool!" she exclaims.

Ava shimmies her bottom on the edge of the tiny seat, but Julia wants no part of sharing and a dispute arises between the two, just as I had predicted. Maria opens the apartment door for us and returns downstairs, leaving us in the empty space that looks larger than I remembered. There is a musty smell in the kitchen, which I deduce is a result of the stagnant brown water on the tiled floor in the vacant space where the dishwasher used to be. The kitchen is unattractive and even more dated-looking without the adornment of cooking supplies. One naked lightbulb hangs from the ceiling.

The girls walk with curiosity around *l'appart*. When I open the large French doors in *le salon*, the girls run to the balcony to join me, delighting in their ability to survey the life unfolding below their feet: the markets, the butcher, the florist, the teashop. Julia dangles her Barbie over the railing, swinging her by her hair and pointing with Barbie's toes to sights of interest. The doorbell rings. It is the *entrepreneur*, Raphael, the contractor who wrote the electricity report. Claire gave me his contact information, and I reasoned that his familiarity with the building, and the apartment in particular, makes him an ideal place to begin and not a difficult choice given my lack of connections.

We exchange introductions. Julia approaches Raphael and asks him a question. His blank, unresponsive stare makes it clear that he does not speak English. Raphael places his things on the kitchen counter. He explains the problem with the outlets and wiring and delineates three options. My limited French remodeling vocabulary necessitates pointing and charade-like hand gestures. Yet, despite the awkwardness of it all, it appears effective and we understand one another. He measures the length of the walls, and as he bends down, his lifted leg cuffs fully expose his expensive Italian loafers. Is that a French *entrepreneur* thing? Fancy shoes?

"*Et ici, aussi?*" He asks me, pointing to the space on the wall where I had proposed an additional switch, interrupting my speculation about his shoes.

"*Oui. Là,*" I say.

I am forced to imagine where I will place tables and furniture in order to anticipate my lighting needs. He says he will prepare a *devis* for the upgrades including installing new baseboards to hide the wires (which is less expensive than opening the walls to run the wires). After thirty minutes, he leaves.

Having gained their mother's appetite for travel and movement, the girls are now running throughout *l'appart* playing airplane. While they clear for take-off, I use two measuring tapes, one in centimeters and the other in inches, and measure the windows so I can have drapes made. Julia returns to the balcony, her toes protruding from underneath the wrought iron railing. As I watch her observing the neighborhood, I imagine the three of us dining in front of this window and sending the girls downstairs to the market across the street for forgotten ingredients while I cook.

"Look! It's him!" Julia shouts, pointing her Barbie toward the street below.

Ava and I join her. The "him" is Raphael, our *entrepreneur* with the expensive loafers, and he is opening the driver's door of a new black Mercedes sedan. "*Chaussures Chics,*" fancy shoes, indeed. I am going to thoroughly examine that *devis*.

We meet my brother and his family at the Jardin du Luxembourg in the 6th. The children love this park, with its zip line and sailboats in the fountains guaranteeing that my absence will not be an issue while I meet with Sachi.

It is humid and hot and feels like rain. I wear a long, sheer sheath dress with a half-slip underneath to cover the core parts. However, between the hot *métro* and my fast-paced walk down the crowded Champs-Élysées, my half-slip has shimmied up to the top of my hips, creating a curious, vulgar ring around my middle and revealing body parts I am trying to conceal. When I arrive at the bank I am sweating and disheveled. Needing to correct the wardrobe malfunction, I reorganize myself in the restroom before I meet Sachi.

Polite and engaging, Sachi is younger than I by more than a few years. I follow her to her office where she offers me a seat. The documents to my dream are meticulously arranged in a series of piles on her desk. She walks me through the *demande de crédit immobilier* where I must initial the bottom of each page and write *"certifié exact et sincère"* before my signature with the date of execution on the final page.

We move to the topic of life insurance, required of all mortgagees (so if I die before the mortgage has been paid, the insurance company will pay off the mortgage and the girls keep *l'appart*). In a matter-of-fact tone, Sachi tells me that I am required to go with the bank's choice and if I am not approved, I do not get the mortgage. My heart races at the suggestion of another issue in this process and, while Sachi continues dispensing instructions for completing the application, I am distracted, "What if I am not approved for insurance? What about that near-death experience? I could not obtain health insurance in the States for years!" My anxious internal dialogue is stopped only by an even more worrisome comment: "You will receive an official offer of mortgage called a mortgage request," Sachi says.

Attendez. Comment?! My mind reels with confusion. I only have an "unofficial" mortgage offer? I have to wait for an *official* offer? The last month was just practice? She continues, "Once you receive the official offer you have eleven days to accept or reject it. It is what French law requires. You cannot sign it sooner," Sachi explains. "Once we receive insurance approval, it is a matter of funding the escrow in time."

Stupidly, I thought that coming to sign papers meant we are approaching the end of this process; instead, I sign one set and I gain two more things to worry about. Sachi turns the conversation to cooking while she staples and reorganizes the document piles. I am grateful for the distraction, and with French law and procedure being what they are, there is no sense in worrying about it anyway. We discuss our favorite preparations and compare our favorite Parisian *bistros*. She tells me that she printed some of the *recettes* from my blog and intends to make them. Flattered, I ask her to tell me how they turn out and thank her for her time and bid her a *bonne journée*.

In the morning Sachi faxes me the English and French versions of the application for life insurance. Once complete, the hotel staff faxes both copies and mails the originals to Sachi. There is nothing more for me to do; I can leave Paris with a quiet mind. We check out of the hotel and Ava, Julia, and I journey south to our summer tradition of friends, *piscine de rosé*, and the Côte d'Azur.

CHAPTER FOURTEEN

Les Grandes Vacances

IT IS EARLY EVENING when we check into the Brise Marine. My senses are inundated with the familiar scent of lavender and the steady background hum of the cicadas. The humid air feels dewy on my skin. Summers in Provence are unhurried and peaceful, and I am immediately filled with a sense of calm. Tonight is the traditional *La Grande Nuit Vénitienne*, the one Saturday night every August when Saint-Jean becomes a Venetian Carnival (time of year notwithstanding). Participants parade throughout the tiny village dressed in full Renaissance regalia and elaborate masks, while troupes of dancers and local bands fill the evening air with music and movement. We walk from the hotel into the heart of the village for dinner. Vendors have already set up their carts, selling disposable toys and sugary snacks; the aroma of the warm, candied almonds greets me before the cart itself is evident.

After dinner each girl fills a small paper sack with her candy selections. Both receive two cans of silly string, the color of their choice, and a Venetian-style mask. We stand on the sidewalk, elbow to elbow with familiar and unfamiliar faces, and watch the parade: larger, louder, and grander than the year before. At its conclusion, the village-wide silly string war ensues, and while its inception and purpose were never understood by me, it is enjoyed by young and old alike, and no one escapes its gooey web. Covered in pink and blue strands, we return to our hotel room where we watch *feux d'artifice* from our balcony. Launched from an anchored boat, they decorate the sky with their colorful bursts, revealing the boats that have gone to bed for the evening as they cascade into the water below. Exhausted from the journey, the girls shed their silly string-laden clothes and give in to sleep, in which I soon join them.

At Paloma, Agat leads us to the second row of *matelas* on the right side of the dock, which enjoys the longest sun (right up to *apéro* time, in fact). We have moved up in the Paloma world. The waterscape is the same, as the same yachts seem to be anchored in the exact spot they were last summer. Occasionally the yacht dwellers solicit Paloma by telephoning the number written on the restaurant roof, and the tiny boat collects them and brings them ashore. Not an early crowd, but by 11:30 a.m., the dock is overrun with children jumping and diving into the water and the careful, and steady, unloading of boat passengers coming to Paloma for *déjeuner*.

Much to the girls' delight, I planned nothing for our time in Saint-Jean. No museums. No trains. Their tanned tiny frames walk about the shore, plastic buckets in hand, searching for crabs hiding in the rocks, and when that adventure is over and the two crabs are returned to their homes, they take a promenade around the edge of the peninsula to "explore" and return to Paloma only to sit on the dock and enjoy ice cream, *chocolat* and *violette* being the preferred flavors. As the afternoon sun melts the dairy treat faster than they can lick, my head is preoccupied with "what's next," and I can only unburden myself of this planning by creating a to-do list for *la vente*:

1. Track market /Convert U.S. dollars to euros.
2. Receive official offer letter from bank.
3. Sign and return official offer letter at precise time

(not before).

4. Fund escrow.

5. Obtain homeowner's insurance (fire, theft, flood).

6. Obtain/review *devis* for electricity and organize start date.

7. Make list of things for my trip in October (what to buy, set up, organize workers).

8. Email Maria.

9. Research utilities (gas, electricity, internet, phone). Set up utilities in Paris.

10. Make drapes (take to Paris).

11. Research how to ship furniture.

12. Organize furniture and figure out what to ship to Paris.

13. Research where to buy appliances in Paris (oven, stove, *frigo*, hood). Purchase. Buy plane ticket for September 30. Progress, even if number seven is to make another to-do list.

Perusing *Elle Décor* and *Côte Sud* magazines, I rip out pages with enviable decorating ideas and sources. My breath is taken away when I cross a full-page advertisement for an oven and stove combination: black enamel with brass fittings, the burners set in stainless steel. The work of art would be perfect for *l'appart*, and I envision myself cooking on it. An unrealistic choice, but I tear this page too and paste it in my Paris *appart* planner, far more satisfying than a Hope File.

THE FRENCH ALPS in the southeastern corner of France are topped with picturesque "hanging" villages (sometimes referred to as "perched" villages) and so-named because the village center—usually consisting of a church, *boulangerie*, and a small market or grocery store—lies at the top of the hill while residences and communal buildings flow out and downward from there. Berre-les-Alpes is such a hanging village, and it is where Alice's parents reside.

As fond as the girls are of Paloma, they adore coming to Berre where they have freedom to roam the rolling hills, weave through lavender bushes buzzing with bees, and run around olive trees with the background barnyard sounds of the neighbor's donkeys and the horses. Alice's father built a small playhouse and a swing in the enclosed "forest" where the children pass hours at a time. Today they are tracking wild boars (which actually do run unfettered in the Alps and are hunted for their meat). On the back patio, Alice and I occasionally catch glances of their tracking procession on the dirt paths and their exuberant proclamations announcing the discovery of tracks of the wildlife they seek. The girls have plucked wildflowers and fashioned them into wreaths for their heads. Crowned in wildflowers, Julia blows on a dandelion bouquet clutched in her hands. The white fibers blow back in her face, causing her to sneeze repeatedly; her little nose is as red as a *provençal* tomato.

While they hunt and sneeze, Alice and I prepare dinner from the bounty she and her mother sourced at the Contes co-operative early this morning. Contes lies halfway up the hill to Berre and once a week, around the time the roosters crow, local growers gather in a large one-room barn-looking building to sell food products they have grown or raised or *fait maison* (made at home), such as jam or desserts. Without contemplation, it is the most flavorful food I have ever tasted because the fruits and vegetables have been left to fully ripen on the vine or branch in the sun and it is this patience and proximity that makes a world of difference. Alice places the sausages on the grill, the meat bright pink. We braise *provençal* zucchini, with its decorated interior flesh, markings absent in summer squash in the States, and serve it as a side. The melons, so fragrant that the sweet smell escapes when my knife pierces its flesh. Evening, but still quite light, we dine outside on the patio, which overlooks the rolling hills. Alice's mother treats us with an apricot tart she prepared. She lightly dusted the unbaked crust with powdered sugar before adding the fresh apricots. This technique, too, like so many others I have gleaned from her cooking over the years, is one I will adopt in my own kitchen.

Darkness sets in as we depart Berre, and I carefully negotiate our much-too-large rental car down the slender mountain road and hairpin turns. Back to our hotel, W9s from Sachi and a *devis* from *Chaussures Chics* await me, both of which I review after I have tucked the girls into bed. Mark (my set-up from John) left me a voicemail message confirming our tentative dinner plans in Los Angeles. We have managed to speak on the phone and our conversations proceed with ease. There is no shortage of discussion topics, but with conflicting custody schedules, dinner plans are challenging. Tentative is the closest we have gotten to an actual date.

Saint-Jean mornings begin early for me. While the girls continue in their summer slumber, I sit at the table on the balcony observing the sun shining on the water with Beaulieu and Monaco behind, appreciative that the familiar view is from where I am, with my daughters, and not a hospital bed. I pull out of my suitcase a draft manuscript of a book I began in culinary school. A manual on food, cooking techniques, recipes, and the integration of that knowledge into daily life. Truthfully, it should be broken down into four books and the magnitude of the project has pushed me into a writer's paralysis. Setting the binder aside, I decide to assemble a smaller, more approachable cookbook using some family recipes and others from my culinary adventures. And, as my beauties continue to sleep, I outline the concept: fifty-two recipes, one per week, correlating to the seasons and holidays throughout the year. Each recipe turning a common ingredient (i.e., day-old bread or canned tuna) into something unexpected by using a unique technique or unexpected flavor pairing.

By 11 a.m. we are back on the Paloma *matelas* and the children are wading in the gentle rushing and retreating waves. Alice sits to my left reading *Paris Match* as I outline my smaller, immediate book and assemble recipes on my iPad.

"What are you working on?" she asks.

"A book."

"Here? Now?"

"Yep."

"God, you are boring," she laughs. "I'm going in the water."

And with that, my beautiful friend sets her gossip magazine aside and takes off into the azure blue while I continue to type, not minding her teasing and not feeling boring or bored at all.

OUR LAST NIGHT in Saint-Jean, the girls and I dine on the beach under the stars at Plage de Passable, the other private beach in Saint-Jean, with Diane. Diane, in her early twenties, lives in Nice and is studying to be a teacher. She has watched the girls on occasion while I took a run, teaching them a little French. They adore her. My friend Chloé and her two children, having just arrived from Los Angeles and staying in Antibes, join us as well. We celebrate the beginning of their vacation and the end of ours. Chloé's son, smitten with pretty Diane, practices his high school French on her with admiration in his eyes and a quiver in his voice, while the three girls chatter amongst themselves at the other end of the table. Chloé and I engage in a fair dose of girl talk with some *provençal rosé* while enjoying the slightly sweet white fish caught nearby. Well-traveled and with a husband who received an international educational experience in his youth, she was able to see the benefit in the three of us leaving Los Angeles for Paris. She was one of the first to convey her condolences when the judge denied my move request.

"Along those lines, I have something to tell you," I say, revealing the Paris apartment secret, which seems more and more of a reality.

She is thrilled for us. "Lisa, even in small doses, Paris will be an experience they will carry with them the rest of their lives," she tells me.

"I think so. I hope so," I say as my thoughts drift to what the future may bring.

PISSALADIÈRE

This is a classic recipe from Nice. I use puff pastry because it is easy to keep the dough on-hand in the freezer. I think it is interesting to compare this with the *tarte flambée* from Alsace. Both are great reflections of the tastes and bounty of the two regions.

Serves 6 to 8

> 2 tablespoons olive oil
> 20 ounces sweet onions (i.e., Vidalia), sliced ¼ inch slices
> 1 fresh sprig of thyme, stripped
> 2 pinches kosher salt
> $^1/_3$ cup white wine
> 14 *olives de Nice* (or black oil-cured olives with the pits removed and olives halved)
> 12 anchovy fillets packed in oil
> 1 sheet puff pastry, defrosted
> A/N fresh French thyme sprigs

Preheat oven to 400 degrees Fahrenheit.

Place an ovenproof pan over a medium-high flame. Once hot, add olive oil. Add sliced onions, thyme, and salt. Cook onions, tossing occasionally, until they are translucent and begin to stick to the bottom of the pan. This takes about 25 minutes. Add wine and cook until *au sec* (when all of the liquid has been cooked out of the pan). This take about 5 minutes. Remove pan from heat. (This can be done in advance and cooled.)

On a lightly floured surface, use a rolling pin to roll out puff pastry sheet until thin. Evenly spread onions and olives over the dough stopping ¾ inch from the edge.

Bake for about 20 minutes on a pizza stone or a baking sheet until dough is puffed and deep golden brown. Garnish with fresh anchovy fillets and fresh thyme sprigs in a visually attractive way. *Pissaladière* can be served warm or at room temperature.

PAN BAGNAT

Serves 2

Sandwich
2 quality individual baguettes or sandwich rolls
2 tablespoons black tapenade
1 beautiful tomato, sliced
2 hard-boiled eggs, sliced
1 handful of mesclun
1 can tuna packed in olive oil, drained, oil reserved
½ cup rough chopped fresh sweet basil
1 small red onion, thinly sliced
3 radishes, thinly sliced

Dressing
~6 tablespoons quality olive oil
2 tablespoons red wine vinegar
2 teaspoons *sel de Guérande* (or sea salt)
1 garlic clove, minced
2 teaspoons Dijon mustard
A/N *piment d'espelette*

To make the dressing, drain the oil from the tuna and pour the oil into a bowl. You will probably have 1 tablespoon of oil. Supplement with additional olive oil until you have 6 tablespoons. Add the vinegar, salt, garlic, *piment*, and mustard. Whisk well to achieve an emulsion.

In a second bowl, combine the mesclun, tuna, onions, basil, and radishes. Slowly incorporate ⅓ to ½ of the dressing into the tuna mixture. You will not use all of the dressing. Reserve.

Slice the baguette in half lengthwise. Add the tapenade to one interior side of the bread. On the other interior half, spread the sliced tomatoes and eggs. Add the sandwich filling. Drizzle with extra dressing to taste.

CHAPTER FIFTEEN

Early Mornings, Late Nights,
and a Few Fires

VACATION IS QUICKLY replaced with the rhythm of daily life. Back in Los Angeles, there is only time to shop for school uniforms and supplies before the girls spend Labor Day weekend with their father. At night, the cicadas' song is noticeably absent and substituted with a persistent owl and the occasional coyote pack enjoying their communal snack.

It takes three weeks to receive the life insurance approval. The nine pages of legal French come in triplicate and, according to Sachi, there is a particular way in which to sign all three copies and if it is done incorrectly, the papers must be re-issued. It sounds like an unfair punishment for an accidental error and the very thought of a re-do makes me shudder. Sachi carefully walks me through the papers over the phone.

My night-time angst is now efficiently focused on the "official" offer letter. Sachi relays that the paperwork is with the "engagement service department" and that I should receive it within the week while she is on vacation. *Comment? Vacances?* Although deserving of a vacation, Sachi's absence from the bank selfishly petrifies me, particularly with the official offer letter still unseen.

And, indeed, the week Sachi vacations, nothing happens. There is no official offer letter nor any news at all. When Sachi returns from vacation, she tries to reassure me, "The offer letter should be ready this week," she says.

But her representation is *not* reassuring. It *should* be in my hand. What happened to it arriving while she was on vacation? Calculating the eleven-day cool-off time, I email her: "Will this be enough time?"

Sachi does not respond. Ten minutes later, she calls me.

"The offer letter was sent today," she says. "You must tell me *immediately* when you get it so we can work together to make it on time before September 30," she says in a no-nonsense, firm tone, a stark contrast to her habitually calm voice.

September 9 comes and goes. So does the 10th. And the 11th. And the 12th. Still no official offer letter. The clock is ticking, and *la vente* is in roughly two weeks. The busy days advance into sleepless nights. When I tell Sachi that I *still* have yet to receive the offer letter, she replies with a tracking number. And, after I drop the girls off at school, I return to the house to wait for DHL. Six weeks after my meeting with Sachi in her office, I finally hold the *official* offer letter in my hand.

My calculations put the eleven-day period at the 24th and, based upon my French bank experience thus far, it seems unlikely the remaining paperwork and funding will be done by the 30th. On the phone, Sachi clarifies that I may sign the offer letter any time, but I have to wait to send it back eleven days after I receive it, which she calculates as 17th. *Comment?* Her calculation does not make any sense to me, but if that is the date the bank is using, and it is more favorable to me, fine with me. Sachi reviews my signed acceptance (ensuring no errors necessitating re-issues) and emails my manager at the Paris bank requesting the conversion and wire of the balance of my portion to my *notaire*.

The telephone wakes me. It is the director of the Paris bank with two witnesses on the telephone to confirm my request. Questions are asked and answered. I orally authorize the conversion and transfer. The daily rate is confirmed, better than yesterday, and I just saved five mortgage payments. Five minutes later, the director calls again. The favorable rate could not be locked in because the "euro is volatile." Ultimately, I save only three payments.

Triple checking that the papers are in order, on the 17th I overnight the papers to a particular address outside Paris, careful to copy and document everything, including the post-mark. With everything on my end done, I buy my plane ticket from Los Angeles to Paris, arriving on September 30 and returning to Los Angeles on Wednesday October 12. *La vente* weekend falls on a "fifth" weekend with a "first" weekend following; the girls will be with their father two weekends in a row and although this court-imposed calendaring is something that I generally dislike, this time the extra alone time works in my favor. My plane will land at CDG at 2:30 p.m., giving me roughly a fifteen-minute cushion after CDG and traffic to make it to the 1st in time to sign. I modify my to-do list for my arrival in Paris:

1. *Notaire's* office at 4 pm. Sign. Get key.
2. Obtain property insurance (*vol, incendie, dégâts des eaux*).
3. Change *les serrures* (locks). Find *un bon serrurier* (a good locksmith).
4. *Appel de fonds*. Due when? Follow-up.
5. Give my contact information to the *gardienne* with envelopes to forward mail and instructions for deliveries.
6. Meet with *Chaussures Chics*. Get electrical done. Begin kitchen remodel, floors, and painting.

7. Purchase necessities, including appliances, bed, table. Arrange delivery.

My list is getting shorter.

The following day my *notaire* unilaterally switches *la vente* from the 30th to the 28th because of his unavailability. *Comment?* The impoliteness is appalling, not to mention I already purchased my unchangeable plane ticket and my bank needs more time, not less. While I protest the change, he, in turn, sends me more French legal documents to review and return. The next day, *la vente* is back on for the 30th due to the unavailability of the seller's *notaire* on the 28th. I do not even bother to question the legitimacy of my *notaire's* sudden availability on the original date.

IN THE LAST WEEK leading up to *la vente*, every day brings with it formalities and paperwork that I did not know existed: my *notaire* must make a legal request to my bank for a funds release; my bank must draft a declaration (the purpose still unclear to me); and now, my *notaire* needs a declaration from my Los Angeles bank, something about proof of the origin of my funds used for the purchase.

Two days before my arrival in Paris and I awake at 4 a.m. to check my email, expecting news of the loan funding. Instead, there are several urgent emails from Jessica. The *syndic* of my future building contacted her in an attempt to prevent *la vente*, alleging that there is damage to the apartment below mine due to my bathroom's "water tightness," which I interpret to mean there is or was a water leak. She outlines four scenarios, which would allow the sale to proceed:

1. Seller proves that she tendered a claim to insurance and that they covered the damage and I am substituted for her;

2. Seller did not tender a claim and will have to do it before signing and if the insurance does not cover it;

3. Seller does not tender it to her insurance company and she has to give my *notaire* an estimate of work that has to be done and this amount will be kept in escrow for the repairs; or

4. I decide to pay for the repair of any leak.

My head is spinning; my heart, thumping. Is this really happening the day before I get on a plane to sign the papers? Pacing my bedroom, I re-read her email, which is written in English, but not a smooth translation. This is the first time I ever heard that there was a leak in the bathroom. I call Jessica and tell her that numbers one and four are a definite "*non*." Number two provides no comfort because there is no protection for me if the insurance declines the tender (and who knows how long that decision would take). Now that the surprise has worn off, I am just angry and I email Claire and demand that the seller give me: (1) proof of insurance for the time the leak occurred; and (2) agree to leave 10,000 euros in the escrow to cover any damages. While I wait for news from Claire or Jessica regarding the "water tightness," the *notaire* emails me with a new issue: he does not need proof of origin of the funds, he needs a declaration from the Los Angeles branch that the funds transferred into my Paris account came from my Los Angeles account. *Comment?* With the end of the French business day rapidly approaching, I have no time to question the levels of stupidity of these requests, and I contact the local branch.

SEPTEMBER 29. At 1 a.m., while I am packing for Paris, Jessica confirms that she received the *facture* (receipt) from the plumber.

"Everything has been repaired and there is no leak anymore," she says. "The *notaire* has authorized the sale to proceed."

An hour later, the bank's transfer has been scheduled. Everything seems to have come together and if there is another problem or a missing document, I will not know about it until I arrive in Paris.

The three of us sit at the breakfast table before school. Julia is picking the strawberries from her breakfast risotto and eating them one by one with her fingers.

"I want to tell you girls something. You know that apartment in Paris we saw, the one I told you I was helping Jasmine with?" "Yeah," said Julia

"Uh, huh," follows Ava, as she puts another spoon of sweetened rice in her mouth.

"'Yeah' is not a word. Anyway, the apartment is not for Jasmine; I bought it for us. I am going to Paris to sign the papers and get the keys."

"Huh?" Julia questions.

"Knew it!" Ava says, smug with her prediction.

"Are we moving? I thought we are going to stay here for school?" Julia asks.

"No. We are not moving. Everything will stay the same, except we can stay in Paris in the summer and when you have vacations. Paris will be part-time."

"You mean I can eat a chocolate croissant in my own bed? We will have two houses?"

"Well, technically yes, but no you are not eating in bed..."

"I already figured it out, you know," Ava jumps in.

"Listen, I did not tell you before because I did not want to get your hopes up if something happened, and I did not want others to know and I did not want to ask you girls to keep a secret. I hope you understand. And guess what? I am going to fix it up—like I did this place—so next summer we will have a nice place to stay. That is why the guy with the fancy car was there; he is a contractor."

"That is really cool, Mom. I wish we could go with you today," says Ava

"Me too."

Extra big hugs are exchanged when I drop the girls off at school. They ask me to say "hello" to our new place. A taxi takes me and my three suitcases to LAX. My carry-on is filled with my laptop and all the legal paperwork and documentation I could possibly need. The large suitcases have clothes, bedding for my nights on the floor, and necessities like a clock, an iPod for music, and ground Italian coffee, all of it packed with the emotional satisfaction that can only be realized after a journey of years.

CHAPTER SIXTEEN

There Is No Place Like Home

WHEN I WAS a child, I would accompany my father to the little airport in Big Bear. Flying was his hobby, and I pretended to be his co-pilot. The bigger the dip, the more unknown the location, the happier I was. When he chatted with his friends or worked in the hangar, I would lie on the hood of the old Oldsmobile—the olive green gas-guzzling machine, big as a building, that he bought second-hand at auction and deemed the "airport car"—and I watched the planes fly over my head. Guessing their destinations, I imagined the pilot's fantastic adventures that were sure to follow, limited only by her need to refuel.

I think of those days as today's plane, much larger than anything my father flew, lands on Paris soil. I think of the difference between my childhood home and Paris. Scanning the attic of my mind, I try to recall what it felt like when I arrived here for the first time twenty years ago, and I conclude that my anticipation and contentment remain the same, but sweeter. Today, I will have a "legitimate" interest in the city that has always felt like home.

Charging through immigration down to baggage carousel thirty-two, I am able to secure a taxi large enough to accommodate all my luggage, making record time out of CDG. From the taxi I call Sachi, crossing my fingers that there were no other issues while I was I over the Atlantic. There were not. She congratulates me on our new home and then gives me the news: today is her last day at the Paris bank and she returns to Tokyo tomorrow. Timing and luck were both on my side, and I smile knowing that *l'appart* would never have happened had it not been for her watching her colleague's files last summer and seeing the purchase through to *la vente*.

Ahead of *le goûter* and *fin de la semaine* traffic, I arrive at the *notaire's* office on Rue du Louvre at exactly 3:50 p.m. *Je l'ai fait!* The driver waits in the taxi with my luggage as I dart across the street with my carry-on suitcase. Jessica greets me and leads me from the reception area to a small room lined with bookshelves, which resembles an old law office when lawyers still used books. A wooden desk sits in the center next to a window. Both *notaires* and the seller are seated at the desk; the gentlemen stand and extend their hands to me when I enter the room. No one looks the way I had imagined them. The seller, ninety years of age according to the *PDV* and, according to Claire, losing her eyesight, looks much younger and quite put together in her navy suit. Her wavy gray hair pulled back from her face which is nude of adornment but for pink lipstick. She greets me with a *"Bonjour Madame,"* which I return.

I take the seat offered me at the desk in between the seller on my left and the *notaire*s to my right. Jessica is moving about the room with papers in her hand. Waiting for the documents, I try not to tap or hum or bite my lip or engage in any of the nervous tics I have, of which I have become keenly aware. I fold my hands and place them in my lap and cross my ankles, trying to appear calm despite the fact I am bursting on the inside with delight and I want to do some sort of victory dance, waving my deed in my hand.

Jessica walks behind the desk and hands me a two-page document and two keys. I take them from her and place them on the desk, waiting for a pen. The weight of the eyes in the room are noticeably on me as I continue to wait. Jessica does not hand me any more paper-work—or a pen—and the silence is now becoming awkward because no one is doing anything but staring at me. Then I read the paper in front of me and when I see my *notaire's* signature, my heart sinks. It is my certificate of sale. They signed the paperwork without me. They did not wait until 4 p.m. The moment I waited years for was stolen from me in some unprecedented French hurry. Disappointment most certainly reveals itself in my eyes, because my *notaire* begins uncomfortable small talk to alleviate the awkwardness of the silence consuming the room.

"It is not a big deal," I tell myself. "It is just a piece of paper." I take the papers and stand up. I thank the seller for the apartment and shake the hands again of everyone present and say "*au revoir.*" There is nothing else for me to do. Or say. The deed will come by mail. And that was the moment *l'appart* became ours.

THE TEN-MINUTE cab ride to the 16th seems an eternity. *L'esprit de l'escalier* sets in as I replay the *notaire* office scene over and over in my head, thinking of the things I should have said or asked. When we arrive at *l'appart* the cab driver carries my bags to the entrance and wishes me well in my new place. My hands shake as I search my purse for my notepad with the "key apartment info," a crib sheet of the basic things I need to know, including the door code, which, despite my memorization on the plane, I cannot recall. At my own door, my shaking hands drop the key. Twice.

I cross the threshold into the dark space, furnished only with my disbelief and joy, and I open the rusted, worn metal shutters to let in the September air and light. I stand on the balcony where Julia stood with her Barbie last month. Residential end-of-the-day rituals are carried out below me: shopping for dinner, enjoying an *apéro* with friends, and walking small dogs. It is said that Maria Callas walked her poodle on this street wearing pearls. I do not see any pearls, but there are a lot of small dogs.

I pull my luggage in from the hallway and close the front door, unpacking my carry-on with my immediate necessities. I plug in my iPod dock, confirming that there is really a grace period as the electricity is still on. Maria Callas, neighbor past, seems fitting and I find an opera playlist inspired by Mr. Monaco. I sit on the blank floor where Ava and Julia played and face the open balcony doors. The soprano sings in the still room, present:

> *L'amour est un oiseau rebelle* (Love is a rebellious bird)
> *Que nul ne peut apprivoiser* … (That none can tame)

Callas' voice and the thumping Habanera-style rhythm saturate the tiny space. All of the worrying, the angst, emailing, faxing, FedExing, the 4 a.m. mornings, the anxiety-inducing phone calls, the years of hoping, planning, and whimsical dreaming, and even the recent disappointment in the *notaire's* office cumulate and are liberated in this honest moment sitting on the blank floor, alone, looking at the Paris skyline and the rooftops I coveted for so long. My tears are visceral and I weep with gratitude and relief. It does not matter that I cannot reside here full-time for ten years because this modest space with these blank, shared walls are mine and my daughters', and with this much-deferred gratification finally realized, *je suis très, très heureuse. Rien ne vaut son chez soi.* (There is no place like home.)

lappart

lappart

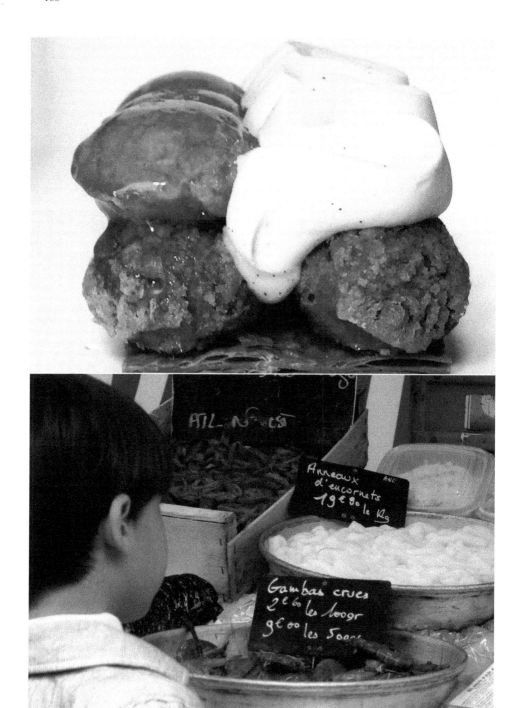

Saint-Jean-Cap Ferrat

Tatoma Beach

Saint-Jean-Cap Ferrat

Saint-Jean-Cap Ferrat

Provence

Luberon

luberon

PART III

CHAPTER SEVENTEEN

You Cannot Make an Omelette Without Breaking Some Eggs

I HAVE TWELVE DAYS. Paris on a part-time basis means that all the remodeling and the furnishing of our little nest must be done at a highly efficient pace and within the parameters of my child-share schedule. While the plan to make *l'appart* a home — while living on a different continent — may seem ridiculous or insurmountable to some, to me it is neither. The harder the task, the more motivated I am. Jumping off of the floor, I take to the Paris streets, armed with two measuring tapes, a drawing pad, and my planner.

Ma cuisine parisienne is a rectangle of seriously small proportions. The longer walls are shared with my neighbor on the left and *le salon* on the right. The original 1920s kitchen door with its panes of antiqued flowered, frosted glass separates the kitchen from the foyer, and there is a large window opening out to the street on the opposite side. Beyond the singular light bulb and the peeling synthetic kitchen counter (*le plan de travail*) and cabinets (*les placards*, as I have learned those are called), is a glass, four-burner electric stovetop which sits beneath a rickety white, metal hood. Other than this paltry-looking appliance, the kitchen is full of empty spaces, necessitating my visit to Darty, the multi-leveled retail haven brimming with reasonably priced kitchen appliances, housewares, and electronics.

Darty in Passy is a ten-minute walk from *l'appart*, which I walk/ run toward with focus until I come across a small appliance store displaying a cream-colored enamel-and-brass stove in its window. Its sheer beauty propels me into the store which is filled primarily with stand-alone mixers, and washers and/or dryers for clothes. While I measure and record the dimensions of the stove in the window, the young *mademoiselle* behind the desk acknowledges the craftsmanship of the culinary work of art as she walks toward me.

"*Oui, je l'adore mais c'est trop ... trop grand,*" I say.

The *jeune femme* explains that it comes in smaller sizes and hands me a brochure, which I open and *voilà;* inside I discover the black enamel stove I coveted this summer on the beach and pasted in my planner. The *quatre-feux* version would fit. Sort of. The *jeune femme* writes the stove's price in the brochure next to its dimensions and I bid her a *bonne soirée.*

In Darty, the diminutive ovens would not fit a twelve pound turkey and the stovetops are dominantly electric. American-sized refrigerators are too large for Parisian kitchens (unless I put it in the foyer like my predecessor), and I measure the compact-sized European *frigos* and even contemplate an under-the-counter refrigerator for additional counter space. I tape-measure my way around the ground floor until my head spins with numbers, choices which I never knew existed, and conversions of length and currencies. An hour in Darty is my limit, and I leave the electronic paradise to explore my neighborhood, which results in the deduction that everything I need —banks, pharmacies, grocery stores, a post office, dry cleaners, manicurist, shoe repair, locksmith, bookstores, and a laundromat—and everything I do not (including *chocolatiers* and specialty boutiques ranging from cigar shops to lingerie) is a ten-minute walk from *l'appart*. Rue des Belles Feuilles, a few streets over from my own, will no doubt be my favorite neighborhood destination, as it is full of food.

My first meal in Paris as a property owner is Italian food on the candle-lit *terrasse* of Di Vino. The irony is not lost on me, but the choice is a convenient and strategic one as the *terrasse* offers me the simultaneous view of *l'appart* and the "Tower" (as its constant presence in my background makes a one-name basis seem appropriate).

The waiter brings me a celebratory *coupe de champagne* and I befriend both him and the owner, the former, Pierre, and the latter, Harold. Famished, I inhale my steak and drag every last one of my *pommes frites* through the remains of the Bordeaux reduction smeared on my plate. My red fruit and gelato dessert is so inviting that the American couple sitting to my left asks me what it is and from there a conversation between the three of us ensues. His work is transferring him to London and both are melancholy about leaving Paris tomorrow; they have lived here for five years. Their goodbye dinner to Paris is my hello. We compare notes on the condition of Parisian apartments when you first move in and when I ask if they have recommendations where I can find reasonably priced lighting, the husband lets out a hearty laugh.

"The joys of the single lightbulb," he says.

"Exactly," I say, feeling fortunate to having been left with two.

When I finish my *café*, I wander the Trocadéro area until I can no longer stand. The stillness of *l'appart* welcomes my exhaustion and I unpack the *faux* fur throw and place it in the center of the bedroom floor and pile an array of bedding on top, which proves surprisingly comfortable. Sleep finds me immediately but it does not last long, and at 3:oo a.m. jet-lag and excitement wake me, and I migrate to the place I always go when I cannot sleep, the kitchen.

Chaussures Chics needs to remove the countertops and cabinets for the electrical work and now observing the actual state of these items up close, there is no reason to try to salvage them, assuming that is even possible. And, with everything out of the kitchen, I am not bound by the existing layout or dimensions, and I find this tabula rasa thrilling, even if I only have two walls and a confined space in which to work.

I consult my planner with appliance dimensions and grab my measuring tape, two colors of masking tape (red and blue), and a Sharpie. There is really only one realistic placement option for the European *frigo* but several options for the under-the-counter *frigo*. Cutting pieces of the red tape to match the height and width of the refrigerator choices, I place the tape on the wall and/or cabinet so I can visualize my options. Using the blue masking tape, I repeat the process for the stove choices. Then I tape the magazine page with the black enamel stove on the wall. Just because. The tiny kitchen resembles a kindergarten art project, and I think of the expression Samy taught me, "*On ne fait pas d'omelette sans casser des oeufs.*" (You cannot make an omelette without breaking some eggs.) It is time to break some eggs.

WHEN I RETURN to sleep, I dream of my Paris kitchen possibilities, and this dream process apparently had merit because when I awake I sketch a proposed kitchen design of the shoebox-sized space with the full length, yet compact, European *frigo* and the black enamel stove. Even better, the combination inspires a *recette* for *l'appart:* an Art Deco theme with black and white as the dominant colors and the kitchen walls, a rich Normandy butter yellow.

Chaussures Chics arrives at 10 a.m. Today his shoes are brown leather. With my *recette* in mind, I ask *Chaussures Chics* for a second *devis* to include the installation of the stove and *frigo* (there is no room for a dishwasher or even a garbage disposal), moving the sink (housing it in a temporary cabinet so that it functions until I select the cabinets), removing and installing a black-and-white tile floor in the kitchen, and collapsing the cabinet in between the foyer and the kitchen for more counter space. The *devis* should also include an estimate to paint *l'appart* and to remove the existing *faux* parquet floors, replacing them with hardwood flooring to be stained ebony with a glossy finish (to match the stove). His eyes light up with enthusiasm at the job expansion as he makes notes on my kitchen sketch. We walk *l'appart*, this time marking the walls with a black "x" where the outlets and light switches will go and arrows indicating which switch will operate which outlet. *Chaussures Chics* tells me that he will return on Monday with the new *devis*. The moment his brown shoes cross my threshold, I set out to make my first purchase. My stove.

The *jeune femme* who assisted me yesterday is not here. Her substitute sitting at the desk introduces herself as Isabelle, the young woman's mother, and asks if she may help me with something. When I open the brochure to the page bearing my stove, Isabelle smiles.

"*C'est magnifique,*" she says and fills out the paperwork.

She asks me if I am sure that I want gas, and I confirm that indeed the four burners must be gas, and I will also purchase the *inox* (stainless steel) wall guard which goes behind the stove and has a rack from which to hang my *poêles* (pans). She shows me the matching black enamel hood but I tell her that I will think about it and, in the interim, there is always the window for ventilation.

The stove purchase puts an undeniable bounce in my step which propels me down Rue de la Pompe to Darty where I purchase the *frigo*. The sales associate, reeking of a cigarette *petit déjeuner*, peers at me from above her bifocals and speaks to me in monotone French, while shuffling her paperwork. She recommends that I sign up for a program Darty has with the utility companies, but I gaze at her blankly because I do not understand what she is saying, which is both humbling and annoying because I thought my French was getting better. She stops shuffling her paperwork and, without raising her head, stares at me from above her glasses, expelling an unsubtle sigh. I request to review the paperwork. It is replete with tiny French print and, from what I can ascertain, it is a contract to lock in a rate for gas and electric for two years. Locking in a rate seems like a smart idea (as I have heard that the price fluctuates greatly in the winter), and I tell her I will sign up. When we are done she hands me my paperwork with account numbers for both utility services. Refrigerator to be delivered on October 4. Appliances, done.

Using my suitcase as my table, I *déjeune* on my bedroom balcony. The sun is out and the weather crisp as an Asian pear. My measuring has confirmed that most of the stored furniture I have in Los Angeles is too large for *l'appart* which means that while I am here I need to not only get the remodeling underway but purchase a few essential pieces. Through the wrought iron I see my post-lunch destination: a home shop across the street, displaying in its window various pieces of furniture and a silver floor lamp with a black shade.

The shopkeeper sits at the counter reading *Le Parisien*, which she puts down to greet me and offer her assistance. Her chattiness is a lovely contrast to the sourpuss at Darty, and I select the floor lamp. She also agrees to sell me a displayed black velvet chair at a discounted price. When she asks me about delivery, I tell her that it is unnecessary because I am moving in across the street.

"*Bienvenue*," she says and reaches for a keychain with a large white tassel and a silver four-leaf-clover charm hanging from the counter display case. She hands it to me.

"For *bon courage* in your new place," she says mixing French and English.

"Merci beaucoup."

One by one, I walk my purchases across the street. The two men working in the produce market next to the home shop watch me traverse the street - back and forth - with the chair and then the lamp. One man arranges the apple display with precision while the other man, juicing oranges, says *"bonjour"* to me as I pass.

Then there are three; two singular lightbulbs and a floor lamp. Opening the lamp box, I climb on top of the kitchen counter and remove the lightbulb from the ceiling. It fits the floor lamp, but it does not work. Annoyed, but pressed for time, I leave the lamp issue for later as tomorrow is Sunday and everything will be closed and I need to find a bed.

Line 1 of the *métro* cuts across the heart of Paris in a west to east fashion. It is the nicest and most comfortable of the *métro* lines because it leads directly to tourist destinations such as the Étoile, the Louvre, and the Bastille. For my purposes, it also conveniently stops at the basement of BHV in the Marais, which resembles a Home Depot while the upper floors are an elaborate department store. My four-leaf-clover keychain appears to be working already as today BHV is having a sale on mattresses. Upstairs I bounce from bed to bed, laying on a few in a fetal position for full effect. The one I prefer has a favorable price tag so I arrange for delivery for Thursday (only five more nights on the floor). The keychain continues to prove lucky because downstairs I find a sale on pillows, towels, linens, and four large plastic bags later, I leave BHV.

Early Saturday evening and Rue de Rivoli is a honking, standstill disaster. The *métro* is jammed and the logistical nightmare of getting my bags through the turnstiles or fitting into a crowded *métro* sends me directly to a taxi stand. Thirty minutes later, the three taxis that stopped did not make a dent in the line. Frustrated with the lack of progress, I trudge slowly south toward the 5th to escape the city-center congestion. The weight of the bags stretches the plastic handles, which are cutting into my hands like fishing wire. With aching hands and still no solution to my transportation dilemma, I alter my thinking: What would a *parisienne* do if they cannot find a taxi and their hands are nearly bleeding from carrying bags of linens through the streets of Paris? A French person would think "*tant pis*" and sit down to enjoy a glass of wine. So that is what I do on the *terrasse* of the nearest *brasserie* I can find.

A young couple sits at the table next to me. The man pardons himself to ask me the time. When I respond, he thanks me and points to the moat of shopping bags surrounding my table.

"Looks like a successful shopping spree," he says.

I laugh. "Yes, but it is nothing exciting. Just linens and hangers."

They ask for restaurant recommendations in the Italian quarter where they are staying. Not very familiar with the neighborhood, I can only offer suggestions of places I like nearby. When I inquire about their vacation I learn that they are on their belated honeymoon. He had to leave for his military tour in Iraq immediately after the wedding. Now on leave from his duty, she flew from the States to meet him here. Their affection is heart-warming, and I am thinking of all the promise and sincerity young love brings when the bride asks: "Do you live here?"

"Yes. Well, partly. I actually got the keys to my apartment yesterday, and I am trying to set up house."

"Wow! An apartment in Paris! That is so cool! You are sooooo lucky!" she says.

And, when I leave them to coo, I do feel lucky, for *l'appart* and also because there is a taxi waiting at a taxi stand directly across the street.

Tonight I try another neighborhood restaurant for dinner, which, despite the French name, is more Italian food. The restaurant is packed with locals, and I do not hear word of English. A man, who appears to be the owner due to his attention to and knowledge of the patrons, takes my jacket and brings me a glass of red wine while I wait for a table. His name is Thierry. Thierry is about my height and wears a cook's white apron tied around his bulging waist. His brownish, straggly long hair does not appear to be kept in any particular way and combed only with his chubby fingers. Thierry is hospitable with me, as he is with all of his guests, and within ten minutes he seats me and tells me of the specials *du jour*, which somehow leads to a discussion of cooking and cooks. In honor of my culinary interests, he brings me a special *entrée*, followed by a *plat* I selected. The combination of the red wine and sitting still after a very full day makes me sleepy, and my head falls toward my plate, only for me to quickly bring it back up again and see Thierry laughing at me. Embarrassed at having been caught falling asleep at the table, I explain that it is jet lag, not disinterest in my meal. He retrieves my *manteau*, and he asks me if I would be interested in doing some catering jobs or working together in some cooking aspect in the future. He suggests *café* in order to discuss. Wondering if he really is interested in cooking with me or just wants to hit on me, I pause, but ultimately give him my French number because saying *"non"* to a potential work connection seems unwise, while making acquaintances in the neighborhood seems welcoming.

SUNDAYS IN PARIS feel like a mini vacation, making Sunday my favorite day. Although France became a secular country in 1905, old traditions remain and most retail stores and restaurants are closed on Sunday, and it is considered a day of rest. Parisians visit the parks (if the weather is agreeable) or go to one of the many movie theaters. Dinner is at home with family and usually consists of roasted chicken or leftovers fashioned into some fabulous *farce* with *pâté* or infused with cream. My friend Lily, who has lived in Paris for years with her husband, told me never to expect an invitation to Sunday dinner as an expat unless you have a close pre-existing relationship with a French family, and even then, the invitation may not come.

"It is just like that," she said. I set my expectations.

JeF is working and Maryam is out of town. Lily and her husband are at their country home in Normandy. With the *très agréable* weather, I run a few loops around the lake in the Bois then head for the Marais with its eclectic shops and its nonconformity to the Sunday usual; some shops are actually open. A tile shop displays a series of black-and-white tiles, all variations of which would complement my Art-Deco-stove theme perfectly. In a home shop I find a long, dark wood dining table with iron legs for eight. It would contrast nicely with the clear Lucite chairs I saw this summer in a French decor magazine (and pasted in my planner). There is also a *faux* leather-wrapped wardrobe trunk, an affordable knock-off of the old Louis Vuitton ones. A consignment store full of stylish oddities has a retro couch made of a series of round, white leather circles held together by a few strategically placed aluminum bars underneath. Not large, but the compact piece would provide an immediate stylish place for my bottom. I note all of the addresses and return to the 16th, where I sit at Café du Trocadéro, taking advantage of the free twenty minutes of WiFi (pronounced, "Wee Fee") and a Kir.

MONDAY MORNING. *Chaussures Chics* arrives with two workers and new a *devis*. The devis is three pages long and for some of it, I am forced to rely upon the context to comprehend what it says. However, there is no language confusion on the price, which has increased eight times. Admittedly, the scope of the work increased, but eight times? That is a lot of euros. That is a lot of U.S. dollars. That is a lot of shoes. I negotiate with him for a reduced price for gutting the kitchen and the painting. Feeling too tired to negotiate the entirety of the *devis* (in a second language) and do the monetary conversions in my head at the same time, as for the rest I tell him, "*Je vais y réfléchir.*" ("I'll think about it.") Then I see the notation on the last page of the *devis* requesting sixty percent as a down payment. *C'est fou!* Offended at the request, I become fully awake and my ever-improving French is clear this time:

"*Et pour les soixante pour cent, c'est non. Je vous donne un chèque pour le matériel électrique aujourd'hui et quand je pars, je vous donnerai un autre chèque pour les travaux à cette date. Je vous donnerai le reste quand tout sera terminé.*"

Looking slightly deflated, he agrees. A materials deposit today for the electrical work, with partial payment before I leave based upon the work done, and final payment upon completion. He knows a sixty percent deposit is ridiculous.

As *Chaussures Chics* leaves, the two workers return with large rounds of wires and white plastic buckets filled with tools. When I ask them how long they will be working today, they stop what they are doing and stare at me. They talk amongst themselves and this time it is clear, they are not speaking French, but Portuguese. Not knowing any Portuguese I resort to the universal language of hand gestures and point to my watch and then to their tools and then to myself to indicate "time," "work," and "Lisa." Using the same method, they respond: 5:oo p.m. Their names are Pablo and Afonso.

A quick face wash, hair in pigtails, cold cream, and a scarf, I step over the wires and leave *l'appart* and make my way to Monoprix for the necessities of an electric water heater for my coffee (a staple in every Parisian kitchen) and light bulbs. After securing both, I proceed back to Victor Hugo to inquire about a chandelier I saw Friday in a home shop advertising a store-wide sale. The perfect size for the foyer and, with electricians already on site, it is an opportune time for such a purchase. The sales clerk tells me that I can take it with me or have it delivered for seventy-five euros, an outrageous sum given the short distance and the cost of the light itself, but she explains that the store does not deliver so employees use their own cars and the delivery has to be worth their while. I tell her that I will return to pick it up tomorrow, and I cross the street to the paint store to purchase six small sample pots of paint, three shades of black and three shades of golden butter yellow.

Pablo and Afonso have shrouded the common staircase and entry way in protective plastic that crunches under my feet as I enter *l'appart*. They are pulling the baseboards off the walls, removing the old outlets, and carrying the debris down to a waiting parked truck. I open my paint samples and brush large patches of each of the three shades of black in the foyer, the living room, and on the doors throughout *l'appart*. I repeat the process with the yellow samples on the kitchen walls. The lightbulbs from Monoprix do not fit the floor lamp and, to add insult to injury, the water boiler is missing its base. Double *zut!* There is a sticker on the lamp with what may be a lightbulb number, so I write it down and return to Monoprix with the number and the incomplete water boiler. My stomach is nervous as I anticipate French attitude and a language difficulty, but the exchange goes without incident, and the woman even apologizes. In my exchange elation, I realize that I forgot to buy another lightbulb, so I cross the street to the *bricolage* store full of domestic essentials including an array of lightbulbs. The woman behind the counter stops her conversation with a young man who looks like her twin and when I hand her the number, she gives me a light bulb.

Lunch-time traffic and the cars and scooters whirl around the Place while pedestrians rush to their lunchtime destinations, allowing me to pass in the busy streets unnoticed with my collapsable ladder and bags. I navigate my way around the mess in *le salon* to *ma chambre* and, full of hope, I place the new bulb in the floor lamp. It fits. *Oui!* I plug it in, but nothing happens. *Non.* I try other plugs. Still nothing. *Putain de lampe!* Fighting the urge to throw the lamp out of the bedroom window, I grab it in my hand and walk with determination back over the mess in *l'appart*, down the plastic-shrouded stairs, and across the street to return to the home shop where I bought it. The store is closed. *Zut!* Undeterred, floor lamp in hand, men at the produce market watching me, I proceed down the street, crossing the Place, Tower in the background, to the *bricolage* store to get to the bottom of this lamp difficulty once and for all.

The twins are still conversing. The girl stops talking when she sees me.

"*Qu'est-ce qui s'est passé?*" she asks.

"*Ne marche pas,*" I respond.

She plugs the lamp in, confirming that it does not work. Her finger runs the course of the lightbulb boxes on the shelf behind her and she pulls another bulb from the shelf, screws it into the lamp and turns it on. The bulb glows, seemingly in a taunting fashion, knowing that I have spent untold time on a project that she did in three minutes. She asks for the box for the first bulb, but I forgot it and promise to return with it later. On my return to *l'appart*, while the collapsed ladder did not garner stares, the shiny, silver floor lamp seems particularly interesting to passersby, and all I can think is that Maria Callas, in pearls, walked her poodle on this very street, and here I am walking a floor lamp back and forth, in yoga pants and pigtails.

Returning to the stores I found in the Marais on Sunday, I find beautiful black-and-white floor tiles for the kitchen (and significantly less expensive than what *Chaussures Chics* quoted me). In the home shop, I order both the dining table and the wardrobe trunk and detour only momentarily to Pain de Suc (a favorite *pâtisserie* among Parisian chefs) for some *financiers*, before returning to a consignment store on Rue Mauvais Garcons where I successfully negotiate a reduced price on the marshmallow-looking *canapé*. I sift through boxes in antique shops and at BHV to find the perfect black and brass enamel door knobs for the interior doors. My lucky tassel continues to work its magic, and I find another sale at BHV on kitchen necessities—wine glasses, knives, Staub cast-iron *cocottes* and even a pull *marché* caddie—all of which I need because a kitchen is not a kitchen without them and how can I be a woman in the 16th without my *marché* caddie? Thrilled with my visions of *l'appart* to be—cooking in these *cocottes* and drinking out of these glasses—I wait in the lengthy line at the *caisse* with patience I never knew I had. When it is finally my turn, the cashier has difficulty scanning some of my items. She leaves her post to find the prices. She returns and calculates my total, which far exceeds my expectation. *Comment?* I review the receipt and see that I did not receive the thirty percent sales discount on more than half of the items. When I ask about the discrepancy, groans emanate from the line behind me. The clerk leaves for a second time to check the prices again, only to confirm that the only things on sale are the *marché* caddie and some tart pans. There is no point in protesting the poor signage because the French do not care about misleading signage; what is on sale is on sale, and the customer is *never* right.

I take the *métro* home, tipping the front of the *marché* caddie down under the turnstiles like a pro. Knowing Pablo and Afonso are

working at *l'appart*, I stop for the free WiFi and a *café* at Café du Tro-
cardéro. David, the waiter who works the *terrasse* next to the *presse*
(and is now used to seeing me), offers me a table. I re-find the clear
Lucite chairs on the internet, but due to that fact that the website is
in French and the internet is slow, my session expires before I can
purchase them. After three tries, and having memorized the process,
when I finally get to the last page, it asks for a bank phone code. *Comment?* I consult my folder with my codes and numbers that the bank
sent me, of which there are several. Not one of them works and my
time lapses. Again.

    L'appart is quiet but there is no food, so I dine at Le Rétro
Bistro in my neighborhood. My cooking magazines and a Kir Royale
are my companions and, while in Los Angeles you do not often see
people dining alone, that is not the case in Paris. The waiter brings me
fennel and onion blinis as an *amuse-bouche* and, just as the sweet but
fresh flavor touches my tongue—*cocorico!*— my French phone rings.
Patrons look around to determine the source, and I reach for my bag
to quiet the noise as quickly as I can, knocking over my Kir Royale.
The glass crashes to the floor, creating more of a disturbance than
the telephone ring itself. The waiter rushes to clean up my disaster,
telling me not to worry about it and brings me another Kir Royale and
a country *pâté* with grainy mustard and bread. Enjoying my time, I
make it a three-course meal and finish with a green salad and creamy,
high-fat-content Saint-Marcellin served in its own little ceramic container. The other patrons who remain appear to be on a first-name
basis with the waiter. In time, I, too, will become a familiar face at the
places in my neighborhood, and I cannot wait.

    DAY FIVE. Two more workers have joined Pablo and Afonso
and *l'appart* is abuzz with activity. While the four of them remove the

decaying and outdated contents from the kitchen, I spend quality time with *Chaussures Chics* and the gas company. The gas company has no record of the account I set up at Darty and trying to figure out this wrinkle takes nearly two hours and results in the creation of a second "unofficial" account number and an appointment on Monday for a meter read.

We move to the gutted kitchen where I write the stove dimensions on the wall with arrows to indicate its placement. I supplement my French remodeling vocabulary with "*truc*," which translates to "thing," and I make comparisons to things I do know the French names for: "*un truc comme ça*" ("something like this"), I say. *Chaussures Chics* appears to understand and, empowered by my sense of his understanding, *truc* becomes my favorite word. With everything out of the kitchen, we realize that there is no gas meter and so nothing for the gas man to read on Monday. The Darty delivery men arrive at the open front door with the refrigerator and pause when they see us standing in a kitchen of sand.

"*Dans la chambre, juste là,*" I say and direct them toward the bedroom (the least-affected room in *l'appart*) where they deposit the appliance while *Chaussures Chics* and I call the gas company requesting the delivery of a meter on Monday instead of a meter read.

At the end of the day, I relax in my velvet chair next to the *frigo* in front of my bedroom balcony. The urban life below intrigues me, and I feel part Audrey Tautou in *Amélie*, part Jimmy Stewart in *Rear Window*, as I observe the private particulars of strangers' lives while they themselves remain a mystery. Growing up in California, I never experienced this urban setting. A wiry, young man with chestnut hair and eyeglasses sits on his bed strumming his guitar, breaking with frequency to smoke cigarettes on the balcony. An older woman opens the door to his room, says something to him, and walks into the *salle à manger.* She looks to be his mother, and I presume she is calling him "*à table.*" I name him Dylan. To the left of Dylan, a middle-aged woman sits in the center of her orange couch; her laptop computer screen illuminates her face as she types. I imagine her to be a writer and I name her Stein. A family of four lives below Stein. Their apartment is minimally and tastefully decorated. A round dinner table sits in front of the window next to a fireplace aglow with dancing flames. The lady of the home sets six folded napkins on the round table which is graced with French *arts de la table*, while her lover decants the wine and sets the glass decanter upon the table. Cleavers, I name them. Relinquishing my chair for my floor bed, I gaze up at my new shiny refrigerator, and it occurs to me that if I can see my neighbors, then Stein, Dylan, and the Cleavers can see me too, particularly with no drapes. Self-consciously I envision the story they create for me: American or English woman, often naked, never sleeps, writes on and paints her own walls, and so hungry she keeps a *frigo* in her bedroom.

DAY SIX. At 6 a.m. it remains Paris Dark, which means the sky abounds in a deep blueish-gray glow before the sun officially wakes from its slumber. I decide to take a street run to explore the neighborhoods south of *l'appart*, taking advantage of the quiet and the blueish-gray glow. I run past Passy, past Maison Balzac, and past the site of Franklin's former residence to beautiful Porte de la Muette, where I decide to turn back and head north. Somehow I manage to turn myself around and end up west in the Bois, exactly the area I intended to avoid in the dark. Even Paris Dark.

The Bois—formerly the Forêt de Rouvray—is where the kings hunted. In the mid-19th century, the Second Empire created two large lakes in the Bois, which today are filled with swans and ducks. Runners and dog walkers circle one lake under the shade of the chestnut trees. Beyond the lakes, forests remain, dissected by numerous roads, some paved, some not, leading to different parts of the Bois. The Bois is so large, it even has a hippodrome and an outside theater where Shakespeare productions are performed in the summer.

One late, warm afternoon last summer I decided to do two things at once: take a run around Lac Inférieur and purchase Shakespeare tickets at the little theater ticket booth. The mission went unaccomplished, however, because on a side road, I saw a near-nude woman run behind a tree. Believing that she had been attacked, my motherly/chef instinct kicked in and I reasoned that approaching her with food and some water would make the situation less awkward, and I ran back to one of the châlets that sells both. Upon my return, I saw quite clearly that she was a he, and he was *not* injured, *nor* alone, but with three other barely clothed men. I realized then that the cars coming and going from the side roads were *not* park-goers and these men were *not* hurt, they were working. I felt stupid and naïve.

At dinner that evening I told JeF about my Bois discovery. He laughed hysterically, "Chef Morgan feeding the working boys in the Bois a sandwich."

It is with this history in mind that I try to avoid those working in the Bois as well as their customers, so I run in the middle of a deserted paved street. Even at this hour there are cars pulling off to the side and figures emerging from the woods. I run on and see signs for Le Pré Catelan, believing I am headed east but instead of finding the Michelin *trois étoiles* restaurant, I reach unfamiliar territory. Lost, yet intrigued, the area is quaint with châteaux next to little homes and islands of grass with small roads in between. There are no blue plaques on the buildings. I had run outside Paris into the posh suburb of Neuilly-sur-Seine.

Taking the *métro* back into Paris, I find my neighborhood quite different than when I left: parents walk little ones to school, *les boulangeries* have lines out the doors, the cafés are filling with coffee drinkers and croissant-eaters, and the *lycée* students are circled and blocking the sidewalk, smoking and gossiping about matters of teenage importance. Pablo and Afonso are already working and dust and noise consume *le salon* and *la cuisine*. My attempt to shower is frustrated, as only yellow water trickles out of the *douchette* (a hand-held spigot secured on a hollow metal pole). Since a shower is not an option, I try the bath instead. Finding no stopper to the tub, I turn a coffee cup saucer upside down and hold it in place for ten minutes until there is enough water to keep the saucer in place. Twenty minutes later, I am able to sponge bathe myself in the yellowish water. Success, sort of. I comb my wet hair, put it in a bun, and throw on a black cotton dress and walk to the *boulangerie* downstairs for breakfast.

"*Une baguette aux céréales, s'il vous plaît.*"

Clutching the baguette, I key the front-door code in the pad. A tall, heavenly smelling dark-haired man in a well-tailored suit passes me and as he continues to walk toward the Place, I cannot help but notice that his behind is just as attractive as his front. As I do, he turns around and catches me appraising *ses fesses. Zut!* Mortified at having been caught, I run into the common area, pass through the second set of double doors to the elevator, and await its descent. Without warning, the nice-smelling, well-dressed man is standing next to me, and his sudden appearance startles me, causing me to drop my baguette.

"*Bonjour. Je vous plais?*"

I am surprised by his boldness and embarrassed by my own indiscretion in looking at his bottom. I also do not know what to think about him sneaking into my building because I do not believe he is a neighbor.

"*Vous me plaisez…Je ne vous connais pas,*" I say.

He laughs.

"*Julien. Enchanté,*" he says as he extends his hand, revealing his cuff-linked shirt.

"Lisa."

"*Vous voulez partager un café avec moi?*" he asks.

I pause. *Café?* I really do not have the time for this as every day of my limited time here is already accounted for, nor do I know what the point would be as I am leaving in a few days, but he is the yummiest thing I have seen in a long time, other than my stove, and a simple coffee might be good for me. A friend's father, who is French, told me recently, in all seriousness, that it is important for a woman to always have a flirt. I reflect on the comment, and I decide he may be right. A flirt does put a bounce in a woman's step, and I do my customary glance at his left hand. No wedding band, but in France that does not mean much.

"*J'aimerais bien … mais, vous êtes marié?*

"*Non,*" he says.

"*D'accord,*" I respond. He says he will text me to set up a plan.

Upstairs I indulge in even more apricot *confiture* and baguette than usual and this delight, in combination with my prospective *café* date, allows me to happily greet *Chaussures Chics* who arrives with wood floor and tile samples. I tell him I found the tile and give him the store address to arrange for delivery. He places the wood samples on the dusty floor of *le salon* and when I bend down to examine them, I see that the workers' removal of the baseboards has exposed what appears to be another floor underneath the *faux* parquet. I grab a strip of the *faux* parquet in the corner of the room and pull it up from the floor. The three men, now motionless, stare at me while I free two more strips of plastic flooring from their glue only to discover the original parquet beneath. And it is in good condition!

The color drains from *Chaussures Chics'* face as I revise my request: remove the *faux* parquet and sand and stain the original floors in black with a high-gloss finish (both of which I will provide him to eliminate any confusion). When I catch a glance at the *devis* for installing a new wood floor, I understand why *Chaussures Chics* looks at if I killed his cat; that would have been a lot of shoes.

Moving from *le salon* into the kitchen, *Chaussures Chics* informs me that not only is there no gas meter and no gas line in the kitchen, but there is no gas line into *l'appart. Comment?* I purchased a gas stove and have a gas account (arguably two) but no access to gas? How was this not discovered when we stood in my kitchen of sand? Annoyance, exhaustion, and a vague sense of panic sweep in the pit of my stomach as I scan my memory, second-guessing myself as to whether there is gas in the building. Wasn't that in the purchase paperwork? Is my over-stuffed brain failing me again? *Chaussures Chics* and I walk into the hallway where, opposite the elevator, we find good news: in-set panels where we find telephone lines and old, capped gas lines. Now I just need a gas line from the hallway through the foyer and then to the kitchen. More limited wall space consumed. More work. Another *devis* modification. More euros. More U.S. dollars. I request *Chaussures Chics* to add a *tuyau* on the new *devis*, careful not to use "pipe" because *"faire une pipe"* in French is slang for a "giving a blow job" and that language debacle I would like to avoid (having previously made a similar mistake with "preservatives" not knowing that *préservatifs* are condoms).

DAY SEVEN. I wake to Pablo ringing the doorbell and a leaking toilet. Only one worker and a leaking toilet seem a step backwards, but today is a day of deliveries, in between which I will write my food blog, take a run, and share a coffee with my stealth-like flirt at 2 p.m., so there is no time to worry. When Afonso arrives, I head to Café du Trocadéro for a *café* and for the free WiFi, of which I manage two sessions before the delivery men arrive with the couch and I run home to meet them.

Dressed in white from head to toe, the delivery men match my couch. One is a dead ringer for Robin Williams' character in *Birdcage* and displays similar mannerisms, mustache and all. I watch as they negotiate the winding staircase, bouncing the small couch and themselves against the stone wall, groaning and sighing as they ascend, and I contemplate whether I should help them. When they reach *l'appart* door, they set the tiny couch down in the hallway, wiping the sweat from their foreheads with cloth kerchiefs as if on cue. The pleasantries on their faces disappear when I open the door and they see the *bordel* inside.

"*S'il vous plaît, pouvez-vous mettre le canapé juste là, dans la chambre,*" I ask.

The path to the bedroom is filled with various construction landmines—wires, wood planks, buckets, tools—much more complicated than when the refrigerator was delivered. I half expect them to leave the couch in the hallway and make a run for it, but they pat their faces and brows with their kerchiefs and press on toward the bedroom. Pablo and Afonso continue their work, unfazed by the sweating, mumbling men in white carrying the tiny leather couch and stepping over their tools. They place the couch in the bedroom, dust off their clothing, fan their faces with their hands, and wipe their foreheads with the kerchiefs, departing with three times the speed in which they arrived.

WHEN I ARRIVE at Chez Francis, the *terrasse* is busy with business-type coffee meetings as well as tourists because there is a straight-away prime view of the Tower from across Place de l'Alma. Julien is already sitting in the second row of bistro chairs *à l'extérieur.* His dark hair goes well with his navy, tailored suit. We order *deux cafés*, and I fumble with mine because he stares at me so intently with those emerald eyes of his that it makes me nervous. He tells me that my eyes are "*magnifiques*" and "*plus bleu que le ciel.*" Smiling, I try to remember the last time a man gave me a compliment, even one that seems an insincere cliché. He tells me that he works in finance and he has meetings nearby, which is why he suggested this location. He was born and raised in Paris and lives in the 16th with his girlfriend and ten-month old baby.

The smile on my face disappears, and I repeat his statement to make sure I heard it correctly.

"*Oui*," he says, unfazed by his living situation. "*Voulez-vous dîner avec moi?*"

I suppose I should have followed up my marriage question with a series of questions such as: "Are you living with a lover? A girlfriend? The mother of your child? And the child?" True, no one gets married in France anymore, and French men are certainly not known for their fidelity, but this is too much. I don't know if he is the most honest or arrogant man I have met, but I feel for his girlfriend because I have been that woman at home with the baby. Definitely *not* my flirt.

Back at *l'appart* the BHV delivery men are delivering my mattress, undaunted by the apartment chaos. When they leave, I lie on the plastic-covered bed, thrilled that my days on the dirty floor are over and my bedroom is now outfitted with a bed, a couch, a chair, and a refrigerator. In a celebratory mood, I return to the home shop across the street and purchase the two black, glossy side tables and little silver table lamps that I noted before to place on either side of the bed, making three trips back and forth across the street. The men at the produce store this time not only say *"bonjour,"* but ask me how I am.

ON DAY EIGHT the morning sun fills my bedroom with warm light and between the sun and my comfortable bed, I do not feel like getting up. However, Pablo and Afonso arrive, interrupting my lazy morning fantasy, so I dress and walk to Béchu for a *ficelle*.

From what I surmise, there are two primary phone services in France: SFR and Orange, and I need a phone and WiFi. There are two Orange stores in *mon quartier*, so I go to the smaller store close to *l'appart*. After thirty minutes I learn that it is not a full-service store and they cannot help me, so I proceed to the larger one on Avenue Victor Hugo, which is packed with customers. After waiting an hour, a salesman walks me through the various service plans and, after choosing one that will suit my needs, I fill out the necessary paperwork. He asks for my address and confirms that Orange can provide service to the residence. He then requests the name of the person who had the service there before me. *Comment? Sais pas. Pourquoi?* I give him the seller's name. That is not it. He researches by the address. The prior account was not with Orange. He cannot sign me up without the information. The entire thing makes no sense to me, and it wasted the entirety of my afternoon, gaining nothing but a headache.

On my way back to *l'appart*, I catch my reflection in a store window. The lack of meaningful sleep and anxiousness to get everything done before I leave, while at the same time, overcoming the learning curve of the French language and manner of doing things, is taking a toll but nothing that a *coiffeur* and *pharmacie* cannot fix. Fortunately, there are two pharmacies at the Place and there are three *coiffeurs* a stone's throw from *l'appart*. With no recommendations or personal knowledge on which to base my choice, I decide on Studio 36 on Avenue d'Eylau as I have seen a constant parade of well-coiffed *parisiennes* emerge from its doors. I make an appointment for color and a blow dry for tomorrow.

I select the *pharmacie* closest to my street; inside I am surrounded with a plethora of lotions, potions, and creams for every complaint and condition, including cellulite, which is approached with all seriousness in France. Every day walking to *l'appart* I cross (at eye level) a large poster in the *pharmacie* window with a perfectly rounded female bottom outfitted in lacy black lingerie advertising a particular cellulite cream. I have never used cellulite cream, but I have often wondered: Does it work? Does it tighten things that are falling? My *panier* is full with three types of masks, two eye creams, an exfoliating scrub, and a large blue tube of cellulite cream. The clerk rings up my purchases and gives me a sack full of samples.

Maria is vacuuming in the lobby when I return with my sack of goodies. I ask her if she knows the prior renter's name. She goes in her apartment and returns with some of their mail, and I copy down the information. Two unsuccessful attempts at Orange is enough for me, so after I deposit my bag in *l'appart*, I take the familiar route to Darty where a young sales associate, fluent in English, helps me find a telephone and WiFi package that best suits my needs. Delivery and installation on Monday. I find a cordless phone set, a TV, and a DVD player, all of which are on sale. Already in the Darty system, I now have warranties and numbers to call if I need help, and the monthly fee will be taken from my account automatically. Probably the most efficient and productive hour I have spent in Paris since being here, making the entirety of the day a success.

DAY NINE. There is an urban rhythm in the Paris mornings, and I have come to find the predictability of these everyday sounds comforting. The trash crews come in three swoops at 5:50, 6:30, and the final truck for glass around 7:00, when the breaking glass falling into the back of the truck sounds like a *fête*. The squeaking sound of the shopkeepers cranking open the roll up metal shutters follows. Thereafter, waiters carry the chairs out to the *terrasse* at the corner *brasserie*, and I can hear the wooden legs hit the pavement as they arrange them. *Les gardiennes* spray down the sidewalks with garden hoses, sweep clean the entrances, and bring the trashcans in from the sidewalk just before the streets fill with the sound of rushing feet, which I join for my daily *ficelle*. When I return, *Chaussures Chics* is waiting for me. My deposit is on his feet in the form of brown suede.

We stand in the sandpit that is *ma cuisine* and discuss my list: paint colors, floor sample, installing the chandelier, fix the broken/leaking toilet, and installation of the gas line. I tell him that I want to put the gas meter in the long cabinet in the foyer that houses the electrical meter, to which he responds, *"C'est pas possible."*

This phrase—it is not possible—is a French staple. It is as common as the croissant. *Chaussures Chics* tells me that it is not possible to place the gas meter in the cabinet with the electrical but offers no explanation for this impossibility. The thought of the ugly meter outside the cabinet is even more offensive than those taunting suede shoes. My head is aching, my stomach grumbling (as I still have not enjoyed my *ficelle*), arm gestures are flying, and the shoes are fancy. I imagine all sorts of *trucs* on my walls. I imagine the place blowing up if they do not put the meter or pipes in properly. Maria walks from door to door delivering the mail and interrupts our conversation to hand me mine. There is a contract from the gas company ... so many French words, but it does not seem to correspond to the contract I just mailed to them with my RIB. Do I have two gas accounts? Does the electric company own the gas company? Why is their name on here? Overwhelmed and confused. I see *Chaussures Chics*' mouth move, but I no longer hear any words, in any language. Feeling displaced, frustrated, and financially and emotionally drained, my need for a quiet, clean space trumps my waiting *ficelle*. I tell *Chaussures Chics* that I will see him on Monday, and I escape *l'appart*, which feels like a tiny, dirty money pit.

Today I skip the cooking magazines and purchase a *Paris Match* from the *presse* in front of Carton, Béchu's neighborhood competing bakery, where I sit and have a leisurely brunch like my Parisian neighbors do on the weekend. I peruse the photos and articles of French celebrity gossip at leisure, and when I have had *café* and quiche to my heart's content, I stroll the streets with no agenda except to return to *l'appart* to accept delivery of the dining table. Once the three boxes have been added to the bedroom, I leave to meet my *coiffeuse*, Lucille.

Lucille is an early thirties, French hipster with bleached-blonde hair cut in a blunt style just below her ears. She wears two layers of tank tops with black jeans that hug her slender hips. She is chatty with the others in the salon, and her French seems consistent with all French-speakers, rapidly paced and punctuated with facial expressions and arm gestures. When she offers me a *café*, I eagerly accept the offer just to keep up with her.

I sit in the leather seat facing the large mirror while a woman next to me is becoming increasingly lighter as the scissors cut inches of her hair and the brown strips fall to the floor. Lucille stands behind me and runs her fingers though my hair. She pauses. Then she looks at my hair while holding a chunk of it in the air, asking me about my hair intentions, which I later discover are part curiosity and part gratuitous because when it comes to my hair, Lucille thinks she knows best. Lucille tells me that for *automne*, I should tone down the red and add some brown. I voice my preference, but it falls on deaf ears. I also tell her that I want a blunt cut. Lucille decides layers. Not sure what the standard is for tipping hairdressers. I assume it is somewhere in between a *pourboire* (a nominal tip for service) and the twenty percent Los Angeles standard. I like the new color, and the layers are a welcome change and leave me feeling a little *parisienne*.

It is morning in California when I call the girls. They sound happy and tell me about their days at school, their friends, the threat of lice, and all the moments in between that I have missed, including the grandmas making them pancakes. *Elles me manquent.* When I hang up I am consumed with their absence in the quiet of *l'appart* and the future happy thought that I will share this space with them in the summer does not ease my present melancholy. I telephone JeF and ask to reschedule our dinner, opting to stay in with my bag of pharmaceutical goodies of the facial kind and decide between: *masque purifiant*, *masque peeling enzymatique*, or *masque hydratation totale*. Comparing the labels I decide that what I need is a real pick-me-up, and I set down the masks and grab the blue tube of cellulite cream. Squirting a generous portion into my palm I rub the thick white cream all over my face because if the cream can tighten a tush, surely it can tighten and freshen up my face. The bath water trickles out of the faucet but at least it is not yellow today and that is a welcome surprise. The candles and the rosewater bubble bath from the *pharmacie* make up for the jungle of hanging damp clothes (yesterday's unsuccessful, yet comical, result of my attempt to wash and dry my black clothes at *la laverie*), and I lie in the water with the cellulite cream on my face. Tomorrow is another day. Hopefully one with a necessary long run and firmer skin.

DAY TEN. Sunday morning and the neighborhood is *très calme.* My BHV research paid off because it is the most comfortable bed I have ever slept in and the rhythm of steady rain provides no incentive to leave *l'appart*, making my lazy Sunday even lazier. Only after two *cafés* and perusing several cookbooks do I get dressed for my run, observing that the cellulite-cream treatment made no noticeable difference.

I run through the heart of Paris, the 7th, 6th, and 5th, with my phone, twenty euros, and two *métro* tickets, just in case I run out of Paris on the east side this time. The Bastille side of Paris is far more lively than the west, and I stumble upon a flea market in the 11th where I gravitate to the tables of *arts de la table* filled with antique *apéritif* and cordial glasses, boxes of silverware, and dishes of all shapes and sizes and for every purpose. The woman behind the table is having a glass of red wine with her friend, and *pourquoi pas?* it is Sunday and just past noon. While they gossip about a Frenchman of great disappointment (at this moment, a redundancy, in my opinion), I find an antique cast-iron chafing dish with spots for candles underneath it to keep the food warm. It is heavy for something the size of a shoebox, but I envision the pots that will grace the top of this unique find. I politely interrupt their conversation, which has become more lively, and just as she reaches for the wine bottle, I negotiate the price from thirty euros to eight.

Running with a ten-pound chafing dish proves a weighty endeavor. By the time I reach the Marais, my right arm is aching. Impulse kitchen shopping has derailed my plan of a long run, so I abandon any notion of exercise and go to Pain de Sucre for a *financier à la pistache* and purchase a chocolate mousse in a *verrine* for later sweet cravings, thanks to my *frigo*. The *métro* ticket is put to good use because the rain has returned, and this time, it is not a gentle rhythmic drizzle.

DAY ELEVEN. The sky is dark gray and *l'appart* is cold. Pablo wakes me with the doorbell at 8 a.m. I begin my *café* ritual and offer him a *café* as well. His daily presence has made him seem like a roommate. He nods *"oui,"* and his smile suggests that he was surprised by my offer. At 8:30 Afonso arrives. He takes a *café* too. Returning to Los Angeles on Wednesday, I have only today and tomorrow to make sure everything is in place to proceed smoothly in my absence.

The clothes hanging all over the *sdb* seem even damper today than yesterday. I pack up the pile to return to the laundromat to finish drying the clothes and, on my way out, I pass *Chaussures Chics.* I ask him to do a floor sample for me with the stain I bought and tell him that I will return in thirty minutes, in time to meet the gas man.

The man from GDF Suez arrives with the *gaz* meter, an unseemly large square metal box with two connections at the top for the pipes. *Moche.* Setting down my basket of clothes, I show him three places in the kitchen that I have determined would be ideal spots for the monstrosity, given my anticipated kitchen design. He rejects all three of my proposals without hesitation. The counter must be *"évident,"* he says. It cannot be higher or lower than eye level, and he demonstrates as such by placing his hands here and there on the wall. His eye level is my eye level, which puts the counter in the very middle of the wall. He suggests that I build a *placard* over it. *Superbe.* A gas man with architectural advice and bad news. *Chaussures Chics* says nothing, but I will not let this issue go. Ignoring *Chaussures Chics'* prior rejection of my cabinet plan, I ask the gas man if we can put the meter in the foyer cabinet below the electrical counter. He ponders the question and bends over slightly to assess the situation. He taps his pointer finger on his lips and says that the meter would be low and not safe with the electrical meter. I persist and ask if we can put a divider in between the two counters for safety.

"*Hum* … [further lip tapping ensues] … *oui, mais* …"

He stops mid-sentence and explains to *Chaussures Chics* the technical requirements. Apparently there must be a steel plate to separate the two meters, and the gas meter can only be installed after the steel separator has been installed and inspected. I recap the gas situation in my head: install barrier, service request to approve shelf, service call to install meter, install meter, attach to gas line still to be installed. I request that he leave the meter counter to install later as I am afraid if he leaves with it, it will necessitate me wasting another morning on the telephone. He looks at me and shakes his head.

"*C'est pas possible,*" he says (unsurprisingly) and explains, because of the theft risk, he is not permitted to leave unattached meters.

As he leaves with the counter, the two Darty delivery men arrive at my door with my electronics. They carry my TV through the disaster and into my bedroom. Wall installation is not included, but they can mount the TV on the wall on the spot for a small fee. I write a French *chèque*, which I am now beginning to get the hang of (although the comma instead of the period to separate the euros from the centimes gets me every time). Hungry, and with no reason to sit and watch them work, I tell them I am going down the street for *déjeuner* and to call me when they are done.

The weather is crisp but no longer cold. I cross the street to Di Vino where I secure a little table on the *terrasse*. Thankfully, my waitress does not know me because it is embarrassing how often I have eaten here in the last week. My ordering is interrupted by the sound of a trumpet and a clarinet and I look toward *l'appart*; on my street are two men in baseball caps and beige sweaters with navy pants filling the neighborhood with live jazz. As I enjoy a glass of rosé with an *Arts & Gastronomie* magazine, the two musical men have switched from jazz to "Hava Nagila" which they play as they walk in the opposite direction toward the kosher sushi restaurant, which advertises bagels as an additional specialty. Di Vino's *terrasse* is filling with Parisians on their lunch break. I take out my camera and photograph Parisian street life as it hums about me. A mother and young daughter walk by my table. The little girl, who resembles Shirley Temple, carries pink flowers with a baguette slung over her shoulder. When she sees my camera, she stops one foot in front of my face and smiles. Her mother tugs her hand to pull her along. I sit and examine the minutia of life. The obvious is beautiful, but it is the details that fascinate me most: beautifully heeled legs crossed at the ankle under a table; the wine glasses on the tray just as the waiter reaches to serve them; the waiter's hand behind his back against his pressed long, white apron; the curves of the vinegar bottle and the wax stamp marking its age; a man dipping his biscuit into a heady espresso; the contour of the metal ashtray and the falling, crumbling ash; the creamy carved-out section of the yellow butter as the knife cuts it. Perhaps that is another reason I love Paris so much, it celebrates the details and the process, not just the end result. My *vitello tonnato* arrives the same time the Darty men call to tell me they are done. The waitress covers my veal with a napkin.

French television is a welcome change to the sounds of saws and drills. Pablo and Afonso have sacrificed two plugs on the temporary outlet connected to the generator for my television and Darty Box, which is my WiFi. The Darty men walk me through the paperwork. My assigned WiFi password is the typical ultra-long combination of letters and numbers. Gushing with gratitude and excitement, I trip over wires in *le salon* as I walk the delivery men to the door. All four men rush to pick my splayed body off of the floor.

JEF IS ON HIS way over. I anxiously try to tidy up *l'appart*, which means creating a path by pushing the plastic buckets of tools and materials against the walls. Despite the half-ripped-up floors and holes in the walls, not to mention the ugly and very green bathroom, I am eager for JeF to see my "piece of stone." I turn on the television for some background noise. *Rien*. I try my computer. *Rien*. When JeF arrives I am in a towel and in an electronic panic because I unplugged and then plugged everything back in incorrectly; all my electronic progress lost. He grabs my whole self with enthusiasm, nearly knocking off my towel, and gives me a double kiss. And there is that smile.

"*Ça va?!?!*" he exclaims, but he knows I am good and, in fact, I am great.

He walks *l'appart*, affirming that the location and bones are indeed excellent, and intersperses his compliments with expletives of "Wow!" and "Good job!" I explain my remodeling plans and then convey my present electronic debacle, and he, being an electronic genius, sorts out the WiFi, gets it working again and even changes the password to something I can remember while I dress.

We sit at the bar at Drouant. Chef Antony greets us and brings us each a *coupe de champagne* with strawberry *purée*. We toast to *chez moi* and nibble on the savory sables with poppy seeds and then I give JeF the reveal: a printed color preliminary draft of my first cookbook that I began in Saint-Jean in August. Three pages devoted to each recipe. The first two a photograph of the ingredients and the final page a photograph of the dish with the recipe in white printed over the photograph. A photo album with food. As he is in the food industry with a talented eye for design, I look to his opinion.

"*J'adore!*" he exclaims "But, why did you do the background on black? You should try it on white for food."

"Because black leaves the focus on the food," I respond. "And just because food is traditionally shot on white does not mean it should always be like that."

"*C'est bien, Lisa. Très bien.*" He looks through the loose pages and flashes me that beautiful smile on his chiseled face, demonstrating his approval, which makes me proud.

"*Santé!*" he says.

Our Champagne flutes touch again and we look one another in the eye, mindful to avoid the French superstition that if you do not, you will not have sex for seven years (and I would not wish a seven-year dry spell on anyone, certainly not myself). We move to a *terrasse* table and laugh and talk over a generous dinner under the retractable awning. Chef Antony joins us for a drink. It is a perfect night and it feels noticeably different than when I was here the last time because now, I have no time pressure to get everything done or see everything I can in a number of days or pack up or ship things to the States because I am no longer transitory. I own a piece of Parisian stone and "stone is solid" as JeF says.

DAY TWELVE. My last full day in Paris and the rooster alarm screams at me to remove myself from my bed at 6 a.m. Coffee in one hand and a Sharpie in the other, I walk *l'appart* writing instructions on the walls in French for things to be carried out in my absence:

> *Noir ici, blanc ici, jaune ici, pas là.* (Black here, yellow here, not there.)
> *Pour les murs, utiliser de la peinture à l'eau au ton mat. Merci.* (For the walls, use matte paint. Thank you.)
> *Les tuyaux à l'huile, laque semi-brillante.* (The pipes in semi-gloss.)

Pablo and Afonso arrive with three other workers. It is a full house; they all get a *café*. Then a plumber arrives to install a new pipe to move the kitchen sink. He gets one too.

The day is filled with last-minute odds and ends: price quotes on the countertop, purchasing a brass faucet for the kitchen, Christmas dresses for the girls, receipt of the Lucite chairs, and a walk to the *bricolage* store for locks for my cave and the ugly large cabinet in my *sdb* where I will store my purchases and electronics while I am gone as I anticipate many people coming in and out of my apartment in my absence (and everyone knows that theft is a problem in Paris). *Chaussures Chics* interrupts me with a new *devis* for the gas line and floors. I negotiate with him in French, pleased that, after just a week, my French has improved and I am more confident in the terms and the process. We agree on a reduced sum and installment payments based upon work done. I do not resorting to using *"truc"* once.

Each *appart* has its own private *cave* in the basement. Maria keeps the basement door locked and provides us with the key for access. Claire never showed me the *cave* and I forgot to ask. *Chaussures Chics* and I descend the winding cement steps to the *cave*, which is damp and musty, but clean. Cement paths are spread out like a maze weaving around stone and bricks. Empty rat traps and moth repellant are strewn about the dusty, cement floor lit by a few singular light bulbs hanging from the ceiling. Each *cave* has its own old, large wooden door. Mine is much bigger than I expected, about the size of my entire *sdb*. Floor to ceiling wooden shelves for wine storage with a vent that leads to the street. I place my lock on the door and give *Chaussures Chics* the key to put the extra paint and supplies in the cave when he is done.

When Maria comes to my floor to deliver the daily mail, I walk her through the contents of a letter I wrote her and show her where to put the deliveries of rugs and lights in my absence. I give her a second key to *l'appart* to let the workers in each morning. I also give her contact information for *Chaussures Chics*, JeF, and myself.

At the end of the day, it is just Pablo, Afonso, and me. I have become accustomed to sharing the small space with them and I offer them some cookies. When they see me struggle with my manual screwdriver trying to install the locks on the cabinet in the *sdb*, they come to my rescue with their automatic tools. My last night I have a quick dinner at Thierry's restaurant and apologize to him for missing his calls and the timing is cowardly convenient because I am leaving tomorrow so there is no opportunity to reschedule that *café*, at least at any time in the next two months.

When I return to *l'appart*, it is still. Pablo and Afonso are gone. I turn on my floor lamp, but it does not work. When I try other electrical things they are similarly inoperable, and I am afraid to turn anything on with all these exposed wires around me. I tread throughout *l'appart* with my little flashlight, looking for the generator switch. The setting sun causes me to panic because I have to pack up this entire apartment and my bags before sunrise, and I cannot get this done in the dark. In my hurried state, I cannot find *Chaussures Chics'* mobile number so I call Claire, apologize for the disruption, and explain to her the situation. She gives me his number, and he tells me how to turn the generator on just as the sun sets.

After four hours of sleep, I wake before my alarm and pack up the bedding and last miscellaneous things, and lock the large closet. At the *boulangerie* downstairs I buy some *pain au chocolat* to take home to the girls. I fall asleep in the cab to CDG and again on the plane. I am thoroughly exhausted but pleased, knowing that I did as much as I possibly could do in twelve days.

CHAPTER EIGHTEEN

Anything Is Possible

WHEN MY ELDEST began preschool, I befriended a recently divorced mother. Talented and kind, she was juggling work, Los Angeles traffic, and single parenthood. Beyond her daily, practical struggles, she shared with me the recurrent uncovering of the numerous deceptions of her recent past. Such revelations seemed to be the acid in an adulterous wound, making her healing a lengthy process. Little did I know, my own experience would soon follow and we would share the commonality of marital duplicity and single motherhood. Now, I know how difficult it is to do everything when there is only one of you, and how isolating it feels when there is no one with whom to share the joy of your child's first lost tooth or today's funny school story. I sympathize with her even more knowing that I do not have the financial struggle with which she was then additionally burdened.

While the girls are in school, I juggle my cooking classes, write my blog and recipes, and see about getting my cookbook published. Wait time in the carpool line is spent with my iPad doing some work or emails. In my spare moments, I try to prepare for the NYC marathon next month (to raise money for a local charity), which I can only do by carrying my running shoes in my car and running for an hour wherever I am. As for dating, I did go on that date with Mark. Actually, two. And, while I found him to be a kind man, devoted father, and a lively dinner companion, there were no genuine sparks between us that were not fabricated by momentary loneliness or a glass of wine. Through it all, the happiest parts of my every day are the evenings when the girls sit in the kitchen and do their homework while I cook them dinner. After I tuck them in, Paris occupies the quiet. The arrangement which I worked out with *Chaussures Chics* has been effective: he emails me photographic proof of the completed work and if I approve, I send him a check. The electrical is finished, the metal partition between the two meters is in. They are now working on the floors.

With the grace period for the electricity soon to end, I turn my attention to *EDF*, the French electricity company. Dealing with French utility companies is just as frustrating as those in the States but with the additional challenge of a foreign language and a nine-hour time difference. This process takes a full week. Three nights in a row I call at midnight, California time. The first two nights I am disconnected after sitting on hold for nearly an hour. The third night, I actually fall asleep while on hold. On the fourth night, I speak with a live person only to run into the same problem I had at Orange: she needs the prior occupant's name to look up the account. Unfortunately, I left the renter's name in Paris, necessitating that I call Maria for the information again. On the fifth night, after forty minutes on hold, I speak with Chantal (who thankfully speaks English). I give her the renter's name, my Darty reference as well as the RIB information to have the monthly electricity bill deducted from my French bank account. Electricity, done.

A few days before Halloween (a non-existent holiday in France but for my American children it is everything) and I am busy creating spooky savory appetizers—canapés that resemble fingers and deviled eggs stuffed from the bottom resembling ghosts. While the dry and wet ingredients combine in the standalone mixer for my chocolate graveyard cake, a lengthy French email from a man I do not know arrives in my inbox. This is trouble. I can sense it.

The letter is from one Monsieur de SAVOY (the use of "de" before a surname indicates French nobility). The noble Frenchman writes on behalf of the *syndic* of my building. Skipping past the customary French niceties, my eyes latch on to certain phrases: "*dégâts des eaux*" (water damage) and "*nous ne souhaitons pas aller au tribunal, ni prendre un avocat*" (we do not wish to go to court or take an attorney). The nobleman alleges that there is damage to the kitchen and bathroom in the apartment directly below mine and that the woman who sold me *mon appart* has applied to a French court requesting the appointment of an expert to determine the cause of the damage. She claims it is not her problem, but that of the *syndic*. The *syndic* disagrees. Monsieur de SAVOY says that it should not concern me since I am remodeling the kitchen but urges me to tell my *notaire* not to pay all of the sale proceeds to the seller. And then adds:

"*Bienvenue dans notre Copropriété!*" ("Welcome to our building!")

I could have done without the sarcasm. I could have done without the entire email. Kitchen? I never heard about water issues in the kitchen, only a leak in the bathroom, which I had been assured had been resolved before *la vente*. Moreover, the *PDV* said that there were no pending legal proceedings. I forward Monsieur de SAVOY's email to my *notaire*.

That night I lie in bed for hours contemplating the water damage and the *notaire*/seller/*syndic* scenario in my head. Putting my lawyer hat back on, I craft a response to Monsieur de SAVOY's email and, knowing that it may be an exhibit in the legal proceeding, I ask Samy to help me translate my letter into proper French, conveying a responsive, neighborly tone:

Monsieur de SAVOY,

J'ai bien reçu votre e-mail concernant les dégâts provoqués dans l'appartement de Madame et Monsieur DESMARAIS (2ème étage, en dessous du mien).

J'ai retransmis cet email à mon notaire à toutes fins utiles, notamment la question de la provision. J'espère que ce problème sera résolu rapidement et de manière satisfaisante. Je me tiens à votre disposition pour toute information dont vous auriez besoin.

Amicalement,

Lisa Morgan

After I send my email to the nobleman, I ask JeF to please stop by *l'appart*. He sends me the requested photograph of the electric meter (which I need to email to *EDF*) and photographs of *l'appart* status, which put a smile on my face. It is the email subject line that worries me:

"We need to talk about your bathroom :) *bisous*."

"What is wrong with the bathroom?" I reply, but I receive no response. He has probably gone back to work.

The girls are with their father for the first weekend in November, and after I drop them off at school, I fly to New York for the NYC marathon. Trying to use my time wisely, I arrange meetings with some possible agents for my cookbook. The appointments, however, do not go as I had hoped and after listening to what they had to say, I suspect that the appointments were made out of respect for our mutual friends. The good news is that everyone likes the book, or so they say they do, but they are not interested in pitching it. Too many color photographs. Too expensive. Moreover, unless I have a pre-established market base, most publishers will not take me on as an unknown cook. One agent tells me that if I do not have a restaurant, a cookbook deal is more likely if I am a television personality. She tells me I should go on a reality show, *Beverly Hills Housewives*, she suggests.

I reflect on these meetings as I run over the bouncing bridges and through the five boroughs. A reality show. Nothing could interest me less, not to mention I do not live in Beverly Hills nor am I am someone's wife. She also suggested the option of "vanity publishing" wherein the author financially guarantees selling a certain number of books, which is not an option either. The news was deflating. However, I refuse to give up. I could always self-publish, and I think of that option as well as Giovanni's admonition that no real money can be made on books. As I approach Central Park at the race's end, I think of the first time I ran this race, ten months after I was released from the hospital. My mother and daughters had come to watch me. It was a good day and the first and only time anyone has come to cheer me on, which was a nice treat. They even made signs.

Back in Los Angeles, the routine of morning drop-offs continues. The girls entertain themselves in the morning's standstill traffic by slapping each other's hands and singing songs they are learning for the upcoming holiday show. An email from JeF crosses my phone screen:

"*13 superbes Photos - Bizzzooooo.*" The images load and there it is …

"MY STOVE!!! MY STOVE!!!!!" I exclaim.

And it is gorgeous, seated in the center of the tiny kitchen on the black-and-white tiled floor. The work of art takes my breath away, and indeed I think my heart skips a beat. The girls mimic my enthusiasm:

"MY STOVE! MY STOVE!" they chant in unison with their arms raised and their hands waving above their heads. They continue to chant until they exit the car and are quick to resume the same chorus in the afternoon when I pick them up.

My grandmother always said that trouble comes in threes. She was right. Since the stove installation, my email has been filled with bits of Paris annoyance or bad news. The New York company I ultimately hired for the door-to-door shipping of our belongings from Los Angeles to Paris promised that if the items are picked up by the 1st of December, they will be at *l'appart* when I arrive in Paris on the 26th. After scrambling to accommodate this deadline, they changed the transit time; our items will not arrive in Paris until sometime in January. Then, the French life insurance company requests the same documents that have been provided to them three times by all means of delivery. This time, however, they threaten to cancel my insurance, which in turn, I imagine will create a problem with my mortgage. The third bit of trouble arrives when JeF emails photographs of *l'appart* progress—gas meter installed, walls painted, floors refinished—all good but for the ugly aluminum kitchen sink *Chaussures Chics* installed in lieu of my antique porcelain one (to be discussed with him *plus tard*). The last photograph steals the smile from my face. It is a photograph of paperwork, which I must expand to read:

"*Avis de Passage.*"

There are attorneys' names. There is *my* name and phrases such as "*Acte*" and "*Nature de L'Acte.*" I am being sued. In France! *Putain!* Maria was apparently served on my behalf, which I cannot imagine is proper service, but it is France so who knows how substitute service works. There is a hearing in Paris on December 16, requiring my presence, to determine if I, as the new property owner, should be officially included in the lawsuit. December 16 is also the day of the girls' Winter Holiday school performance and the day Winter Break begins and the first week they are with me. JeF puts me in touch with his lawyer.

The weeks leading up to Winter Break are routinely exhausting and this year, I am not my usual holiday-happy chef self. Rather, I am a chef with sharp knives, an adopted French attitude, and a sharp tongue. My *notaire* is on the top of the naughty list and after a few sleepless nights, I send him another letter putting him on notice of the lawsuit, demanding assurances that a portion of the sale proceeds was retained, and reminding him of their representation that any problem was resolved prior to *la vente* (in a firm, yet polite, French-like manner). His response, calling my attention to things I already know, and offering no solutions or suggestions, is annoying and hardly surprising. More maddening is that he did not retain any portion of the funds and justifies his failure to do so on a "certification" from the plumber that the repairs had been done and there was no issue. He includes a copy of the certification and *facture* for the repairs upon which he relied; it was *Chaussures Chics* who did the repairs.

Red is the color that landscapes my field of vision. Not one of them even makes the naughty list—not the *notaire*, not *Chaussures Chics*, and not the realty company—they are only deserving of coal and only *if* it is used to fuel the fire under the spit on which I would like to roast each one of them. By all appearances, they did what they could to cover themselves and push the sale through at my cost. The *notaire* should have retained a portion of the sale proceeds as a precaution, and it was inexcusable that he did not. He knew of a dispute between the parties and a one-page *facture* from a plumber hardly seems due diligence. The seller's strategy of including me in the lawsuit was no accident. It all leaves me feeling like a cliché; their actions justified by the well-accepted French perception that Americans are spoiled, entitled, and have money so they can better bear a financial burden than a French citizen and most certainly an elderly French widow of 90. I have a fine French acronym for her!

While the girls sleep, the hush of evening does not quiet my anxiety. Beyond the complication to my Paris dream and feeling duped, there is also the practical matter: how much is this all going to cost me? At 2 a.m., I speak with JeF's attorney, Christophe. He assures me that he will appear on my behalf on the 16th and report to me the outcome. In the interim, I send him all the documentation I have and wire him his retainer (which is three times the amount of the alleged damages). *Zut!* Worse yet, I know how quickly the retainer will erode, especially once an expert becomes involved. This is going to cost me.

I WAKE TO to a complete copy of the French summons and complaint:

Avis de Signification d'un Acte de Procédure
Assignation en Référé en Ordonnance Commune Devant le Président du
Tribunal de Grande Instance de Paris.

Filed in front of the President of the Tribunal of Paris means it is no "small claims court" matter. And according to the allegations in the document, the water leaks began a year before I even looked at *l'appart,* and the owners of the apartment below tried to get the seller to make repairs. When she did not, the *syndic* got involved. About the time I was looking at the property, in June, and unbeknownst to me, the leaks continued in the foyer and bathroom and the renters' management company so informed the *syndic.* The *syndic* hired a plumber who said that the tiles in my bathroom were not waterproof and the shower/tub hook-up under the tub needed to be redone. I assume this "plumber" who performed the work in my *sdb* is *Chaussures Chics.*

In September, while *la vente* was pending, humidity problems continued in the kitchen. On October 13, *the day after* I left Paris for Los Angeles, the owners of the apartment below mine sued the *syndic* and the seller. All of the allegations occurred prior to me taking ownership; however, a singular ambiguous allegation in the complaint implicates me:

"*A ce jour, les infiltrations dans l'apartement ... persistent au niveau de la salle de bain et de l'entrée, et l'appartement continue de se dégrader.*"

A leak in the foyer and bathroom exist to this day. *Merde.*

Christophe fashions a stern letter to my *notaire,* demanding the evidence upon which they relied to assure themselves that there was no issue with the apartment. He closes the letter with: "*En toute hypothèse, je vous remercie de séquestrer entre vos mains une partie du produit de la vente que nous déterminerons d'un commun accord.*" ("In any event, I thank you for withholding a portion of the sale money in an amount to determined by mutual agreement.")

CHRISTMAS IS twelve days away. My email inbox is consumed with bits of bad news rather than holiday joy. The French insurance company denies my tender. Christophe says that plaintiffs are acting through their Legal Protection Insurance, which he describes to me as an "infernal machine," meaning this nuisance will not be going away any time soon. Moreover, he has been unable to reach the infernal counsel for any type of discussion but plans to speak with them at the hearing tomorrow. The court has appointed an expert to determine the source of the alleged leaks. He proposes an inspection of *l'appart* and the apartment below mine on January 3 with all parties and their counsel present. I tell Christophe that I cannot be in Paris on the 3rd because the girls begin school in Los Angeles on the 2nd.

Then there is *Chaussures Chics*. He is both my enemy and a percipient witness, which makes for a tricky situation. The questionable disappearance of my antique kitchen sink is one thing, but his involvement in the apparent water cover-up conspiracy makes it worse. However, as the remodeler of my kitchen, not to mention the alleged "fixer" of the bathroom leak, I need to play nice with him as he likely will be a witness in the lawsuit. Yet, I cannot seem too familiar with him or his testimony will appear compromised. I already regret using the informal "*tu*" in prior emails. Samy helps me write a carefully worded letter to *Chaussures Chics*. Believing that more expensive shoes are an incentive, I bait him with future work and ask him for a *devis* for the bathroom remodel and remind him that we need to close out any issues with the work he did in the kitchen. JeF has already promised me the name of another contractor to finish the remaining work in *l'appart*, but perhaps if *Chaussures Chics* thinks he may be getting additional work he will stay cooperative.

My head aches with French legal details so I go to my happy place. The weather is chilly and overcast, and I decide *pot-au-feu*, a French beef stew, would be perfect for this winter weather. The simmering pot fills the house with a beef and vegetable aroma and the comforting smell even lures Coco into the kitchen from her slumber. Coco, who turned eighteen in October, sleeps all the time. Since the coyote nabbing, she has aged significantly. She moves slowly and her eyesight and hearing continue to decline. Her sense of smell, however, remains strong and when it comes to eating, she excitedly moves toward her food dish every time. She lies at my feet in the kitchen, waiting for her share, and I put some in her dish with some steamed rice and when it has cooled enough to eat, I give her the bowl. She gobbles it all up as if it is her last meal and then wobbles back to her bed.

At 4 a.m. my inbox is full of emails from Paris. Christophe reports that the hearing went as expected and I am now officially part of the lawsuit. And this inclusion makes me the recipient of even more legal letters with idiotic French niceties such as: *"Croyez, Mon Cher Maître, à l'assurance de mes sentiments dévoués."* ("Believe me, my dear sir, I give you all of my devoted sentiments.") *Bah!* This morning alone I am the recipient of six such letters. Infuriating because each one costs me more euros. The only good thing is that Christophe was able to move the inspection date to January 23, 2012, an extended weekend the girls will be with their father, and I have frequent flyer miles.

At 8:30 a.m. I sit in the third row of the auditorium seats, waiting for the holiday show to begin. Every grade performs three to four songs, and I have already been instructed by the girls as to where on the risers they will be standing. I force the lawsuit out of my mind; it is this show, not the lawsuit, I will remember in the future years, and I ready my video camera to make sure. When the show is over, elated children scurry from the auditorium to their Winter Break freedom. The girls and I take Julia's bestie home with us for the afternoon. The weather is warm and sunny, and the only hint of snow this winter lies in the plastic snow globe that is now leaking on the coffee table because it has been dropped so often. The three girls play soccer in the front yard and request snacks. Coco has gotten sick (as is often the case these days) and needs to be outside. I avoid putting her in the front yard with the girls playing as I worry they will bump into her or accidentally let her out, so I put her in the backyard where I set up my photography area for this week's blog. I have thirty minutes before the sun disappears and my consecutive meetings with Samy and Tim, who helps me with my website, begin. Coco paces around the pool, like she always does while I go inside to retrieve my camera.

When I return to the backyard, an eerie silence consumes me. Coco is not pacing. I look on the sides of the house, but she is nowhere to be found. I look in my bedroom to see if she has returned to her bed. She is not there. Then from the window I see her, floating on her side in the pool. I run and scoop her out of the cold water, cradling her body to my chest. She is foaming at the mouth and not breathing. Frantic attempts to press on her little chest and give her mouth-to-mouth are futile, and I hug her ten-pound body into mine wishing my love and warmth could somehow will movement back into hers. But it does not, and I curse myself for letting her out of my sight. How could I? All the times she avoided harm—the several yard escapes from our Hollywood home and ending up on a busy street or befriending neighbor Bob Barker, her tangles with skunks, the coyote dognapping. I have heard that the last sense to go when you drown is your hearing, and I wonder if the last thing Coco heard was me calling her name. The thought makes me feel worse. Overwhelmed with grief and weeping from every fiber of my being, I swaddle her in a towel and hold her in my left arm. The girls continue to play soccer in the front yard. I email Samy and Tim from the phone in my right hand, canceling our afternoon meetings.

When Julia's bestie leaves before dinner, I deliver the sad news. Ava cries into her hands while Julia, sobbing, folds herself into my lap. They have known Coco the entirety of their lives. The girls write goodbye letters to Coco, which we will read and bury with her, and I ask Martin, our gardener, if he can dig a hole under the large olive tree in the backyard from where I watch the sun bow to meet the ocean in the west. I have forgotten about the Paris lawsuit, the *notaire*, the expert, the seller, and *Chaussures Chics*. Coco has been with me since law school. She survived the bar exam, boyfriends, a marriage, and gently and curiously greeted the girls when we brought them home from the hospital. The kitchen is usually where I find solace, but not tonight. Coco's bowl sits in the center, and the kitchen remains quiet and dark.

THE BIG EMPTY, as I call it, begins at noon on Christmas Day. Before that time, the days and nights are filled with the usual holiday madness; the rush to prepare for Christmas and all the nuances that it entails, including school obligations, parties, and festivities. The week prior to Christmas the girls are with me and we are busy with shopping, baking, and holiday merrymaking. On Christmas Eve, our house fills with the warmth of the people we love the most. Santa comes and goes. Wrapping paper is torn. Toys and dolls revealed. Then, in an instant, the merrymaking is over and the guests leave. At noon on Christmas Day, the girls leave to repeat the Christmas process with their father, and I am left with a quiet home. Passing the legacy of divorce to my daughters feels like a personal failure, especially at Christmas time, and my mind drifts to my choices and the circumstances that led to a repeat of the past I sought to overcome and never wanted for them. This year, without Coco's toenails tapping on the hardwood floor, the emptiness is profound.

When I was first separated, my father tried to comfort me. He assured me that time heals all wounds. Despite his sincerity, I do not think that is true. Time is *not* a healer. Rather, time is both a thief, taking years and people too quickly, and a warrior, continuing without pause, marking those grief-stricken and stolen moments as historical. Time does not heal; it only gives us distance. For me, Paris eases the Big Empty. At 1 p.m., I leave for LAX, with two pieces of luggage, two large boxes, and my bubble-wrapped curtain rod, which looks a lot like a shotgun. I arrive at LAX resembling someone who is either moving or going hunting.

Terminal 2, from which Air France departs, is nearly empty. I load my luggage on the scale. The clerk pauses when she sees my bubble-wrapped rod. I assure her that I cleared the drape rod dimensions with Air France previously. She is suspicious and calls over another clerk to discuss. Measuring tapes are drawn, and they acknowledge that the offensive and dangerous-looking package indeed meets the requirements.

We move from the subject of size to weight. I knew I was going to have to pay extra for the boxes and the rod, but I should have read the fine print, or at least remembered that I had read the fine print. It is $75 for the first and then $200 for the second and $200 for the third. Not $75 for each! *Putain!* Tears of frustration well in my eyes. The harder I try to be economical and stick to my budget (stove being the exception), the quicker my budget erodes. How did I get this so wrong? I keep telling my doctor that I need an MRI or something similar because my brain, cloudy and forgetful, just does not seem to function like it used to. He says it is just being a working single mother. My friends say it is paramenopause. Neither explanation provides me relief nor solves my problem. I stand at the desk wiping tears from my eyes and type into my phone a to-do list for my return: "GET MRI FOR NON-FUNCTIONING BRAIN! EXHIBIT A: BAGGAGE DEBACLE - LAX." As I type my note, a woman behind the desk sees my tears and offers me a homemade Christmas cookie from a round tin bearing a Santa Claus and three bears on the lid, but the kind gesture causes the tears to fall faster, because I do not feel like an empowered woman going to her happy place to make the most of her forced fucking "me time." Instead, the absence of my children with whom I usually fill the same Christmas tins consumes me and this empty terminal seems devoid of oxygen. A supervisor passes by and observes the spectacle of the boxes, bubbled-wrapped curtain rod, the two clerks, one bearing cookies, and the bawling passenger. She looks at the computer screen and sees the luggage fees. She changes my seat to some fancier and roomier version of economy.

The Christmas kindness results in extra room for my legs and my bottom, and this practical autonomy eases the baggage sting. So does the *coupe de champagne,* which I sip while settling into a French movie. I miss my girls but remind myself what I tell them, that we will be sleeping under the same blanket of sky, and with that thought, they do not seem so far away. The Big Empty.

Joyeux Noël à moi.

Putain.

POT-AU-FEU

This beef stew is easy to make and perfect for those cold months. There are two things to note when making this dish. First, you must skim often or the broth will taste greasy. Second, to create a more flavorful broth, I cook the mirepoix and brown the meat as I would a braise. This extra step bumps up the flavor of the broth. You can add marrow bones or ox tail to the broth as well.

Serves 6

Meat and broth
3 pounds rump roast, trimmed and tied
A/N kosher salt
A/N freshly ground pepper
1 tablespoon unsalted butter
½ cup chopped leeks
1 cup chopped onions
1 cup chopped carrots
½ cup diced celery
1 tablespoon tomato paste
¼ cup dry red wine
A/N cold water
1 *bouquet garni* (fresh Italian parsley, thyme, and 1 bay leaf)
1 tablespoon sea salt
1 teaspoon black peppercorns

New vegetables
16 baby fingerling potatoes
16 baby carrots, trimmed
4 celery stalks, cut *bâtonnet*
10 baby bok choy, trimmed
12 Tokyo turnips, trimmed
12 pearl onions, trimmed and peeled
A/N sea salt
A/N freshly ground black pepper

Season the meat generously with salt and pepper. Set on a plate and let it come to room temperature (about 1 hour before cooking).

Place a cast-iron skillet or a dutch oven over a medium-high flame. Once warm, add butter. When butter has melted, add the meat to the pan. Brown the meat on all sides. Remove meat from the skillet and set aside. Add the leeks and onions to the skillet. Add a pinch of salt. Cook until tender. Once tender, add the carrots and celery. Cook until tender. Add tomato paste to the vegetables and toss the vegetables in the tomato paste.

Add red wine. Toss the vegetables in the wine, scraping any meat *fond* from the bottom of the skillet. Reduce *au sec* (until the liquid has been cooked out of the skillet).

Return the meat to the dutch oven (or, if using a skillet, place the meat and vegetables in a large pot). Add enough water to cover the meat and the *mirepoix* completely. Add salt, pepper, and *bouquet garni*. Bring to a boil. Once a boil has been reached, reduce heat to a low flame. Use a large, metal spoon to skim foam and impurities that rise to the surface. Partially cover the pot with a lid. Simmer the meat and vegetables for 1 hour and 30 minutes. Skim often.

Use tongs to remove the meat from the broth. Set the meat on a plate and cover with aluminum foil to keep warm.

Strain the broth into a clean pot by pouring it through a chinois (or a colander lined with two layers of cheesecloth). Discard the *bouquet garni* and cooked *mirepoix*.

Skim the fat from the strained broth. This is important or the broth will taste greasy and unpleasant. (If you are having difficulty removing the fat, you can ladle out some of the broth into a fat separator and use that to separate any grease from the liquid.)

Place the strained broth on the stove over a medium flame. Reduce broth by cooking for about 15 minutes. Return the meat to the broth. Add the new vegetables (baby carrots, celery, pearl onions, and potatoes). Simmer for about 5 minutes. Add the bok choy and baby turnips. Simmer for another 2-3 minutes. Adjust seasoning. The vegetables are done when a fork can easily be inserted into the carrots and potatoes. Turn off the flame.

Remove the meat from the broth and cut the string from the meat. Slice. Place meat on a serving platter. Remove the new vegetables from the broth and place them on the platter with the sliced meat. Pour the broth into a tureen. Table side, serve each guest some vegetables and meat. Ladle the broth over the meat and vegetables.

Serve with crispy bread.

CHAPTER NINETEEN

Quarante Cocottes

THE CITY OF LIGHT is clothed in festive attire and accessorized with holiday-themed lighting and decor. My taxi passes by the Étoile, and I peer down the Champs-Élysées toward the Place de la Concorde. The famous avenue has been taken over by the Christmas Village, small white wooden châlets on both sides of the street brimming with holiday cheer in the form of artisanal culinary treats while cups of *vin chaud* warm chilly hands. When I crack open the taxi window, eager to feel the chill of the season that is absent in Los Angeles, my nose fills with the aroma of spiced wine and nutty *marrons chauds*. I wonder if Jean, who has been selling roasted chestnuts from his beautiful little cart in front of Les Deux Magots for as long as I can remember, is back at it again this year. With Christmas come and gone, Paris is quiet. Many restaurants and businesses are closed and there are likely more *bûches de Noël* in Paris than Parisians. Parisians are skiing in the Alps.

A rush of warm air and smell of pine welcome me from the four-degree chill. The lobby has been transformed into a winter wonderland; a large white-flocked Christmas tree trimmed with hand-sized white ornaments and blinking lights dominates the space. A miniature Santa Claus on a scooter is underneath the tree.

It takes two elevator trips to accommodate my nesting essentials. Chasing the elevator filled with my luggage, I count the doors I pass bearing a *Joyeux Noël* sign (three). A flip of the new switch in the foyer and the crystals from the new chandelier spread circles of light throughout the dark space. Even in the dark, *l'appart* is quite transformed and more lovely than any email can convey. The black paint on the interior water pipes that scale the foyer walls to the ceiling (my Art Deco nod to Le Centre Pompidou) look fantastic against the clean white walls with their artistic panels. *Ma cuisine parisienne*, still a work in progress, but dramatically changed, while the single light bulb dangles nostalgically from above, spotlighting the stove. I run my hands over the stove's glossy black surface. The burners ignite with the ferocity of a jet fighter plane taking flight. *Whoa!* I play with the flames, high, low, and repeat, it has a responsiveness that would have been completely lost on an electric stovetop.

Freeing my feet from their long boots, I slide across the glossy ebony floors in *le salon* in my stocking feet, delighting in the lack of cords or tools for me to trip over. With the metal shutters open, the winter gray light allows me to better survey the rooms. The electrical lines are hidden in the baseboards, and the switches are all where I requested. While I admire the *chic* contrast of the eggshell walls with the ebony floors, I realize that the wrought iron curtain rod, perfectly curved to match the architectural bend in the bedroom wall, is nowhere to be found. Another item to add to *Chaussures Chics'* punch list, and foiling my hopes for a bit of privacy.

Pulling my belongings inside from the hallway, I remove my jacket and hat but put them back on within minutes because *l'appart* is so cold. *Très froid.* Turning the radiator knob in both directions is futile as the pipe and radiator remain cold. The radiator in the *sdb* similarly offers no sign of life. I turn on the bathroom faucet to warm my hands, but after several minutes, the water remains cold. At the kitchen sink, the predicament is the same. Pulling my boots back on,

I proceed downstairs to inquire about the water and heat situation only to find a note taped on Maria's door: She is in Portugal for the holidays, returning on January 4. *Merde*. No heat. No hot water. No Maria. Living the Paris dream.

The good news is that I have electricity and a floor heater. The bad news is that the floor heater is in the large bathroom closet, the contents of which are held captive by the unassembled dining table leaning against its doors. Deciding to conquer two tasks at once, I decide to assemble the table pieces: a twelve-by-four-foot wooden top, two solid iron legs in the shape of a curvy capital H with an extra cross bar on the bottom, and one long iron bar that screws into the legs to stabilize the table. The legs are too heavy to lift, so I am forced to slide each one from the *sdb* to *le salon* partially resting the leg on a towel and partially on my lifted foot. I use the same method to slide the large, solid wooden table top. After one iron leg falls on my foot (causing me to break momentarily to wipe my tears and assess if my toes are broken), then re-assembling the table a second time because the first time I had the legs facing the wrong way, the table for eight is assembled and sits in front of the balcony windows.

In no time, the small heater takes the chill from the inside air. I break from my domesticities for an outing to Béchu for my favorite nut and raisin bread with its crispy, well-baked crust. The compression of my boot eases the discomfort of my right foot, and I head out into the Paris air where puffy down jackets resembling walking comforters bounce down the damp streets. Well-tied scarves hide all necks, and gloved hands carry umbrellas. Every so often, a full-length fur jacket crosses my path, something I'd never see in California. At Béchu I request *deux tranches,* and the woman behind the counter takes her serrated knife and cuts two healthy slices. Next stop is Halles des Belles Feuilles, my favorite produce market. The same elderly couple is working; he is operating the scale and she, the register. Today's special, bundled bright pink fresh lychees sold on their branches, is too good to pass up, and I request one bundle for no reason other than I have never ever seen fresh lychees, and I am curious to try them. The man selects a bundle and places them in a paper bag, while I add some winter staples to my *panier* as well as some *mirepoix* for stock: an onion, a large carrot (still covered in dirt, a detail I love), and two stalks of celery. In France you can take as much as you need; you are not forced to buy a bundle of celery if you do not need it, and that practicality I consider perfect in many ways. After the husband weighs my selections, he hands the bags to his wife at the register who asks me how I am.

"*Très bien, merci,*" I say.

Her recognition feels like a personal success.

At Au Poulet de Bresse, *la boucherie* for *volaille*, the prized, feather-headed fowl are prominently displayed. I approach the counter filled with poultry varieties of all shapes and sizes and skin tones. A man with an accumulation of years in a butcher's white jacket peers from behind. A ring of white hair circles his otherwise bald head, and he wears thin wire spectacles. His little white mustache dances on his upper lip as he asks what I would like.

"*Os de poulet, s'il vous plaît,*" I say.

Chicken bones. He stares at me politely, yet perplexed. Admittedly, my pronunciation of "*os*" needs work.

"*Pour faire du bouillon de volaille…*" I continue, hoping that an explanation of my intended use will bridge the language gap.

It does. A look of recognition flashes across his round face. He explains to me that there are no chicken bones. It then occurs to me that such a request is ridiculous because in contrast to the States, where the chicken breasts and other parts are commonly sold "skinless" or "boneless," in France, chicken is cooked on the bone, the skin is used, and all parts have value. I alter my request: two chicken legs (sold with the thighs). He wraps the meaty parts in butcher's paper, concluding my first experience in Paris purchasing chicken.

The local Casino *supermarché* is four times the size of the local Monoprix. Large display cases of Champagne, chocolate, *galettes des rois*, and *foie gras* (in every shape and size — *cartouche*, *bloc*, *terrine*, or *tranche*) leave no doubt that it is the holiday season. I buy a variety for comparison purposes and find whole truffles not far away.

Overwhelmed, yet delighted, I have never seen so many dairy selections in my life, and I toss three variations of Normandy butter in my cart with several selections of pre-made doughs — *pâte sucrée*, *pâte brisée*, and *pâte feuilletée* — just to have on-hand in the freezer for emergencies (and to test the quality). The produce section is filled with pear and apple varieties, which are not available in the States. The temptation too great and my curiosity piqued, I grab two of each variety, Reines des Reinettes (used for *tarte Tatin*), Calville Blanc d'Hiver, and by the time I am finished, I have four varieties of apples and three of pears.

At the checkout stand, the cashier shakes her head when she sees my selections and sends me back to the produce aisle to weight and tag each variety of fruit. *Zut*. The scales have a screen with a photograph of each variety of vegetable or fruit and I select the appropriate button, place the corresponding fruit on the scale, a price tag is spit out, and I place it on the bag. To avoid the head-shaking cashier, I stand in another line. This cashier asks for my *carte de fidélité* (which I do not have) and then my address. The young man assisting her begins placing my groceries in a large, hard plastic bin. *Zut! (Encore!)* I am in the *livraison à domicile* line. A second line fail, requiring me to explain to her that I do not need delivery, I just got in the wrong line.

She overlooks my mistake, but the young man unpacks my things from the bin and walks away.

Back at *l'appart* I continue unpacking the closet, amazed at the sheer quantity of food products and housewares I managed to accumulate during my twelve-day stay and efficiently stuff in this closet. My premature desire to outfit a future kitchen—the heart and soul of a nest—resulted in a large larder of everything from various mustards to Puy lentils. I still have no place to put all of these pantry items, which makes me laugh a little at myself. Soon the electronics bring the place to life (minus the WiFi, which I have managed to mess up again), and I assemble the Lucite dining room chairs with ease, except I am missing one set of legs, leaving me with five chairs and a half.

Once the bottom of the closet has been emptied, I focus my efforts on the top section which can only be accessed by standing on the top rung of my five-foot ladder. The bedside tables are closest to me in this Chinese puzzle of small furniture, and I begin by pulling on the leg of one of them, gently at first, then with more force, loosening it from the stack. Trying to avoid the top bar of the ladder, slowly I pass the table over my head, but the maneuver causes me to lose my balance and I fall off the ladder and land on the bathroom tile. The table garnishes my splayed body like a flower arrangement on a coffin. I reach through the table legs, and feel my face for blood or missing teeth, then push the table off of me. The entirety of my body aches; my foot does not feel so bad by comparison. Staring at my surroundings from this unfortunate vantage point, I wonder if my ultimate demise will be to die of internal wounds here in this avocado bathroom bearing my Sharpie instructions on the walls. I contemplate walking downstairs to floor "zero" to visit the doctor, but he is probably gone for the holidays too, and four floors away seems too far, even with an elevator.

I roll over on my side and instinctively crawl toward the bathtub and turn on the water. No longer yellow, nor trickling, but it is cold. I sit with my hand in the running water, hoping that by some good fortune it will eventually warm up, but it remains cold and my body begins to shake from either the cold water or the shock of falling. My need to ease my aching body in a hot bath takes on primitive means.

Unpacking the four cast-iron *cocottes*, I carry them one by one from the bathroom to the kitchen where I fill each one with water and place them on the stove. As soon as the water begins to boil, I carry one *cocotte* from the stove across *l'appart* and pour the hot water into the tub. Four gas burners. Four *cocottes*. I repeat the process ten times. *Quarante cocottes*. The water temperature in the half-full tub has cooled from a boil to a simmer and after a thirty-minute soak, I find the Advil in my running bag and crawl into my unmade bed, wrapping the blankets around me like a cocoon. I forget about the fact that I cannot hang my drapes, my neighbors can see me sleeping, that I have to boil water to bathe, and can only warm myself with a small floor heater. Mark Twain once said that "truth is stranger than fiction." And I think about that expression as I fall asleep filled with gratitude for the comfortable bed and the Advil.

WHEN I WAKE, the skies remain gray while my foot and my torso are noticeably black and blue. I unpack the luggage and boxes I brought from Los Angeles filled with housekeeping niceties, including my espresso machine *grâce au Père Noël*, which I had wrapped in the carefully folded drapes. With no countertops, I place the machine on a cutting board on top of my stove. A frothy cappuccino is the perfect way to begin this day, and I plan to treat my black and blue self to coffee in bed next to my heater with some French magazines. The milk foamed, I press the button for a double, my coffee cup readied underneath to capture the heady goodness coming my way. Nothing happens. When I press the button a second time, a loud, abbreviated buzz followed by an explosive sound and a puff of smoke causes me to jump away from the machine. Fearing that something has gone terribly wrong with the electrical, I cautiously examine the electrical panel; it appears unaffected, so I focus my efforts on the kitchen plug. It, too, is unaffected, and then I realize that my converter is not a converter but an adaptor, and I electrocuted my Christmas gift. *Putain!* With my winter gear covering my sore body, an umbrella in one hand and my *marché* caddie in the other, I make the familiar trek to Darty for a replacement machine, determined to have that leisurely (now, late) morning in my new bed. The air feels like Sancerre—crisp and dry—and the vintage temperature so rejuvenating that I slow my usual pace and even stop at Isabelle's shop for the companion hood to my stove (as it is evident that my idea of using the kitchen window for ventilation is not such a grand idea in winter).

JeF, having just returned from his holiday celebrations in Burgundy, arrives at my door with a trio of Bourgogne wines and a holiday grin. Grinch he is not. He picks me up off of the ground although I warn him not to hug me too tightly, but in truth, all people should hug the way he hugs, bruises or not. While I look for wine glasses so we may enjoy his thoughtfulness, he spies the mess of wires on the floor. He fixes my electronic challenges for a second time, and I abandon the glass search to assist him, tagging each wire with masking tape to identify where it goes should I disconnect them again. We have not seen one another since October, and we walk to dinner where there is no shortage of wine or conversation. When I finally fall into my exposed bed, I do not feel black and blue anymore.

WHEN THE MORNING light finally makes an appearance, it reveals more gray skies. My four-minute eggs cooking on the stove, my heater going full blast, I consume my cappuccino and a stack of new French cookbooks in bed with a view of the Parisian rooftops. It is a perfect morning and I only interrupt my contentment to walk across the street for my appointment with Lucille who makes me an espresso and fires one question after another at me: *L'appart?* What am I doing to it? What have I been cooking? How was my Christmas? While she tells me about the dreamy *foie gras entrée* she devoured last night at a dinner party, she has her way with my hair color and cuts my mop in any way which she feels inspired to do.

"*Plat ou avec volume?*" she asks.

"*Plat.*"

And once she has blown my hair flat I see that it is a tad darker, but my *coif* is only to be enjoyed momentarily because when I leave it is drizzling.

With my hairdo undone, I decide to take a run to the 17th in search of a bathroom showroom I found on the internet, entertaining myself by counting the *pâtisseries* and *boulangeries* en route with which I am unfamiliar. The window at La Petite Marquise bulges with mini *bûches de Noël* ("*buchettes*") and large *bûches de Noël* made of dark chocolate with deep red chocolate ruffled strips folded to resemble a dahlia. Stunning. The artistic yule logs lie next to the *sapin au chocolat* (another French holiday tradition) made of crisped rice or flakes covered in chocolate the shape of branches and stacked together to form a tree, dusted with powdered sugar "snow." *Boules* stacked in the baker's rack behind are carved with 2011. Baking inspiration gained, I continue running north but by the time I reach the Étoile, the dark clouds relieve themselves of their heaviness and the drizzle becomes a deluge. Umbrellas unfurled to ward off the rain obstruct my view of the holiday decor on Avenue de Wagram, consistently fetching this time of year. I find the showroom tucked away on a side street with a small hand-written note on the door; it is closed for the week.

The damp weather intensifies my desire to cook. Stock preparation is a necessity and a ritual in French homes and likely the reason why French *supermarchés* carry only bouillon cubes (which I find wholly unsatisfying), quite in contrast to the aisles of prepared stock found in American stores. My dining room table serves as my prep station, and I chop in front of the large windows facing Stein who is sitting on the same place on her couch with her computer on her lap. Soon the smell of the simmering stock pervades *l'appart*, and the heat from the kitchen is steaming the windows, giving me some privacy. My stove to the rescue again.

Taking a break from skimming the simmering stock, I walk across the street to the *boucherie* where milk-fed veal and beef from the Limousin region are the advertised house specialties. The butcher, about my age, is bent over a three-inch-thick chopping block, used so often, and in the same spot, that there is a one-inch crescent-shaped depression worn in the center. He trims a roast for six, because in France you order meat by the number of people you are feeding, not by weight, and this method always works: there are rarely leftovers and everyone has the appropriate portion. He spools the glossy white string around the meat and ties it as if he is wrapping fine jewelry. When it is my turn, I decide on the house specialty. There is no tying or trimming involved: veal *escalope. Une personne.* He does not bat an eye at my singular request and places the thin slice in between a plastic sheet and wraps it delicately in butcher paper, calling out the amount to the woman with the wavy hair standing behind the register. She has the same round face and soft brown eyes as he, and I deduce that it is another family business.

The windows are now sweating. When I deem the water to have sufficiently taken on the flavors of the ingredients, I carry the stockpot to the bathtub where I strain the stock into a clean pot, cognizant of the fact that food in a bathroom is *très dégoûtant*. However, the task could not properly be carried out in the kitchen, given its current state. With no ice nor an ice wand to cool the stock, I violate even more kitchen protocol and place the container of hot stock on the balcony to cool, battling with the maddening *film fraîcheur* because the plastic wrap sticks to nothing, not even itself, despite the "*très adhérent*" claim. Twisting a lengthy piece of plastic wrap into a belt, I tie it around the pot to secure the plastic film on top, poking holes in the cover to release steam, giving my neighbors yet another oddity to witness.

A cutting board on top of two wooden wine cases turned on their sides becomes my temporary counter upon which I set my cooking essentials. I fire up a burner and caramelize apple chunks of different varieties and experiment with the pre-made dough, creating an assortment of miniature *tartes Tatins*. I then fire up a second and a third burner, steam fennel, brown both sides of the veal, remove, add shallots and capers, a little wine, stock, reduce, add butter, return the veal to the pan and spoon the sauce over it. I purée the steamed fennel. Dinner. My tray of tarts cool on a rack on the other end of the table while I enjoy my veal with *Règal*, a French food magazine. The apartments across the way light up for the evening mid-week rituals. Three of the windows are filled with Christmas trees. Dylan and his mom are dining while the French Cleavers are setting up their table for dinner.

The bathroom has a lingering smell of chicken when I begin my *cocotte* bathing ritual. JeF told me about a craftsman, Henri, whom he hired to remodel his bathroom. Henri lives in Boulogne, just outside Paris, and when his time is not occupied re-working Parisian hotels, he takes on various jobs in and outside of Paris. Pleased with his work, JeF suggested that I speak with him. So I did and we made a *rendez-vous* for tomorrow morning to discuss finishing the kitchen. Lying in the warm water, examining the ugly green walls, I decide that I will speak with Henri about redoing the bathroom too.

It is early evening in California when I telephone the girls to wish them a goodnight. They both join in on the conversation, their questions overlapping: How cold it is in Paris? Is it snowing? What does *l'appart* look like? I tell them about the holiday decorations in the city and changes in *l'appart*, falling off a ladder, heating water on the stove to take a bath, and the little tiny heater. They laugh heartily to the point of snorting. Ava asks about the stove and if I have used it yet beyond heating bath water. Laughing, I tell her that I have and it is perfect and I look forward to cooking something for them on it.

HENRI ARRIVES at 8 a.m. He is wearing faded denim overalls. His shoes are not fancy and when he introduces himself, he takes his cap off, folding it in half in his hand at his side. Hair has disappeared from the entirety of Henri's head but for a small tightly trimmed triangular Velcro-looking patch on his chin. He has large brown eyes that look directly at me when he speaks. I invite him in and offer him a *café*, which he takes with sugar. Born in Tunisia and raised in France, Henri does not speak any English, as I have learned is often the case with tradespeople. He tells me that he was raised in Marseille, where his family remains, except for his teenage son with whom he lives. We begin discussing the kitchen project at hand, and when we move to the tiny space his face lights up at the sight of my stove.

"*Oh là là!*" he says.

And with that, construction conversation is quickly redirected to cooking about which he is quite passionate, and I find this shared joy endearing. Henri tells me how he and his sisters were taught to cook by his mother and grandmother, and as a teenager he worked in his uncle's restaurant on a Marseille beach. Marseille is known for its seafood and in particular bouillabaisse, a fish soup with tomatoes in a broth of water and olive oil served with crispy French bread and *rouille*, a mayonnaise spiked with *piment*. It is delicious and I love it in no small way, but just when I am hoping to glean some authentic Marseille tips on bouillabaisse, Henri tells me that he does not care for it and he prefers to make puff pastry stuffed with finely minced meats. So we discuss making *pâte feuilletée*: forty turns for *sucrée* and eight turns for *salé*, he says. However, Henri's favorite thing to make is sushi, and he pulls his phone from his pocket to show me photographs of his extensive knife collection, purchased just for this hobby. His own kitchen is indeed a space created by someone who loves food and loves to cook.

On his notepad, Henri draws some suggestions for the cabinets and the placement of the sink. He tells me that he will think of various options and, because prefabricated cabinets are far less expensive than custom, he will determine if there is a way to make them work in the space. The addition of French remodeling terms to my vocabulary allows our meeting to proceed much more smoothly than my initial meeting with *Chaussures Chics*. Henri says he will prepare a *devis* setting forth a few options and can begin working on the kitchen the week of January 20th. He does not ask for a deposit and, as we exit the kitchen, the back strap of his overalls catches on the kitchen doorknob, ripping it at the side. His cheeks show embarrassment while I am apologetic. So went my first meeting with Henri.

Moving from construction to law, I meet with Christophe. He had an appointment nearby so he offered to conduct our *rendez-vous* at *l'appart* (which is a good idea anyway as he needs to see the space firsthand to knowledgeably discuss the allegations). Christophe is tall and slender. His disposition is pragmatic and easy-going and his fluency in English, combined with my prior legal experience, allows our meeting to be efficient. Over a *café*, he tells me settlement is not possible at this time. Water issues in Paris are taken seriously and there needs to be an understanding of where the leak is coming (or came) from and assurances that the problem has been definitively resolved. That, I understand. He says that there is not much to do before the inspection on the 23rd of January and asks if I can be present. I tell him that I will be here and we conclude our meeting. Never in my Paris dreams did I anticipate such a wrinkle—involved in a French lawsuit within months of property ownership—but then again, I assumed I would have heat and hot water too, so what the hell do I know.

The lack of news from *Chaussures Chics* does not disappoint me. I anticipate an unpleasant conversation over the final amount and the missing sink and drape rod. Their disappearance only adds to my to-do list and my costs. I shuck some Perle Blanche No. 3 oysters purchased from the *poissonière* around the corner and pour myself a glass of white wine from the trio JeF gifted me. The wine pairs wells with the mildly sweet oysters. The *Chaussures Chics* annoyance, forgotten. When I was a child, my mother was a devotee of the television show *Little House on the Prairie*. As I set my *cocottes* on the stove, preparing to fill my bath, I think of her and that show, which I feel I am living out in spirit. Little Kitchen by the Tower.

BONNE FIN D'ANNÉE. Happy end of the year. To say goodbye to 2011, I wake early, and with my layers of clothing, run through the heart of the sedated city. The familiar sights of silently creeping barges, lovers smooching on Pont de l'Archevêché amongst the locks, and waiters at La Frégate setting up the *terrasse* seating for the day invigorate me. The air smells like melting butter and rising dough. The green metal box display cases of *les bouquinistes* remain closed, decorated in recent graffiti, written in English and quite misspelled. I scale the metal barricade at the Louvre and walk around the large pyramid. City workers sweeping the barricaded area bid me "*Bonjour Madame*" when I climb over them to look at the architecture unobstructed by tourist lines. On my return, I run on *rive droite*, the north side of the Seine, and, by the time I have returned to the welcoming wings of the Trocadéro, the recently vacant streets are filled with double-decker tour buses lined up in front of Cimetière de Passy collecting and stacking passengers.

At 3 p.m. the streets are busy with my neighbors gathering and buying items for their celebration of *le réveillon de la Saint-Sylvestre* because Parisians primarily celebrate New Year's Eve with a dinner party with friends (at least those who did not celebrate the occasion the night before). I take to the streets for some gifts of the *chocolat* variety for two special blondes. Lines extend beyond the doors of the Monoprix and *les fromageries*, and at *le poissonnier* at least twenty people wait patiently for their turn in front of a large display case filled with s*aumon fumé*, blinis in various sizes, and caviar. A fishmonger cuts thin strips of the smoked flesh of a very large salmon on the counter, smoked salmon "*sur mesure*." The other fishmonger is packaging langoustines and live blue lobsters. There are substantially more oysters today than there were yesterday including the rare Huitre Plate Bélon No. oo from Brittany (known for their meaty, robust flavor and hefty price tag). *Boulangeries* box up *bûches de Noël* in all flavors and sizes including the tiny *individuelle* ones. Parisians walk with bouquets of flowers turned upside down while baguettes are tucked under their arms. Hostess gifts of Champagne or dessert are carefully wrapped.

Once my *chocolat* and caramel purchases have been made, I call the girls to wish them a *bonne fin d'année*. They are in Palm Springs where they always are this time of year and the same place I was every year when I was married. The thought of the ritual makes me smile. Life does not allow insincerities, conscious or unconscious, and their father and I found ourselves in places where we are most at home. For him, it is playing golf in the desert; for me, Paris. Our comfort zones are not even on the same continent, and it goes to show you that things eventually work out the way they are supposed to.

I cannot think of a better way to end an adventure-filled, prosperous year than with JeF and, donning something black and festive, I meet him at George Cinq for some Champagne. He does not go to the hotel and teases me for my *américaine* request, but I love the fireplace and generous, comfortable chairs, and it is the perfect walking distance from *l'appart*, so he obliges. The hotel is predictably packed and bursting with lights and holiday decor. After some Champagne and our New Year's peck, JeF offers me a ride home, but I decline, opting to linger in the night air one last time. Taking the cigar from my purse, I light it as my father's admonishing words ring in my head—"ladies do not smoke cigars"—and think that perhaps that the definition of a "lady" should be revisited and written by the woman herself.

The Tower, usually a bright, blinking beacon in the night sky, has been decapitated by the fog and there is a slight drizzle. Although prohibited, people drink Champagne in the streets without recourse or discouragement, and I am offered a few glasses on my way home but decline. Chants of *"Bonne Année"* ring in the air. The same five homeless men are outside the Musée Guimet asking for a light and this time I have some matches to give to them. A couple strays off course and ask me how to get back to the Trocadéro, and I am proud when I can give them directions.

The kitchen must be emptied to allow Henri and the plumber to work, so I pack up *l'appart* in the early morning hours. The kitchen contents and anything of value go back into the ugly bathroom closet. The linens and furniture can stay out, and that little bit of progress is something. Dylan is having a *soirée*, his mother noticeably absent. There is a rotation of smokers—three at a time—on his small apartment balcony while Parisians sing in the street below, raising Champagne bottles in the air. *Santé! Bonne Année!* I take a break from my packing to sit on my chilly balcony watching the escapades around me, content in this moment, and very happy to be exactly where I am. I send a text to myself from my rooster phone to my duck phone: "This is going to be a good year." I will receive the text when I land in Los Angeles. The streets reach a hush about 5 a.m.; Dylan's *soirée* is over.

Two hours later, I walk to the taxi stand next to Café Trocadéro. The streets are filled with trash, broken glass, bottles, food, and confetti. I peer out at the mess from the taxi window knowing that in a few hours' time, Paris will be swept clean, leaving no traces of the shenanigans of the night before. Despite a rainy week filled partly with business meetings, partly with bruises and kitchen injuries (and lots of boiling water), my quiet time slowly creating our Parisian space was exactly what I needed. Waking up to the Parisian rooftops, listening to the rain in the comfort of my own space and cooking in my own kitchen with everything I need a five-minute walk away is a dream to which I look forward to becoming accustomed. Although I will be happy to see my girls, I am not ready to leave. I would love to stay and cook myself through the winter gray until it meets the spring green and all the seasons thereafter.

À bientôt, Paris.

BASIC CHICKEN STOCK

5 pounds chicken bones
3 carrots, diced
4 celery stalks, diced
1 small fennel bulb, diced
2 yellow onions, diced
Handful of fresh Italian parsley
1 bay leaf
1 teaspoon black peppercorns
Kosher salt (optional)
Freshly ground black pepper (optional)
A/N filtered water

Place chicken bones and vegetables in a large stockpot (or large pot with a built-in colander). Add cold water (there should be enough to cover the bones). Add parsley, bay leaf, and peppercorns. Once bubbles start to rise, reduce flame to a low flame.

While simmering, use a large metal spoon to skim impurities off of the top of the stock (impurities have the appearance of foam or greasy bubbles). Simmer for about 4 to 6 hours until flavorful and golden in color. DO NOT boil.

Place a china cap inside a chinois. Place both in a large, clean container. Gently pour the stock into the china cap. Discard everything caught in the china cap (or in colander).

Place container in an ice bath to cool. Season to taste with salt and pepper. (It is preferable not to season the stock so it may be used for a variety of recipes.)

Once cool, place in refrigerator. Stock can be stored in refrigerator for a week or in the freezer for about 6 months. When chilled, the fat will rise to the top and solidify, forming a "fat cap" on the top of the stock. Carefully remove the fat cap before use. (For home use, I pour the stock into quart-sized containers and freeze.)

VEAL SCALOPPINE WITH A SHALLOT-CAPER WINE REDUCTION AND FENNEL *PURÉE*

Serves 2

Fennel purée
1½ pounds rough-chopped fennel bulbs, core, stalks, and fronds removed
$^1/_8$ cup fresh lemon juice
¼ cup olive oil
A/N kosher salt

Place water in a large pan. Place steam basket inside. The basket should be above the water. Place the fennel in basket and cover the pan with a lid. Steam the fennel over a medium flame until the fennel is tender.

Carefully remove fennel. Place fennel in a food processor. Add lemon juice and olive oil. Blend until very smooth. Season to taste with salt. This can be made in advance.

Veal
A/N all-purpose flour
A/N kosher salt
A/N freshly ground black pepper
2 veal cutlets, ¼ inch thick
1 tablespoon unsalted butter
4 tablespoons capers, rinsed and drained
4 tablespoons minced shallots
¼ cup dry white wine
¼ cup chicken stock
1½ tablespoons unsalted butter, cold
1 tablespoon minced fresh Italian parsley

Season veal with salt and pepper. Dredge in flour and tap off excess flour. Place a frying pan over a medium-high heat. Add butter to pan. Melt. Add veal to hot pan and cook each side for about one minute. Remove veal from pan and place on a plate. Keep warm with foil.

Sweat minced shallots. Add capers and wine to pan to deglaze. Reduce by half. Add chicken stock. Reduce to achieve desired consistency (about half). Add cold butter. Add parsley. Adjust seasoning.

Add veal back into pan and cover in sauce. Serve warm.

CHAPTER TWENTY

Coeur d'Artichaut

Before my hope transitioned into acceptance, and with nothing to meaningfully offer in return, I bartered with God to allow me to stay here on earth awhile longer. I wanted to watch my daughters grow. I wanted to teach them and show them as much as I could. That endowment of *la vie quotidienne*, with its equilibrium of delights and difficulties, has proven far better than the alternative. For a fourth year in a row, January, in particular, with the predictable appearance of *galettes des rois*, seems like Christmas to me. And, for four years now my mission of experience and completion has proceeded with urgency, and without pause. But as I delight in the moments with my ever-growing daughters and check the items off of my list one by one, occasional quiet moments make me miss a lover's touch. The longing thought seems selfish as I have been given so much, and it does not really seem fair to ask for that too. Notwithstanding, a part of me has at times longed for a romantic connection because when you are in love, the sky appears brighter and the stars, closer, and even your heart feels fuller.

My text message to myself from my Paris balcony was not in fact the first in my text string when I arrived in Los Angeles. It followed another:

"Happy New Year from L.A! I wanted to be the first to wish you a HNY. How about that belated birthday celebration?"

The text is from Prince, not the singer, but someone I met in December, and Prince really is his nickname, not given to him by me. Michael is his given name. The unexpected appearance of the text on my phone causes me to smile spontaneously. When we met, he stopped what he was doing and stared at me as if he had known me his entire life. It was both flattering and unnerving. A conversation ensued between us, and when he saw my NYC marathon cap, he volunteered that he, too, is a marathon runner. He asked if I would like to take a run together the following weekend.

"No time. January?" I said.

He looked at me inquisitively, prompting me to explain that my birthday was the following weekend and I was spending it with my daughters and my girlfriends, and birthday celebrations were immediately followed by the holidays, and then my week in Paris. He asked for a raincheck.

I read his text again and then my own, deciding that 2012 is the year I will make a better effort at some semblance of a social life. In reality, I hardly have time to blow out my hair, and I will be back in Paris in seventeen days for the inspection of *l'appart,* but I decide to make time for both: a date and a blow dry and think perhaps I am the recipient of even more than I bartered for.

"Happy New Year to you," I text back. "How about the run you promised?"

"Run. Then belated birthday dinner?" he replies.

"Deal."

Friday night arrives. The girls are with their father for the weekend, and I drive to downtown Los Angeles, where Prince lives. DTLA is now considered trendy due to the bevy of eateries, art galleries, and sleek artist lofts popping up in spades, making it much different than what it was when I made the drive for college or my first law job. Prince's fifteenth-floor loft has two walls of glass offering a panoramic view of the city and testing my fear of heights. The sleek furniture with clean lines, the eclectic art pieces carefully curated through gifts or inheritance (as he explains), and the minimal electronics make it the most stylish male living quarters I have ever seen (not that my points for comparison are great). The pristine kitchen causes me to tease him. He laughs and opens his refrigerator door, exhibiting a topless bunch of sad-looking carrots and almond milk.

"That is really pathetic, you know. Our rabbits and chickens eat better. Isn't your best friend a chef?" I say.

"Hey, now. Time for that run," he says, smiling.

We run the sidewalks in a city transformed by gentrification. The Art Deco bank and theater buildings have been restored and residents walk the streets. The evening air feels refreshingly cool after the Paris chill, and I am thrilled with the need for only one layer of spandex. After a quick five miles, which passed even faster with conversation, we clean up at his apartment and then head to dinner.

Our dinner venue is a transformed bank building bustling with weekend diners and quite loud as a result of the crowd and high ceiling's poor acoustics. We sit across from one another at a small table. His eyes are as black as coal and they match his hair, which approaches the top of his forehead in a slight widow's peak. The dim light casts a glow on his creamy olive skin and over the top of my menu, I see him nervously and discreetly tugging at his French cuffs, which extend the perfect length beyond his dinner jacket sleeve. His elegant hands are exquisite and they do in fact look like the hands of a Prince, much in contrast to my large, weathered hands, with scars and burns from cooking. I try to focus on the menu, but my mind now wanders and follows my eyes to those hands of his and all the things he has touched. A part of me hopes to be next.

The usual first date small chat ensues. I ask what he recommends on the menu and in doing so I learn that he is a vegetarian and although I am not, I find the lifestyle choice familiar as I was raised vegetarian myself. We decide to order some of his suggestions and share them, and when I close my menu the draft it creates sends a waft of his cologne across the table, which makes my heart speed up a little. My glass of red wine is not helping to temper that sensation. First date. So far, so good. I tally the factors in my mind: I am dining with a good-looking man who: (1) ran with me; (2) chose the restaurant; and (3) ordered his favorite things, which means I do not have to make a food decision (priceless because I am around food so much I have palate fatigue; when I dine out I usually ask the chef to make me anything s/he feels inspired to make). I catch myself staring at the pronounced curves of his lips. His calm, low voice is soothing and a charge of electricity shoots through my core when he speaks to me.

Our first plated dish arrives: a salad with spiced nuts and beets. The waiter splits the salad on two plates and as we pick up our utensils, I offer reassurance that his choice is a pleasing one: "This looks good ... I love nuts."

He does not hear my compliment as the restaurant is louder than it was when we arrived. I repeat myself, louder this time, "*I said, yum ... I love nuts!*"

Out of my peripheral vision I see the couple sitting to my immediate right. The man is grinning at me while his female dining companion is not as amused. Saturday Night Live flashbacks with Alec Baldwin's skit about holiday (Schweddy) balls dance in my head. My face becomes warm, and as my children would say, an "awkward silence" ensues between Prince and me. He heard me this time and smiling, he breaks the silence by asking if I would like some water.

We return to his apartment after dinner for tea and take in the view. Despite my most carnal urges, and the bliss of his tender mouth on mine, I drive home after our tea, promising a second date.

Prince and I continue to see one another, squeezing in a dinner or lunch when we can. We laugh like children and spending time with him is the perfect dose of fun and romance that I was craving: we dance, go to burlesque shows, and he even reads Rumi to me in the bath. The fact that my heart speeds up whenever I see him, *c'est la cerise sur le gâteau* (it is the icing on the cake). Prince's office is not far from Surfas, where I teach group classes in the test kitchen, so I bring him food after my class if there are leftovers beyond what the students take home. His appetite for my food earns him the affectionate nickname "Hungry." The *macarons* are his favorite because he also has a sweet tooth.

Prince is four years younger than I. Previously married, he is without children but wants them, and I congratulate myself for finding this brilliant combination of a demonstrated ability to commit without the burden of balancing two families. What I failed to appreciate is that his bachelorhood also makes things harder because Prince does not nor can he comprehend parental responsibilities nor the unique juggling of a divorced parent. A bachelor with no responsibility to anyone or anything, he knows only the luxury of time and spontaneity, apart from his work obligations, which, thankfully, keep him extraordinarily busy. Although he grew up partly in London, Prince does not know Paris at all. We talk about him coming to Paris at some point, but our schedules make it impossible and I do not have time for visitors anyway as my current Paris visits are filled with necessities. When I tell him that I have to return to Paris for the inspection and I will be gone over the extended Martin Luther King, Jr. holiday weekend, that, in combination with the many French emails I receive between midnight and four a.m, leads Prince to ask me if I have a lover in Paris. His question is serious, but its improbability makes me laugh, and I assure him that I do not and if he knew what I actually did on my last trip to Paris, he would think I am boring and maybe nuts.

"You know, if I could have you physically in both places, life would be ideal," I say.

He smiles and his slight dimples compete for notice with the fleshy curves of his mouth. His black eyes shine in a way that makes my heart thump and he draws my face to his own imparting a kiss that lasts for days. He may not know Paris, but the entirety of my being revels in our sheer physical connection and my heart feels safe and full. The way he looks at me, I know he adores me, bestowing a certainty of desire and love the likes of which I have never known. Sentimental me.

CHAPTER TWENTY-ONE

Too Many Cooks In My Kitchen

EACH MORNING, while the chickens (seven), rabbits (two), French frill canary (one, "Jean Valjean"), and both girls slumber on our Los Angeles "farm," Paris is wide awake, and I spend hours every morning on one French issue or another. Our furniture and household items apparently reached the Normandy port and are due to arrive in Paris "on or about the 24th" of January (when I will be there). My French contact, Alain, emails me an assortment of inventory sheets (down to the number of clothing pieces), various statements for French customs, and even requests a copy of my utility bills. I never anticipated that shipping a minutiae of items would be so time-consuming, although I am not sure why I am surprised. After nine months of being lost in the mail, the life insurance company has "confirmed" that they have received the documents they need. *Chaussures Chics* and I make an appointment for the 23rd of January, right before the inspection, which he agrees to attend. Henri researched cabinets and sinks, and prepared various options and estimates for me to review. We make a *rendez-vous* for the 21st of January, two days before the inspection. It is all progress. The legal emails continue with their redundant, nonsensical niceties; each one costs me more euros and imparts nothing but grief. My frustration builds when some French expressions do not translate to English smoothly, and the context does not ease my struggle. And, then there is the seller. If this deceptive character did not give me enough grief before, now I find out that she did not pay an *appel de fonds* (or two) and the management company is trying to stick me with these bills as well. *C'est trop!* (It is just too much.) How dare she sit next to me at the *notaire's* office, smiling at me in that grandmotherly *gentille* kind of way, when in truth, she was nothing more than a spider waiting to entangle me in her web of monetary and legal problems and suck my money and Parisian apartment bliss out of me. I shut my computer. Dwelling on the injustice and stupidity of it all is getting me nowhere and I once again decide to think like a *parisienne* and change my perspective: I accept that this lawsuit will proceed for quite some time. I accept that water leaks happen and this will not be the last. I decide that I'll read the letters and collect the documents for my lawyer *when* I am able and have the desire and it is this sense of non-urgency and acceptance that allows me to greet the day and sleep at night. *C'est la vie.*

PARIS GREETS ME me with an eleven-degree temperature and overcast, drizzling skies. The Epiphany has come and gone and the festive holiday decor has been traded out for Parisian winter normalcy. Prince was not happy that I was leaving for Paris and he gave me the cold shoulder to make a point of his displeasure, a technique not well-received by me.

A whoosh of warm air hits my face when I enter the lobby. I push and pull the boxes and roll the suitcase through the space to the elevator and then *l'appart*. Sadly, the lobby temperature was not indicative of my own space, which is still freezing. I step over the three rolled *tapis* (rugs) and the box of *papier peint* (wallpaper), which were delivered in my absence and head straight for the bathroom closet to retrieve my floor heater. I check the internet and turn on the television for background noise. All electronics are working; should there be a hot water issue, I do not want to know about it yet.

The following day, Henri arrives just as the men delivering my wardrobe trunk leave. (Four months late and after several follow-up phone calls from the States.) Henri recommends IKEA for its pre-fabricated cabinets, which come in 5o- or 6o-centimeter sizes. We drive twenty minutes outside of Paris to IKEA, the practical destination for everything household, which is bustling with weekend shoppers weighing decisions of domestic importance. I select one cabinet line I like, a sink, and find some stainless-steel *étagères* (shelves), which will be perfect for dishes, *cocottes*, and S hooks to hang my ever-growing battery of kitchen supplies. The time difference has caught up with me and when we arrive back at *l'appart*, it is *l'heure du goûter.* I purchase some treats from La Pâtississere des Rêves down the street which Henri and I enjoy with our *cafés*. When we finish I leave him in *l'appart* to hang the drapes in *le salon*, the chandelier in the bedroom, and drill holes in the solid walls to hang framed pictures and menus. I visit Lucille.

LAZY DAY SUNDAY begins at 3 a.m. when the girls call me (6 p.m. California time). They excitedly tell me about their weekend. Ava asks if the water is hot and she laughs hysterically when I tell her the news, which she shouts to her sister: "Mom is still cooking water to take a bath!"

It is true. Despite my sternly written French letter to the *syndic* and Monsieur de SAVOY's promises of hot water, the water remains cold.

The morning slips through my hands like superfine sugar. JeF and I made plans to lunch together, but as lunch time approaches, I cannot reach him. So, I walk to Musée d'Orsay where the permanent collection of impressionist art is formidable and the temporary exhibits are always well-curated, taking a minor detour to Les Cocottes where the food, not bath water, is served in *cocottes*. I sit next to an American journalist from Chicago with whom I strike up a conversation. He is lovely, but I am focused on my *pavé de cabillaud*, followed by my *tarte au chocolat* with its shiny, smooth ganache and flaky, buttery tart crust. After I have eaten, JeF calls, frustrated that I ate without him, but I remind him that it is now 3:oo p.m. and he has no right to complain.

Chilly, overcast weather is the perfect excuse to stay in and roast that Bresse chicken—the A.O.C. treasure, raised on grain and dairy with a specified grass perimeter in which to exercise and eat worms for a particular period of time—which I purchased yesterday on impulse after my hair appointment. I have always wanted to cook the prized *poulet* and indeed the mere purchase of it was filled with pomp and circumstance befitting the expensive treasure. After the butcher displayed the fowl to me for inspection, he placed it on the block, took out a meat cleaver, and removed its feet and white feathered head. He plucked stray feathers from the dimpled flesh and passed the flame of a blow-torch over the legs and the fowl's bottom and carefully wrapped it in butcher's paper. Unwrapping the paper, the physical difference between this tagged-leg fowl and chickens found in a grocery store in the States is immediately evident. This chicken has small breasts (unlike the top-heavy chickens in the States). I imagine that my little poultry treasure is probably what our free-range chickens at home in Los Angeles would look like if we made them into dinner (but we will not because we named them).

The taut, thick skin forces me to work a bit in order to place butter pats and black truffle slices between the skin and flesh. I season the cavity and stuff it with *mirepoix* and then place it in the preheated oven which has heated *l'appart*. Diced black radishes and sunchokes I toss in olive oil, *sel*, and fresh thyme and roast them as well. When I pull the chicken from the oven, it is a beautiful golden brown and the skin is super crispy. The sharpness of the vegetables mellowed with the oven's heat, and flavored with woodsy thyme, are a perfect companion to the chicken. As I dine on my chilly-weather creations, I take notes for future recipes.

INSPECTION DAY, January 23. I do not wake with my usual eagerness to face a Parisian day. I am annoyed that Alain and my furniture are both missing, and I anticipate an unpleasant conversation with *Chaussures Chics* as well as the management company about my lack of hot water and the seller's unpaid *appel de fonds*. Then there is the infiltration of my private, happy space with people I do not know about a subject I do not want to be involved in. To occupy my mind, I pass the morning with domesticities including a fast-paced walk across the Seine to the home improvement store Zola in the nearby 15th in search of wallpaper paste. When I cannot find it, I solicit the assistance of a sales clerk and struggle with various French words that will help convey my need—*adhésif*, *mur*, and, even resorting to "*truc*"—with arm gestures to demonstrate hanging something on the wall to get my point across. It works, and he walks me to where I can find the paste. When I arrive home I only have time to toss my purchases in a closet and put on something more professional looking than what I wore to Zola.

The doorbell rings. It is *Chaussures Chics*. His shoes are tan leather. He hands me his *devis* for the bathroom (which is as high as I anticipated) and I thank him, saying that any work depends on the inspector and the lawsuit. When I inquire about my missing bedroom curtain rod and antique kitchen sink, he tells me that they were thrown away with other *"débris."* I doubt his veracity and envision both items being salvaged and sold. Nevertheless, they are gone and I inform him that the items will be discounted from his bill, but before I can sit to write *Chaussures Chics* a check, Christophe arrives. Introductions are made, and *Chaussures Chics* excuses himself and goes downstairs to my neighbor's apartment where the inspection will begin. Christophe and I remain in *l'appart* to discuss the inspection until we are interrupted by Monsieur de SAVOY knocking at my door. Finally, I meet the face behind the emails, and in fact, I am allowed quite a good look at his face because the Monsieur stands six inches from mine. The expert is here and ready to begin.

While the plaintiffs own the apartment below mine, they rent it to a woman who looks to be about my age. She is petite and casually dressed in jeans and a button-down white shirt. She has dirty blonde hair and nondescript eyes, mostly because she looks down at the ground the majority of the time. She politely invites us in and offers us seats in the living room. The layout of her apartment is the same as mine and as we pass through the foyer I look up at her significantly stained and peeling *plafond*. Chairs are drawn from all corners of the apartment to accommodate the collection of *maîtres,* all of whom are now arranged around a modest wooden coffee table. The room is lined with IKEA bookshelves that I recognize from my recent shopping adventure with Henri. The renter and *Chaussures Chics* stand behind the chairs, tangentially and hesitatingly involved in the matter. Monsieur de SAVOY also stands.

The expert is a man in his late fifties dressed in a suit with an average build. His face is unremarkable. He has gained his expertise as a partner in a Parisian architecture firm. There are five lawyers present, including Christophe. The lawyer for the *syndic,* a slight, blonde woman, says little, in stark contrast to the male lawyer for the management company who is both abrupt and cross when the opportunity presents itself, and often when it does not. Plaintiffs' counsel is a woman in her late thirties who talks endlessly, but she represents the plaintiff, who, is the complaining party and has the burden of proof, so I do not blame her for her very vocal participation. The seller's lawyer is a young, mid-twenty-something annoyance. Granted, it could be that I have likened her to her blood-sucking spider of a client and that has prejudiced me against her. When she interrupts the expert for a third time, the collective of the group looks away when she speaks, and I confirm that she is annoying on her own merit. Monsieur de SAVOY steps up to the back of Christophe's chair so closely he could stand on Christophe's shoulders. He introduces himself to the group as a retired attorney, here on behalf of the *syndic* in an "unofficial" capacity. His repeated interjections seem to annoy the expert and between Monsieur de SAVOY and the seller's lawyer, no one else has much of an opportunity to speak. The expert looks up and down at the various voices while taking copious notes. The lawyers for the plaintiffs and the seller want to add the insurance companies, particularly the insurer of the person who rented my apartment before I purchased it. I whisper to Christophe, "Ask exactly when the last damage occurred ... before or after September 3o." Other than that obvious point, which I am sure already occurred to him, I do not say anything unless the expert asks me a specific question about the remodeling or condition of *l'appart*. Lawyers themselves make the worst clients, and I try to be mindful of that.

We sit there for an hour and a half before the actual inspection begins and to that end, the expert pulls out a little yellow handheld gadget from his briefcase. He walks to the foyer and places the yellow gadget on my neighbor's wall, running it up and down the length of the foyer wall, section by section. It looks like a stud finder.

When it beeps, lights flash, the expert declares the section "*humide.*" The more humidity, the more lights, the louder the beeping. The living room wall, in between her kitchen and living room is *sec,* but the walls and the ceiling in the kitchen and the foyer are *humides.* We follow the expert and his humidity detector to the bathroom where I almost let out a laugh. The damage to my neighbor's ceiling is about 4 inches long, and I fail to understand why I heard about the bathroom damage when the damage in her foyer is far worse. The humidity detector does not beep or flash. The bathroom ceiling is declared "*sec.*"

My turn. The cast of characters shuffle in a huddled mass up one flight of stairs to *mon appart.* The expert runs the humidity detector on the walls in my foyer.

"*Humide,*" he proclaims.

I am both displeased and curious because I have never seen any evidence of a leak nor dampness. The expert moves to my kitchen. He asks *Chaussures Chics* if he did an undercoat in the kitchen under the *carrelage. Chaussures Chics* confirms that he did. The expert tells me that he will need *les factures* for the work so he can see what work was done in the kitchen. He proceeds to my bathroom. When the expert sees the large cast-iron *cocotte* sitting in the plastic bathtub, he turns to me requesting to know the reason for the cooking vessel in my bathtub, suspecting it is there for some water leak. Seizing the opportunity to let the *syndic* and management company know of my displeasure about the lack of hot water, I tell the expert it is because I have not had any hot water in *l'appart* for weeks, and I am forced to heat water on my stove, sending a sharp look to the attorney for the management company and Monsieur de SAVOY. The expert is satisfied with the explanation. Monsieur de SAVOY and the lawyer for the management company, uncharacteristically silent, look away.

The expert asks *Chaussures Chics* some additional questions about the work he did in the bathroom for the prior tenant and then excuses him from the meeting.

As we return to my neighbor's living room, my neighbor *à gauche* arrives home. The group continues on downstairs while I take the opportunity to introduce myself to her. Her name is Katy, she works for a French bank and as a result, speaks English. Katy lives with her eleven-year-old son. She says that she is not having a problem with her water and she offers to let me use her bathroom to shower, which is kind, although I will not take her up on it (as it seems awkward to shower in a stranger's space). We exchange contact information and I rejoin the group.

My head aches as we approach the third hour. I can only focus intently on French for so long and we seem to cover the same things over and over. The entire ordeal is like watching a bunch of French teenagers negotiate with each other for cigarettes and wondering if they should bring in others to join the party. How many times do we have to discuss the insurers? How many times do I have to hear the expert opine that the source of the humidity is a *mystère?* Then suddenly the expert switches gears and indicates that he does not think I have any responsibility in the matter. My ears perk up. He says that he will prepare a preliminary report and then he says no more. The meeting is done. The parties scatter. So goes my introduction to the French legal system.

Christophe and I reconvene in *l'appart*. With the inspection over, and my bathroom deemed *sec*, Christophe confirms that I can begin work on the bathroom as long as I keep all of the *factures*. This is good news and as soon as Christophe leaves, I keep this hiccup in perspective, put on a little black dress, and set out into the Paris night.

I PURCHASED an opera ticket to Tchaikovsky's *La Dame de Pique* just to have something to keep my spirits up, and I only bought one ticket because I did not know how long the inspection would last. While not familiar with this opera, I am particularly excited to see the inside of the Opéra Garnier, with its red velvet seats, Chagall-painted ceiling, and old-fashioned boxes. However, when I arrive, the opera house seems quiet, oddly so, even with the drizzle. I walk the partial circumference of the building; only the restaurant has a semblance of life. I pull the computer-printed ticket out from my purse: Opéra Bastille. *Merde!* The new opera house is across the city, and the light drizzle has become a steady rain. With my purse over my head (cannot take the California out of the woman, apparently), I run away from the opera house as the immediate taxi stands are filled with tourists stranded in the rain. Wet and close to calling the whole night off, I finally secure a taxi on Boulevard des Italiens, arriving fifteen minutes before intermission.

It is nearly midnight when I arrive home, and I am starving. I use the left-over chicken and thanks to my anticipatory pantry, make a chicken Basque with some jarred peppers. The inspection sparked my interest as to what is actually underneath the plastic planks in the bathroom, which are now wavy due to the leaking toilet last October. Once I have finished my late-night chicken dinner for one, and still in my opera dress, I walk into the bathroom, remove the doors to the cabinet housing the plastic tub, exposing the edge of the planks. I can now pull up one plank from the floor, then a second, then a third. The task is not difficult due to their warped condition, and the physical exertion feels therapeutic. Exchanging my heels for running shoes, I lean five or six planks on the edge of the bathtub and jump up and down on the middle, breaking them into smaller pieces which I toss into the bathtub. The process is repeated until the entire floor has been removed, exposing the original white tile. It's in decent shape but unusable due to a strip of non-conforming blue tiles lining the circumference of the room and then dividing the space in half. My house recipe calls to use the space as a whole and the bright blue clashes with the stove.

The elation from my therapeutic floor demolition and my subsequent conversation with the girls make sleep sporadic. The glow from the street lights below shines on the box of wallpaper sitting on the bedroom floor. Empowered with newfound remodeling confidence, at 4 a.m. I spring from my bed to tackle the wallpaper project. It takes five minutes for me to tire of the lengthy, small-print French instructions before I toss them aside and dump a cup of the powder in a bucket, add some water, and mix it to obtain a paste consistency. After measuring and cutting the paper to fit the space, I return my attention to my bucket of paste only to discover it is hardening with pea-sized lumps — admirable for flaky butter biscuits, not in wallpaper paste. A wave of panic sends me running to the kitchen and grab my balloon whisk and return to the bedroom where I whisk the paste vigorously, but the effort only manages to incorporate air, and the lumps remain. With more drastic measures needed, I run back to the kitchen, grab the immersion blender, add more water to the bucket and purée the paste into a fine wallpaper *velouté. Et voilà!* The lumps are gone.

I spread a thin layer of wallpaper paste *velouté* on the white wall and wrestle with the velvet-embellished wallpaper which is so weighty that the top collapses over my head while the lower section is twisting and in danger of wrinkling. Pinning the back of the sheet against the wall, I reach toward the top and pull the squeegee carefully down the length of the paper to remove the air bubbles but not to damage the black velvet flowers. Yet, despite my gentle approach,

I cut not only the paper but also the tip of my left thumb because, unbeknownst to me, the squeegee has a sharp blade hidden behind the rubber edge. My bleeding thumb has decorated the paper with red dots and the flowers look like they are weeping red tears. The paper falls away from the adhesive, collapsing over my head, and the puréed paste is hardening in the bucket. *Quelle catastrophe!*

With my left thumb bandaged and held in the air, I repeat the process with a fresh strip of wallpaper, and abandoning the lethal squeegee, I seize Guy Martin's cookbook *Cuisine* laying on my bed and run the bound edge of the cookbook down the wallpaper strip. Too unwieldy to use with one hand, I toss it aside and grab a smaller book, and soon the lumps are gone. It takes four more strips to cover the space, and just as the bubbles are removed from the last strip, and as if on cue, the doorbell buzzes.

"*J'arrive!*" I shout.

I pull on my jeans underneath my nightgown and run to open the door. Henri pauses when he sees me. My bare arms are smattered with wallpaper paste, my left hand is dotted with dried blood, and my thumb is wrapped in a bloodied paper towel.

"*Ça va?*" he asks.

"*Ça va. Et vous?*" I respond.

I wipe off my arms and make us both a *café*. We discuss the five-centimeter cabinet-space issue and his proposal of moving the stove toward the refrigerator, solving the space issue and allowing me to purchase the pre-fabricated IKEA cabinets. We move into the bathroom. Henri chuckles when he sees the broken floor pieces in the tub. He writes down the tile quantities I need to order for the bathroom floor and for the walls. The plan is to finish the kitchen and then begin the bathroom. When Henri leaves, I head out to order the tile and the bathroom fixtures and tub.

JEF REQUESTED a "stove demonstration," and I am happy to oblige. I purchase two beautiful fillets from the *poissonnerie* and a baguette and a chocolate tart from the *boulangerie*. Dinner is in the oven and I straighten up *l'appart* in a tornado-like fashion, cleaning up my *mise en place* on the dining room table and setting the table for two. *L'appart* is filled with the fragrance of creamy butter and woodsy thyme. A bottle of wine breathes on the table. JeF arrives, a bottle of wine and cookbook in hand, and a smile from ear to ear.

"Lisa, the entire hallway is filled with the good smells coming from your place. What are you cooking?" he asks as he enters *l'appart*, removing his coat and scarf.

Cooking for someone, besides myself, makes *l'appart* seem like a home, and I excitedly show him around. He is noticeably shocked by its transformation and even compliments me on the one papered wall. We walk back into *le salon* and he touches the gold and black taffeta drapes, which hang behind the dining table.

"*Superbe!*" he says.

JeF sits down while I place our dinner on the table. I agree with him that I should have opened up the wall between the kitchen and *le salon*, and I most likely will, but I am not yet ready for the bureaucracy, architects, and additional cost right now. As I sit down to join him, he runs his hand across the top of the dining table.

"*Et cette table, c'est cooool!*" he says.

He pours us each a glass of wine and as he does, I relay my adventure of putting the table together. He stops pouring the wine.

"*Attends...*You put this together? Lisa, it's iron! This table is iron. And this wood..." he says grabbing the width of the table's top edge. "You are crazy!" His guttural roar of laughter consumes the room.

"*Oui, je sais...*"

"*Craaaazzze américaine girrrl!!!* " he says as he continues to laugh, running his fingers across the solid dark wood. He continues pouring the wine and stops laughing only to try his food.

"*C'est magnifique!*"

"*Merci,*" I say, genuinely flattered.

"The apartment is already your own," he says.

"What do you mean? I am not even half done."

"Lisa," he says with arm gestures to match, "the professional stove, the food, copper pots, cookbooks, books and pictures of the girls ... This apartment is all you."

Although far from finished, he is right about that: *l'appart* is a reflection of all that I love and the things most important to me. His recognition of that fact makes me proud.

"*Merci, mais fais attention dans la salle de bain, c'est un bordel!*" I say using the slang he previously taught me and quite applicable to the bathroom as it is a complete disaster.

He jumps up from the table to sneak a peek at the bathroom and returns, laughing hysterically, declaring the *sdb* to be a "war zone."

"What happened to the floor?" he asks.

I tell him about my post-opera floor demolition project, and when I reveal that I executed my plan in my evening dress and running shoes, he laughs even harder and returns to his seat.

"Lisa, I don't like fish because most of the time it is overcooked, you know, but this is cooked perfectly. It's good."

"*Merci.*" I smile.

I love cooking for JeF because he not only likes my cooking, but I am flattered by his French-palate appreciation. He was raised knowing what good food tastes like so when he compliments me on something I have made, it seems like a triple compliment. We talk until midnight and when he leaves, I clean the kitchen, which must be done in stages. Tonight that means seven of them and afterward, I go to bed, pleased with the weekend's events and knowing that this will be the first of many dinners I will be cooking and hosting here.

TURBOT WITH ROASTED SUNCHOKES
AND BLACK RADISHES

Satisfying and simple, this dinner will be a go-to on your busy days. This simple method of preparing fish can be used for a variety of fish, including, Branzino, sea bass, cod, and salmon.

Serves 2

    2 Turbot fillets, with skin
    A/N olive oil
    1 handful sunchokes
    1 bunch black radishes
    2 to 3 sprigs fresh thyme, stripped
    A/N kosher salt
    A/N freshly ground pepper

Preheat oven to 375 degrees Fahrenheit. Wash sunchokes and radishes well. Dry. Cut radishes and sunchokes into cubes. Toss in olive oil and thyme. Add a pinch or two of kosher salt and a few turns on the pepper mill. Roast vegetables in the oven until golden brown. Adjust seasoning as needed. Cover with foil to keep warm.

Place a sauté pan over a medium-high flame. Once hot, lightly coat bottom of sauté pan with olive oil.

Season fish with salt and pepper.

Place fish skin-side down in the pan. Turn down heat to medium. Cook until skin is crispy. (The skin will release from the pan.)

Flip fish with a fish spatula. Turn off the heat and let the fish finish cooking with residual heat in pan.

CHAPTER TWENTY-TWO

Packages, Presidents, and Princes

HALLMARK-INSPIRED or not, Valentine's Day is my favorite holiday and this year it is made even more enjoyable by the fact I actually have a love interest, beyond my daughters, with whom to celebrate the day. The girls and I decide to host a small family Valentine's dinner. They do their homework at the kitchen counter while I chop; dinner will be early as it is a school night. And, because a large family dinner seems an easy way to make an introduction, I invited Prince. The girls draw hearts in the air with their fingers when they hear me on the phone with him, and everyone is eager to meet the man I actually make time for when they are not around.

Prince calls to tell me that he is detained at work and, thereafter, he continually updates me on his status which progresses from "late" to "very late." Truthfully, I understand. The girls' father worked all the time, as did my own father. My brother, sister-in-law, and I drink Champagne and talk in the kitchen while snacking on charcuterie, and the four kids run about the house, stopping every so often in the kitchen for something to eat. Prince's moving ETA (and my Champagne consumption) results in an overcooked paella, which could be quite honestly the worst dinner I have ever made. When he does arrive, four pointer fingers making hearts in the air appear in my peripheral. Julia spies the orange box tucked under his arm and proclaims:

"Oooo! Mom is going to like that!"

"Is she now?" Prince says in a low hum, which causes Julia to blush. When he extends his hand to hers, she loses her words but maintains her smile. There is no denying the man is charming, and everyone likes him as I knew they would. By the time we all sit down for dinner it is 9 p.m., an unheard of time for dinner in Los Angeles. The children are tired and have already consumed emergency pasta. I take a bite of my own rice atrocity and laugh, suggesting that we forget dinner and move straight to the chocolate dessert. There is no disagreement to the modified plan.

THE MORNING I leave for Paris is filled with last-minute packing, bubble-wrapping, and unnecessary drama. Prince and I had a disagreement last night (again) about my lack of time (which I find ironic due to his Valentine's Day *faux pas*). His point is not without merit, but our discussion devolves into reactive texts that continue right up until my taxi ride to LAX. Without marriage vows and the overriding desire to keep a family intact, my tolerance for childish disagreements or perceived bad behavior in a romantic relationship is slim. More accurately described, it is zero. I delete our text exchange and decide to table the matter until I can reflect on it in a less reactive way.

Henri sends *un petit coucou* via email, attaching progress photos of the kitchen. My plan is to have *l'appart* finished by the summer, and with Henri on board I am confident the goal is achievable. (I wish I had as much confidence in the shipping and the lawsuit matters, but *c'est la vie*.) Henri has installed the lower cabinets and the hood. He warns me not to knock my head on the corner of the hood and instructs me *not* to cook or place anything on the nude counter. The thought of his request, which is, essentially, that I not use the kitchen now that it actually resembles a kitchen, makes me giggle, and I catch the taxi driver looking in the rearview mirror to see what is so funny.

I ARRIVE IN PARIS hungry and tired as I could not sleep on the plane and entertained myself with French movies, including the timely and relatable *Mon Pire Cauchemar* about a woman remodeling her apartment, and, funnily, her contractor also suggests IKEA. Immigration is empty, and I charge around the endless winding ropes and approach the window, handing the agent my passport. He looks through the stamped pages and then asks me why I travel to France so frequently. I respond that I purchased an apartment in Paris and am conducting repairs. Pale pallor, thick brown hair, and Gaelic features, the officer's blank stare offers no hint as to his follow-up question: "*Vous êtes avec votre mari?*"

Am I with my husband? Odd question, but again I dutifuly respond, "*Non.*"

"*Prendriez-vous un café avec moi?*" *Comment?* Coffee? Is he asking me out? Can he do that? Is he joking? He is not smiling. Why am I answering questions that have nothing to do with immigration? What is wrong *with me?* Annoyed at the situation, but I manage a strategic and nonchalant response, "*Non, merci, j'ai un petit ami,*" believing the status of being in a relationship will free me from the uncomfortable situation.

"*Ça va,*" he says shrugging his shoulders. He does not care if I have a boyfriend or not. An awkward chuckle escapes my lips, and I tell him that my boyfriend would not appreciate me sharing a coffee with a stranger, but "*merci*" and reach for my passport, which he places in my hand.

When I open the door to *l'appart,* I go straight to the kitchen. My stove is hugged by cabinetry and crowned with a black enamel hood. Everything is in place minus the countertop. A stench of mildew leads me out of the kitchen to *le salon*, which is filled with my un-crated furniture, and boxes of housewares. My things arrived a few days early and this unexpected surprise thankfully allows me to check shipping and Alain off of my list.

Lucille is chatty and happy *comme d'habitude* and eager to update me on her move to the 15th. She is pleased with her decision and does in fact seem to be lighter in disposition without the worry of a meddling roommate. We talk about *l'appart* and my quick visit. We do not discuss our romantic relationships; we do not know each other well enough and the topic would be inappropriate. Instead, she asks me what recipes I am working on, then interrupts her own question to ask me if I make *bœuf aux carottes*—beef braised in stock and wine with carrots—a classic dish that was reportedly so good last night that she is still thinking about it today. I tell her I like to make it on cold days and like to plate it over well-whipped *pomme purée*.

"*Miam!*" she says and laughs as she blows out my hair.

I do not have several hours for a braise, so I opt for potato and leek *velouté*, far more enticing than the wallpaper paste *velouté* of last visit. Henri's admonishment not to do anything on the temporary countertop made of pressboard is an unfair request to make of a cook. But respecting Henri's work, I protect the surface by covering the temporary surface with worthless French plastic wrap and lay some cutting boards on top. I place a saucepan on the fire but, forgetting how powerful the fire is, I let the butter brown and I have to clean out the pan and start over. Sauté the leeks (white parts only) in melted butter. Add diced potatoes and toss with leeks. Add chicken stock. Simmer with a bay leaf. Remove leaf and purée soup with immersion blender. I swirl some grated Beaufort cheese in the puréed soup as an extra treat. Twenty minutes later I dip a wedge of my *boule au levain* from Béchu in the creamy indulgence and chase it with a sip of my Bordeaux. *Parfait.*

With a happy belly, I arrange furniture and after two hours of my organizing and sorting, and having worn out my well-coiffed self, I lie in bed admiring the progress. Wallpaper flanks either side of my bedroom. Henri insisted on finishing the second wall after he saw the mediocre job I did on the first one. Admittedly, Henri's wall looks more professional than mine, but I like the fact that my wall shows its seams.

At 3 a.m. the girls call "just to say hi" after which I fall back asleep until 10:00 a.m., unheard of for me, but I deem it a lazy Sunday and cut myself some slack as I roll around in my covers, contemplating whether I will forgo *petit déjeuner* or actually put on clothes and walk downstairs for a croissant. JeF calls and asks me if I would like to have brunch, relieving me of this weighty decision. Even better, he is bringing brunch *chez moi.*

When JeF arrives, he backs away from my kisses warning me that he is coming down with a cold.

"Now you tell me?" I tease him and feel his forehead, which indeed is a little warm.

"You got your things!" he says. The living area is noticeably more home-like with chairs, my desk, and stacks of things to hang on the blank walls. JeF walks into the kitchen and admires Henri's work.

"*Superbe!*" he says. I agree. Henri is quite a find.

I push JeF out of the kitchen, thrilled that I have a surface upon which to work, and insist that he sit while I make us a *café*, juice the blood oranges, and slice the loaf of brioche with its terrifically high butter content. The deep ruby red of the juice, the apricot confiture, and the pale creamy white of the cheeses is a beautiful collection of color, contrasting with an otherwise dreary day. JeF reaches into his bag and hands me a book of short biographies on the fifty best French chefs in Paris. I scan its contents and see that some of my favorites are included: Yannick Alleno (Meurice), Guy Martin (Grand Véfour), Pascal Barbot & Christophe Rohat (L'Astrance), Alain Passard (L'Arpège), and Frederic Anton (Pré-Catelan). Someone gave it to him at the studio while filming something cooking-related, and he thought I would like it. And, I do.

"*Merci, Chéri,*" I say and kiss him on the cheek, ignoring his warning. I pour him more juice and when I insist that he drink it, he smiles at me.

"*Maman!*" He teases me, but I know he means it as a compliment. I touch his warm cheek and return the smile as I push the full juice glass in front of him. We linger at the table, eating and joking. I voice my frustration with my attempt to date, and we laugh about our perpetual single-dom in a cursory way. In all the time I have known JeF, very infrequently have we discussed our dating lives, past or present. The French are private. Sometimes I think that it is too bad JeF and I are like brother and sister because he would be a good boyfriend. He is passionate about everything, smart, fun, well-traveled and read, and I love how devoted he is to his son, six years older than Ava. There must be something wrong with my head. And his. So, we talk about love in a philosophical way as we tend to do.

"Love makes you stupid," he says.

I know what he means. Blind, stupid. My view is different.

"No, love makes you *hopeful*," I reply, realizing that our views likely reflect his French realism and my American optimism.

When he asks me why I am returning to Los Angeles so soon, I remind him of my child-custody schedule, and he responds negatively about American divorces. He thinks the notion that courts, not the parents, create a child-share schedule dictating when a child can and cannot see a parent or that a parent needs to be reminded to financially care for his or her child is ridiculous. "Stupid" is again used by JeF in this context, and this time, I agree.

It is *après-midi* when JeF leaves. I clean up the dishes, and I sit down to revise my weekly blog. The recipe is not working so I move to plan B, a simple *endives au gratin*; cream and breadcrumbs with vegetables always sound comforting in the cold of winter. My mind drifts to America. No news from Prince. My heart and ego are both insulted. I do not like bad air between us or anyone, actually, but I don't understand why he thinks, particularly after just six weeks, that he has the right to object to how I apportion my time. He knew going in that I am a mother with children, work, and goals that I have been working toward long before I met him and all of which are important to me. My thoughts work me up into a fit of my rightness, and I exchange my *au gratin* recipe for my running clothes.

I run past Trocadéro, under the Tower, through the Champs de Mars, past the American Church, past Invalides, cross in front of Notre-Dame, and take the path north of the Seine toward the Bastille where the uneven cobblestones twist and turn my feet. The more I reflect on the things that happened with Prince before I left, the more indignant I become, and I run a bit faster. When I think of all of the brioche and cheese and jam I just consumed for brunch, I run faster yet. By mile nine, my anger is gone. Thank goodness for my running, which I began after my separation from the girls' father. Hurt and sad, I would take to the streets and think of all the vindictive, angry things I wanted to do and say, and, without fail, by the time my run was over, all the nonsense in my head was dispelled and I could approach various difficulties without anger, even if the hurt remained a dull gnaw. When I return to *l'appart*, I write Prince what I deem to be a constructive and thoughtful email. Pleased with my adult communication skills and feeling quite evolved, I press "send." Thirty minutes later, he replies: "Very lengthy email...at work...will read on my day off :) and respond."

Comment? His day off is in a few days. His dismissive response offends me, and I close my computer. *Quel con!*

SUNDAY NIGHT and I need to escape my organizing and recipe writing. I put on a sleek pair of long black boots, and with my gifted book from JeF and a cigar I find in my little humidor, I head out of the sleepy 16th toward the 8th. It is too cold to smoke my cigar on the café *terrasses*, so I take a cab to the Hôtel Costes, the genius concept of the Costes brothers who have spread their atmospheric restaurant magic all about Paris, including La Societé in the 6th, Café Marly (in the Louvre), and Café de l'Esplanade in the 7th.

I discovered the Hôtel Costes in 2003. The girls' father and I took a long weekend away from the girls to attend a work conference organized and hosted by a Parisian law firm. It was the first time I was away from the girls and I justified this absence as the romantic getaway we needed. Romantic it was not; his mind was elsewhere. Nevertheless, one gathering was at the Costes, a stark contrast to my diaper-and-bottle environment in Los Angeles.

Decorated like a swank old French bordello, at least what I would imagine one to be like, I was taken with the indulgent space: red velvet chairs dripping with fringe, oil portraits hanging on the walls, and red roses standing at attention in beautiful vases in dimly lit rooms. The sexy smell of perfume permeated the entirety of the building and all public areas pulsed with seductive lounge music. Everything about the place was sensual. Four years later, when Giovanni and I met in Paris, he made us a reservation here. I never told him about my prior experience or the memories I associated with the hotel, and they soon became moot. Giovanni and I dined late into the evening, danced until dawn at Les Bains Douches or Le Chapeau, swam in the underground pool where we enjoyed *petit déjeuner* by ourselves, and every night I went to bed exhausted and feeling loved. Four years can change everything.

It is nearly midnight; the open to the sky interior *terrasse* is a quarter-full. My centrally-located table offers me a strategic view of everyone and everything around me. On my right there are two men in their early fifties looking *chic* in their cashmere sweaters, blazers adorned with silk kerchiefs in the front pocket, and leather loafers the likes of which would make *Chaussures Chics* envious. One is smoking a cigar. There are two men sitting at the table directly in front of me, speaking English with American accents, loudly, and overly impressed with their salmon dinner. On my left there is a group of six French men, in their forties I estimate, and I recognize a couple of them as actors, but their names are unfamiliar. Chimneys of cigarette smoke rise from their table as they roar with laughter. As I admire my cumulative surroundings, my phone quacks. It is my mother; inquiring as to the status of my furniture and *l'appart*. We chat for a few minutes and as I hang up the phone, the waiter approaches me.

"*Madame, en français ou en anglais?*" he asks, referring to my choice of menu.

"*Comme vous voulez,*" I respond.

He then tells me that the gentlemen would like to buy me a glass of Champagne and asks if that would be okay.

"*Lesquels?*" I inquire as I do not know the group of men to which he is referring.

He tells me the men on my right—the duo with the fancy loafers—asked before the others. His charming, yet I imagine false, flattery makes me laugh. I tell him that a glass of Champagne would be fine. *Merci*.

Five minutes after I am given my *coupe de champagne*, one of the gentlemen approaches my table and asks if I would join them at theirs. I decline. He then asks if they may join me at mine, and I agree.

The man with the kerchief and the cigar introduces himself as Abdul, a Prince of a "small country," which he refers to as "a mistake on the map." The man who approached my table first introduces himself as Robert, and he appears to be the Prince's assistant/friend. Robert does most of the talking and asks me what I am doing in Paris and other basic questions. The Prince remains rather quiet, puffing on his cigar, then interjects that it is rare to see a woman smoking a cigar. Never having been to the Middle East, I have no response for the comment that would not be conjecture and likely cause offense based upon my understanding of women's rights there. When he sees what I am smoking, he offers me one of his, correctly implying that mine is substandard. I accept and thank him for the Cohiba. Robert leans over to light my cigar, and I reflect on how bizarre my life is right now: fighting with a *faux* Prince on the new continent while smoking a cigar with a *vrai* Prince on the old. And, as it is the case that I have not met a real Prince before, I take the opportunity to ask him questions and begin with how many children and wives he has, which he answers without hesitation: one wife, three kids. They are at home. He says he travels all the time and is here because he is remodeling his place in the 8th. His hushed, smooth voice conveys a melancholy overtone and I imagine that his privileged life is isolating. Speculation on my part, but I sense something of the sort nonetheless. Robert says that anytime I would like a ride from CDG, they will send a car to pick me up. Robert's offer comes seemingly from nowhere. Maybe this is how the Prince keeps from being lonely, fetching women from the airport. I thank him, but decline. The suggestion of a married man, Prince or not, sending a car to pick me up from CDG does not remotely interest me.

Our conversation moves to travel and the mutual places we have visited in France and some of our favorite restaurants: La Colombe d'Or in Saint-Paul-de-Vence is high on both our lists. They suggest Le Grand Venise in the 15th, which I've heard has great Italian food. Robert suggests a second drink, but I decline. The Prince then invites me to join them for dinner tomorrow night. I thank them for the invitation and tell them I will think about it, knowing I will not go, but it is well past 2 a.m. and I would like to end the evening in a quiet way without protest from them, so I give Robert my requested French cell number.

We walk out of the hotel together. Their Quattroporte is waiting in front at the valet, and they offer to give me a ride home. I decline that too.

"It has a Ferrari engine," the Prince interjects. I smile. Men. Princes. Fancy cars. Frogs…

"*Non, merci. Je prends un taxi,*" I say good night, and walk to the taxi stand around the corner.

The Grand Venise reference ignited a pasta craving, and at *l'appart* I head straight to my kitchen. Thankful for my premature pantry items, I gather *farine type 55, sel,* an egg, and a little water, and I create a well and use my fingers in a swirling motion to combine the ingredients in a large bowl. Once mixed, I knead the dough and roll it out, which is not very easily done on the protective, glass cutting board, but a generous dusting of flour makes it possible. I slide my hands with spread fingers across the powdered, smooth dough; it feels like a caress on my palms. Nothing compares to the feel of dough in one's hands, a cathartic sensation I first experienced while making noodles with my grandmother when I had to stand on the plastic step stool to properly reach the counter. This memory accompanies me as I toss in additional pinches of flour, roll out the dough, and cut the thin sheet into tagliatelle-sized strips. My grandmother's noodles adorned her famous potato soup. Tonight, I cook the thinner, wider strips *al dente* in salted water with garlic cloves. Tossed with virgin olive oil, toasted walnuts, *sel de Guérande*, and truffle shavings from the remaining truffle in my refrigerator. *Le salon* is too far a walk, so I sit on top of my plastic-covered *plan de travail* in my little kitchen. The cigar and Champagne have long worn off, as have all thoughts of Princes, fake or real. Henri replaced the singular hanging light bulb with a brass three-light *bistro*-inspired light fixture. When JeF came over for brunch he reached up and slightly twisted the light fixture to a forty-five degree angle, rather than parallel to the stove, giving the kitchen a much better flow and reminding me that sometimes the slightest adjustment can change your entire perspective.

WHEN I RETURN to Los Angeles, the *faux* Prince and I reconcile. I begin dinner while he makes a fire in the living room fireplace. When I walk into the room with some wine and snacks, I find the furniture rearranged and a blanket spread out in front of the fireplace, a picnic inside. As we sit on the blanket with our wine, he apologizes and promises to be more understanding of my schedule. My apology follows, because when I hear his low voice, any annoyance or anger I have dissipates. I am convinced it is some sort of hormone-chemistry thing or maybe it is because I know that life is just too short to argue.

POTATO AND LEEK SOUP
WITH BEAUFORT CHEESE

Simple and satisfying for the colder months (when leeks are in season). This recipe calls for very few ingredients so take pride in the ones you use. Fresh leeks. Golden yellow butter. Beaufort is an unpasteurized cow's milk cheese from the French Alps. If you cannot find it, you can substitute another alpine cheese such as Gruyère.

Serves 2 to 4

    2 tablespoons unsalted butter
    8 ounces leeks (white parts only), chopped
    1 pound potatoes, peeled and diced
    3 cups chicken stock (or vegetable stock or water)
    1 bay leaf
    A/N sea salt
    A/N freshly ground black pepper
    A/N Beaufort cheese, grated
    A/N fresh Italian parsley, minced

Place saucepan over medium heat. Add butter. Melt. Add leeks and a pinch of salt. Cook leeks until softened. Add potatoes and toss in leek-butter combination. Add liquid (stock or water). Add bay leaf. Simmer until flavors come together. About 30 minutes.

Using a food processor or immersion blender, purée until smooth. Strain puréed soup through a chinois and put in a clean saucepan. Discard bay leaf. Adjust consistency (if too thick, add more liquid). Add grated cheese. (I usually toss in a handful.) Adjust seasoning with salt and pepper. Garnish with parsley.

VALENTINE LAVA CAKES WITH HEAT

These spicy, chocolatey cakes are perfect in the chilly winter months. They are easy to make but elegant enough for a special occasion. Serve with a quality vanilla ice cream.

Makes 6

A/N unsalted butter, for ramekins
10 ounces quality bittersweet chocolate
9 tablespoons unsalted butter, room temperature, divided
1½ cups all-purpose flour
1 teaspoon kosher salt
½ teaspoon baking powder
½ cup light brown sugar
½ cup granulated sugar
2 fresh eggs
1 teaspoon vanilla extract
¼ teaspoon ground chili d'arbol (no seeds)
¼ teaspoon ground *piment d'espelette*
½ teaspoon ground cinnamon
⅛ teaspoon ground allspice
¼ teaspoon ground cayenne pepper
2 tablespoons brewed instant espresso
¼ cup buttermilk, shaken
24 semi-sweet chocolate chips

Preheat oven to 325 degrees Fahrenheit. Butter the interior of the ramekin dishes. Set aside. Chop the chocolate. In a *bain marie* or a double broiler, melt 5 tablespoons of the butter and the chopped chocolate. Stir constantly until smooth and completely melted. Remove from heat. Set aside.

In a bowl, mix together flour, baking powder, and salt. Set aside. Combine the eggs, spices, brewed espresso, and vanilla extract in a separate bowl. Set aside.

In a standalone mixer fit with a paddle attachment, mix together the remaining 4 tablespoons of butter and the sugars on low speed until blended. Add melted chocolate to creamed butter-sugar combination. Mix to combine. With mixer on low speed, slowly add the egg combination. Once combined, add the dry ingredients and the buttermilk, alternating between the two, until both have been incorporated.

Divide the batter into the 6 ramekins. Press 4 chocolate chips into center of the batter. Place the ramekins on a rimmed baking sheet. Bake until puffy and slightly crusty on edges, but still soft in center.

CHAPTER TWENTY-THREE

Ouf!

MARCH CAME and went. So, too, the first half of April. With the kitchen *finie*, Henri has moved on to the *sbd*, which has not been without complication. Henri and his assistant hand-carried sixty bags of debris down four flights of stairs to empty the *sbd* of its contents. The tile delivery is delayed week after week and still MIA. Now, the bathroom store requests a check for the balance (contrary to the credit card plan we discussed), and they use this opportunity to clarify that "delivery" extends only to the street. *Comment?* Who delivers a bathtub to the middle of a *rue?* Nevertheless, Henri intervenes and tells me that he will deliver the requested checks and accept delivery but needs my approval to hire six men to help him carry the cast-iron tub from the street to *l'appart*. Six men? It is that heavy? Could this tub fall through to the floor below? What if I get into another lawsuit? I convey my concerns to Henri who reassures me (twice) that the floor can adequately support the heavy tub. And, within the week, the delivery plan is executed: the checks and bathroom items are exchanged in the *rue* in front of the produce market. When it is done, Henri, usually long on words, simply writes: "*Ça y est, tout s'est bien passé…. OUF!*"

As I read Henri's email, I envision him uttering "*ouf*," (phew) in exasperation and a few other French three-letter words as well.

In Los Angeles, May brings summer-like weather, making it hard to focus on my present task of inventory sheets and menus. The girls are with their father for the weekend and Prince is busy. The sunny weather beckons me, and I go to Mulholland Drive for a run. The two-lane road lines the crest of the Santa Monica mountains, and weekends up there are quiet. With the clear blue sky above me and a view of the San Fernando Valley on my left, and the ocean and Catalina on my right, it is an inspiring place to run despite the occasional speeding car. Four miles out, my head in some sort of warm-weather whimsy, I slip on gravel and broken glass on the side of the road. My left hand instinctively extends to break my fall, and while this maneuver saves my face and teeth, it sacrifices my left side which is now bleeding from shoulder to foot. My left wrist is swollen and painful. I remove the elastic-bound, expandable pouch holding my keys from around my hips and tightly wrap it around my wrist and run back to my parked car with my left hand in the air.

When I arrive home, limping and bloody, Tony, both my friend and masseur, is waiting for me on the porch. Tony is the only masseur I will let touch me as a result of my first spa experience. I was a twenty-five-year-old first-year attorney at a law firm retreat. Each lawyer was given two free spa treatments. One of my selections was a massage, and I was a first-timer. At dinner that night I learned that my masseur spent a considerable amount of time on my tush, while the behinds of my colleagues seemed to have been neglected. My colleagues suggested that perhaps my masseur thought I was the only attorney who sat in a chair, laughing loudly while their glasses clinked to the suggestion. I have been suspect of masseurs ever since. Tony, who worked with my chiropractor, has been the only exception. I asked him to do me a favor and come over tonight to give me and my friend, Sophia, who is going through a difficult time, a massage. Girls' night in. I provide the masseur. She is bringing the Brunello.

"What happened to you?" Tony exclaims as he helps me into the house

I tell him.

"You are really a klutz," he says laughing. It is not the first time I have fallen while running; he has seen the scars on my legs.

"Thanks a lot. As if my body does not hurt enough. You have to add on?" I say.

"You're lucky this did not happen last month in Boston," he adds.

"True," I say, acknowledging that falling in the Boston marathon, with my daughters waiting for me at mile twenty-five, would have been a bummer. The record heat was enough of a challenge.

We clean the dirt and blood off of my leg, arm, and shoulder, revealing how scraped up and bruised I really am. A wrap-around wine bottle cooler serves as an icepack for my wrist. Sophia arrives with wine in hand. The three of us decide that my wrist is not broken because I can still move my fingers and I reason that the girl time and aged Brunello will heal any discomfort.

But heal it did not. At 3 a.m. my wrist is very swollen and unbearably painful, so I drive myself to the UCLA emergency room where it is confirmed: an intra-articular distal radius fracture. They give me a temporary cast, which extends from mid-finger to my elbow and several prescriptions for the pain. No running today and, worse yet, no cooking.

DR. WARREN is an orthopedic surgeon referred to me by friends who have dealt with broken bones before. He and his wife are parents at the girls' grammar school. They were kind to put me on the schedule for today and even work around my afternoon carpool duties. At his office, Dr. Warren lets me choose my cast color. Black, of course, yet traces of white plaster peek out from underneath the black gauze on either end. Before heading to the girls' school, I stop at home and, with the aid of a glue gun, I adhere black grosgrain ribbon over the white edges and accessorize the cast with a white silk Camilla flower from a shopping bag. It does not look so bad anymore. The girls even think my decorated cast is "cool."

Yet despite its "cool" appearance, it is awkward doing anything with a plaster tube on my wing, accessorized or not. Cooking with a cast presents its own challenges. For sanitary purposes, I place a disposal latex rubber glove on my left hand and pull it over the cast's edge. Then using (thankfully) American plastic wrap, I "cater wrap" my cast and glove edge so no food can seep under my cast and the cast itself is kept clean. Sanitary, but not attractive. While I was appreciative that I did not break my dominant hand, I now realize how significant my left hand is to cooking. Slicing and dicing food has become a tedious challenge. Gutting a fish, trimming lamb chops, both are exercises of frustration and result in a sloppy product. By the time I am finished with my prep work, I am too annoyed to begin on dinner. Prince brings Japanese food and flowers for me.

"How can I sign your cast if it is black?" he smirks. "You know," he continues, "breaking your wrist is a sign that you need to slow down."

"Grrrrr."

"Did you just growl at me?" he asks.

"I did," laughing at my own response. "Maybe you're right."

He smiles at me and cradles my face with his hands. He brushes his thumb across my lips and then leans into me and bestows on me one of those kisses, making the pain in my wrist nonexistent. In fact, my limbs do not feel connected to my body at all.

THE SHEER frustration of trying to type has kept me off of my computer for days and this avoidance has Henri in a real panic as our electronic correspondence had been daily. So accustomed to my immediate replies, my silence causes him to ask JeF to check on my whereabouts. I sit down and punch out responses to Henri's seventeen emails with my right hand, explaining my absence and agreeing with his suggestion of purchasing a refurbished Art Deco *radiateur* for the bathroom. In my silence, someone bought the first one Henri found, but he found a second that he will retrieve in Quimper (known for its butter).

The tenth day with a broken wrist proves the most challenging thus far. Three friends host a book signing for me in Alice's backyard as summer has come early this year. After the disappointing publishing news in New York, I decided to self-publish my little cookbook. I did not expect to make much money on it; the profit margin was tremendously small due to the color photographs, but I was proud I had something tangible to show others, especially in France. As planned, I prepare many of the recipes in my book for the guests. My wrist wrapped in plastic, the preparation of the lunch dishes takes twice as long. However, I am blessed with help and the company of wonderful people, and the event goes well.

JeF stops by *l'appart* and emails me a photograph of the installed bathroom floor with the heading: "that is gonna be beautiful." Henri's email, however, which follows shortly thereafter, is not as positive. He says that he has eighteen days of work to do before my arrival on June 12 and it is *"trop court pour finir le chantier."* He asks me to postpone my visit to Paris. *Comment? C'est pas possible!* The plane tickets are nonrefundable, not to mention I have been looking forward to this visit for months. So I assure Henri that he does not have to finish everything; primed walls and a functioning bathroom are all

I need. Henri thinks it is a concession, but I know that running hot water and a non-leaking toilet is a step up. Last winter did not set a high bar.

PARIS-BOUND in four days. The end of the school year has dizzied into its customary frenzy of activities, and as each year passes my parental responsibilities and obligations seem to increase, not decrease, making the time pass even quicker. I wake to a slew of emails from France and open Henri's first:

"*Voilà! Tout est prêt pour ton arrivée le 12 juin, si tu as besoin de quelque chose d'autre dont tu aurais besoin, nouriture, petit déjeuner, boisson ou autre? N'hésite pas!*"

I have a primed, functioning bathroom thanks to Henri who even offers to purchase something for me to eat or drink upon my arrival. *Sympa*. We make a *rendez-vous* to meet the day after my arrival. The same day I have a *rendez-vous* with Christophe (because after a three-month hibernation, the lawsuit has re-emerged). Despite Christophe's letters, not to mention the addition of two insurance companies with deep pockets, the infernal machine continues. I remain in the lawsuit. The expert requests that I produce all of *les factures* for the work in *l'appart*, so I gather the requested information as well as photographs of the before, during, and after, and put everything on a flash drive for Christophe.

I am faring no better in the relationship category than the legal one except, instead of a machine, my romance is a rollercoaster. Prince and I are either making love or arguing, and the latter exhausts me. With my impending departure, it is more of the same; the tension between us is high, and my patience is at a low. I've had enough of the rollercoaster ride and feel resentful that he is upset that I am leaving rather than being supportive that the girls and I will finally reap the benefits of years of hard work and dreaming. Yet, at the same time, I understand his frustration. He misses me. And, who would want to have a relationship with someone who wants to jump on a plane to Paris every chance she gets and is planning a life there? Especially since it is clear his life will remain in Los Angeles. At the outset, I tried to set expectations and be honest about my plans and limitations, but maybe it is just an unfair ask of anyone and perhaps this is the cost of my unwillingness to compromise my priorities of motherhood, work, and Paris? Maybe I should forget about dating, or at least a relationship, until the girls go to college? Or, maybe it is just stupid to try to date men who do not live (or want to live) in Paris? While I contemplate these queries and their possible answers, I knew what my gut was telling me: this is not the long-term relationship for me. I relay my thoughts to Prince. He agrees. Expiration: five months, one week. Already I know that I will miss him; the sound of his low voice and the way he loves me with his whole heart. His love, however frustrating at times, made me a better woman and despite my resistance, he did teach me to occasionally slow down and look up from my lists. So, in that respect, Prince was a *vrai* Prince after all.

TWO DAYS BEFORE I leave for Paris, I host a cooking demonstration at Surfas. Edgar, who manages the test kitchen, came up with the title: "How the French Eat So Well and Stay So Slim" and whether it be the title or the free food, the demonstration is well-attended. All forty chairs are full, leaving others to stand. Ava and Julia attend, and while Ava wants nothing to do with cooking, she sits in the first row. Julia, my *sous chef,* eagerly helps.

Admittedly, the more accurate title would have been "How the French Used to Eat" because the traditional French ways to which I became accustomed have been gradually slipping away with globalization. The younger generations are quite fond of McDonalds and such instant gratification eateries are everywhere in Paris—including one in my neighborhood—and it is always full. Obesity is rising in France and, as a result, admonitions are issued on the bottom of advertisements for things such as sweets or cheese, reminding the consumer to consume such items in moderation and to eat five fruits and vegetables every day.

Before the actual demonstration, I discuss the genuine appreciation the French have for food and their knowledge of quality, fresh, and regional products. I reason that consuming flavorful food leads to eating less because you are satisfied and, thus, not chasing elusive taste. The logistics of space and the convenience of Parisian life enables them to purchase fresh food on a daily basis with ease, and I give them examples of the size challenges of *l'appart* and the differences between life in Paris versus Los Angeles that I have experienced. We discuss French general eating habits: smaller portions and less dessert (and that fruit is often dessert and non-fruit desserts are not as sweet as traditional American ones). In France, butter, milk, and jam are breakfast items only. Food items that Americans consume for breakfast—waffles (*gaufres*), *crêpes*, or French toast (*pain perdu*)—are considered dessert items or for *le goûter*. Someone asks about all "those sauces" and "the cheese," and I acknowledge that the French do enjoy them but in moderation, and cheese is eaten in small portions. Absent is the cheese platter decorated with several large wedges. Dressings are vinaigrettes, not mayonnaise-based. Dips and *purées* are made with vegetables and proteins such as tuna, sardines, or tofu, not with mayonnaise or buttermilk as is common in the States. The sour cream toasted onion dip of my youth, nonexistent in France (except maybe next to the peanut butter and ketchup in the U.S.A. section of the International food aisle of a grocery store).

When I move behind the work space, the slanted mirrors above me permit the audience to view what I am doing on the counter. More often than not, my wrapped black cast hits the counter or the oven door, because when I am not cutting or chopping I am using my hands to illustrate my point. The French's curiosity and knowledge of food make preparation easy and packaged foods unnecessary and, to demonstrate such ease, I focus on two seasonal ingredients: tomatoes and peaches. While I am talking, Julia passes out illustrative snacks: peach and prosciutto wraps, peach mousse, and tomato and radish salad in *verrines*. Audience members are called up to make various *entrées* and *plats* with tomatoes and peaches, using different techniques to demonstrate the range of the two ingredients. A little girl comes up and together we make a green bean and tomato salad with a slice of *terrine de foie gras* (which I made this week and brought as a treat). She is so helpful that we also make a peach and arugula salad with a balsamic glaze. Julia, with other assistants, plates the salads and passes them out. Those standing in the back row complain that they are not getting a fair share of the samples and Julia rushes to their rescue. Two more volunteers prepare a Mediterranean *sauté* with cherry tomatoes, olives, fresh basil, and chunks of swordfish. Then we roast monkfish fillets and grape tomatoes. Moving from sautéing and roasting to baking, I demonstrate the *tarte Tatin* technique, and additional volunteers come up to the stove to practice. One makes a savory cherry tomato *tarte Tatin*, another makes a sweet one with peaches. Young and less young, all take turns at the stove and the oven.

THE GIRLS, worn out from the day, fall asleep in my bed halfway through our favorite movie, *Ratatouille*. I pack for France and, when finished, nestle back in between them with my laptop to read emails. To my surprise, there are several from guests at today's demonstration. A few tell me it was the first time that they tasted *foie gras* and thank me for the opportunity, while others tell me how much they learned. Many are simple thank you notes. Then there is an email from a woman who thanks me for the class and goes on to say how endearing it was to watch Julia so eager to participate: "She is so proud of you," she writes.

Words can be powerful. Proud of me? I was proud of her today, but the converse never occurred to me; they see me cook all the time. *Sous chef* sleeps peacefully against my side, and I wipe the blonde tresses away from her cheek and give her a kiss.

When the girls leave for vacation with their father, I stop at Dr. Warren's office before heading to LAX. He comments on how well my wrist has healed, surmising that it must be the cooking. He saws off my permanent cast and gives me a removable one because the six-week mark will occur while I am gone. He asks that I return in July for a check-up and begins to tell me about a physical-therapy regime, but stops himself mid-sentence.

"You won't go to therapy, will you?"

"No," I say chuckling at his suggestion, "but I do plan to cook and knead a lot of dough."

"That'll work." He smiles and wishes me a *bon voyage*.

SWORDFISH MEDITERRANEAN *SAUTÉ*

Serves 4 to 6

>20 ounces fresh swordfish
>A/N kosher salt
>A/N freshly ground black pepper
>A/N *piment d'espelette*
>1 to 2 tablespoons olive oil
>2 garlic cloves, minced
>¼ cup capers, rinsed and drained
>2 dozen olives
>1 to 2 beautiful heirloom tomatoes or 2 dozen cherry tomatoes
>1 to 2 tablespoons minced fresh Italian parsley
>A/N fresh basil leaves or fresh French thyme

Trim the skin off of the swordfish steak(s). Cut steaks into ½ inch to 1 inch cubes. Season with salt and pepper and a little *piment d'espelette.*

Remove the pits from the olives and cut olives in half. Drain and rinse the capers. Cut the tomatoes into wedges (or cut the cherry tomatoes in half).

Place a large sauté pan over medium-high heat. Add olive oil. One oil is hot, add garlic. When you can smell the garlic, add the swordfish. Use tongs to turn the swordfish in the pan to evenly cook all sides. Remove partially-cooked fish from pan and set aside on a plate covered with foil. Add the tomatoes, capers, and olives to the pan. Sauté until the tomatoes have softened and half of the cooking liquid has been cooked out of the pan. Return the fish to the pan. Gently toss the ingredients and cook for another for 2 to 3 minutes to combine the flavors and finish cooking the swordfish. The fish is done when it is opaque in the center.

Salt and pepper to taste. Garnish with fresh herbs and serve warm.

TARTE TATIN

You can use peaches, nectarines, or pears instead of apples. For savory renditions, such as cherry tomato, cauliflower, or zucchini, eliminate the sugar and butter, and use a little olive oil in the pan instead.

Makes 1 *tarte*

    8 to 9 apples, peeled, cored, and halved
    A/N fresh lemon juice
    4 tablespoons unsalted butter
    1 cup granulated sugar
    A/N kosher salt
    1 sheet puff pastry
    Fresh French thyme, optional garnish

Defrost puff pastry sheet in the refrigerator.

Preheat oven to 400 degrees Fahrenheit.

Peel the apples. Cut in half. Remove the core and seeds. Squeeze lemon juice on the peeled apples to prevent browning. If apples are large, cut into quarters.

Place an ovenproof sauté pan over medium heat. Add butter and melt. Pour sugar over the melted butter. Combine. Add apples. The pan will be crowded, but apples will shrink as they cook. Continue to cook the apples until they are soft and the butter-sugar mixture is thick and bubbly. This takes about thirty minutes. (Be patient.) Turn off flame.

Roll out the the puff pastry sheet on a lightly floured surface. Cut puff pastry into a circle large enough to cover the pan. Arrange the apples in pan with flat sides facing up (or, if cut, arrange them in a decorative way). Cover the apples with the pastry dough. Tuck the pastry inside the rim of the sauté pan. (Do not let the pastry hang over the edge of the pan.)

To caramelize the applies, place the pan in the oven. Bake for about 15 minutes until the pastry dough is puffed and golden brown. Carefully remove the pan from the oven using an oven mitt or kitchen towel. Let the *tarte* slightly cool in the pan for about 10 minutes so the caramel can settle.

Place a plate over the pan (with the bottom facing up) and carefully invert the *tarte* gently onto the plate. The apples should be a deep caramel color. Remember to do this carefully and use a towel as the pan handle will still be hot. The *tarte* is best enjoyed warm and generally served with real vanilla ice cream. Garnish with fresh thyme if you would like.

CHAPTER TWENTY-FOUR

Tellement Magnifique!

THEN THERE IS the June gloom—*la grisaille*—yet despite its cloudy-with-drizzle exterior, Paris bursts internally with life in anticipation of warmer days. Winter's spindly, bare trees are now resplendent with leaves and hide the stone buildings. Flower beds of organized color and shape explode from the ground with precision in all public spaces. Peonies dominate the florists and marchés with their colorful pompoms of white, pink, and magenta. Store windows announce the impending *Fête des Pères* and *l'école est finie*, the passing of which are synonymous with summer's arrival.

My chatty taxi driver deposits me and my moving boxes at the lobby entrance. As I negotiate the wrought-iron door with my body and push my possessions over the threshold with one functioning hand, an exiting neighbor sees my cast and my dubious method and carries my boxes through to the elevator. In *l'appart* the light from the windows illuminates the sheets covering the furniture; they resemble ghosts. Bright pink peonies explode from a glass pitcher on the table and next to them a note from Henri: *Bienvenue chez toi*, it reads, Welcome to your home.

Ma cuisine parisienne stuns me. No doubt the smallest kitchen space I have ever worked, but it is efficiently organized and the countertop is a perfect complement to the stove. I scale the boxes in the foyer and make my way to the other end of *l'appart* to the bathroom.

Magnifique! The tub sits majestically at a slight angle at the room's far end, facing the window, giving the soaker a city view. Instinctively I walk to the tub and turn the *chaud* knob. Clear, hot water gushes into the porcelain vessel while a single lightbulb still hangs above—"the joy of the single light bulb"—just to remind me of how the space has changed. The black-and-white Art Deco space I imagined, with its intermittent rich golds, buttery yellows, and aubergine, exudes Paris romance and whimsy. And, it all began with the stove.

If the heavy clouds are to be believed, rain is imminent. While eager to unpack my baking goodies from Mora and hang my copper pans, not to mention immerse myself in scented bubbles while soaking in a hot bath, I defer these treats to *faire du shopping* in the neighborhood I have missed.

The streets are a murmur of activity and filled with the familiar, pleasing odors of roasted chicken and herbed potatoes. Lucille stops blow-drying the red hair on the head in front of her to greet me with a double kiss. She puts me in the books for tomorrow morning and returns to the red head. The *presse* has new cooking magazines and I select several and hand the stack to the *madame* who is standing behind the counter in the magazine-lined hut. She wishes me a *bonne journée* as she gives me my change. At Béchu I secure some feel-good carbs and then visit the Monoprix where I proudly hand the cashier my *carte de fidélité* before my eggs, milk, and yogurt pass the scan. Two doors down, white asparagus and cherries take center stage at Halles des Belles Feuilles. The asparagus boasts the impressive girth of a globe artichoke stem. The husband asks me how many *asperges blanches* I would like.

"*Huit, s'il vous plaît.*"

He pauses momentarily before counting out eight, which fill the paper sack, making me feel a bit greedy and slightly perverse because they are *très chères* and *très grandes*. Although Freud may have something to say about my impulse purchase, I am mentally planning my culinary experimentation. The husband also scoops the requested two kilos of the deep red *cerises* (which are my favorite). The cantaloupe and figs from the south are making a first appearance, but I will wait until after I return from the Luberon, this year's culinary excursion where I will spend the upcoming weekend. His wife totals my items and asks how I am. Four months felt like an eternity while I was away, but nothing has changed, the familiarity is reassuring, and the recognition by my neighborhood vendors makes me feel like a full-fledged local.

The younger man is working today in Androuet. Coat-hanger thin with dirty-blond straight hair he looks to be about eighteen years old, and I wonder if he is doing a *stage* (internship). He, too, recognizes me from a prior visit, which adds to my contentment. I choose something new and two favorites: a Napoléon Brebis, a sheep's milk cheese from the Basque region; a Graine des Vosges, soft rind, creamy cow's milk cheese that comes in a small wooden *carré* (square) box; and a small round of Banon de Banon, uniquely wrapped in chestnut leaves (historically a preservation method) and tied perfectly with raffia. The cheese has a unique taste and blond color due to the leaves, and it is said to be best at this time of year. My *carte de fidélité* is stamped and filling rapidly, part-time status or not, making me a cheese over-achiever.

Back at *l'appart*, without the patience to prepare a meal and an urgent need for something in my growling stomach, I pit some cherries and cook them in a saucepan to a jam consistency with a little lemon juice, sugar, and *piment*. I pass my serrated knife through the center of the *ficelle* from Béchu and generously line one side of the airy interior with thin slices of the Napoléon Brebis, and the other side I slather with the impromptu spiced cherry jam. My sandwich looks like it is bleeding but the appearance does not hold me back: *Miam!* How do the French eat well and stay slim? Not like this.

HENRI ARRIVES and I gush with gratitude for his work and the thoughtful peonies. We walk through *l'appart*, and I show him in the bathroom where I would like him to install the chandelier, mirror, and sconces. It is 7:30 p.m. when Henri finishes. We sit down at the toe-assaulting table and he opens his file to pull from its tidy interior a *facture* for the work. As I am spelling out the amount in my most legible cursive French, double checking each letter, he hands me another *facture. Comment?* My surprise at two bills—neither a small sum—reveals itself on my non-poker face. I knew the plumber had a separate *facture*, but when I previously asked Henri the total, I meant the total for everything, not just his work. While the misunderstanding is no one's fault, I am looking at two bills totaling twice the cost I was anticipating. My attempt to explain my confusion in French fails and makes everything awkward. Tired and unsure of some of the vocabulary, my inarticulateness frustrates me and confuses Henri. I dropped a stitch for sure, and the atmosphere feels somber as I write out the second *chèque*. The idea that I have hurt Henri's feelings is far worse than paying two bills.

My two days in Paris before my departure to the south is filled with organizing *l'appart* and spending time with visitors from the States. The first, Pierre, lives in California and is passing through Paris en route to a wedding in Italy. We have weaved in and out of each other's lives as convenient dates for six years, with enough sexual tension to make it exciting, but enough respect for our friendship to leave things as they are. Fluent in French, he knows Paris well and is utterly charming. When he arrives at *mon appart,* he brings wine and a large bouquet of white flowers as a house-warming gesture. *Génial.* Not having seen one another since last fall, we spend hours at Hélène Darroze with lots to catch up on and plenty of gorgeous wine with which to do it. When we close down the restaurant, we take a taxi to the Costes for Champagne and *fromage,* which at the time seemed like a fine idea, but when I fall into bed, it is 5 a.m.; it gives me only three hours of sleep. When I awake, I write an earnest email to Henri, apologizing for the misunderstanding. He is receptive to my email, and he wishes me a *bon week-end* and gives me his tips for my time in Gordes, one of his favorite places. Damage repaired.

My *petit déjeuner* is a *café* with Lucille who again has her way with my hair. She makes it a tad darker yet, despite the unrequested change, *ça me plaît.* I race from Lucille to Le Flandrin, a five-minute walk from *l'appart,*where I meet Mark, who is in town on business, for *déjeuner.* I have not spoken to him since last fall, but I promised we could get together.

The cloudy weather does not discourage Parisians from enjoying the fresh air on the *terrasse,* drinking wine, smoking, gossiping about lovers and enjoying classics like *œufs bio "mayo"* and *salade de champignons de Paris.* Mark and I secure the last table on the *terrasse.* Our gangly, blond waiter overhears our accents and introduces himself as a fellow "yank" who is apparently eager for a little American companionship as he launches, unsolicited, into his twenty years living in Paris, how he worked in the fashion industry, including the house of Christian Dior, and lives nearby. Mark appears bored with Andy's tales and name-dropping. I don't mind as much because I understand his eagerness to talk with us; a connection with your roots lends a sense of comfort because no matter how long you have been an expat living in France, you will always be a foreigner, even if everyone recognizes you in your favorite spots.

VENDREDI. Sleep was intermittent, and I woke at various points throughout the night to write down white asparagus recipe ideas. Troubling. I actually spent time with two men in the last two days, yet I am preoccupied with asparagus recipes. My expensive purchase will not last until my return from the south, but three hours is enough time to experiment in the kitchen until I need to be at the *gare.*

Every nook of the kitchen is accounted for. Asparagus is roasting, shocked in an ice bath, and macerating with the aid of lemon juice and sea salt. A *velouté* is simmering on the stove, and I creatively cut some spears for a garnish. Thrilled with my own inventiveness, I leave various dishes to cool while I pack for the south. I print my train ticket. *Zut!* I am not leaving Paris at 11 a.m., I am arriving in Avignon at 11 a.m.! I crash about *l'appart* in a whirlwind of speed—stove off, windows closed, food on ice, rinse dishes, clothes in weekend bag, food in the refrigerator—how do I do this to myself? Wrong train. Wrong time. Wrong date. I run down the street pulling my trolly behind me and take the *métro* to Gare de Lyon. Forty minutes, an impressive time to get across town, but I still missed my train by nearly two hours, and because I did not change the ticket before it departed, I ate the cost of the ticket.

The line for new ticket purchases wraps around several turnstiles. I opt for the big yellow automated machines where there is no waiting, and I soon discover why: two of them do not work and the third one works but then the screen freezes when I insert my credit card, necessitating that I re-join the line, which is now even longer. Thirty minutes later, I explain to the ticket agent that I missed my train because I was busy testing white asparagus recipes, which had to be done before I left. He does not bat an eye or question my story; it is too ridiculous to be untrue and my awkward French in a desperate, frustrated tone adds to his amusement. Not to mention that in France, all things food take precedent.

"*Pas de problème,*" he says, smiling at me.

He types a few things on the computer and finds me a seat on the next train, which is leaving in fifteen minutes. He also exchanges my ticket without charging me for a new one.

"*Merci beaucoup, Monsieur! Bon week-end.*"

When the train pulls away from the covered station, rain drops smear across the window, and the large streaks distort the urban view. *À bientôt la grisaille!* I sound like my Parisian friends who vow that weekend breaks from the Paris gray are necessary for one's healthy emotional state and key to living in Paris. I settle into Millay, with whom I share sentiments of trains and travel, while the landscape changes from industrial to expansive green with white dots of the grazing goats. Avignon is calm and sunny. I exit the station and follow the tiny asphalt path across two single-lane streets to where my green Mini awaits me, the smell of lavender and adventure in the air.

RAW WHITE ASPARAGUS SALAD

Serves 4

> 8 ounces large white asparagus spears, trimmed
> 2 handfuls of wild arugula
> ½ teaspoon *sel de Guérande* (or ¼ teaspoon kosher salt)
> 2 ounces quality parmesan cheese, thinly sliced
> A/N quality olive oil
> A/N quality balsamic glaze*
> Thin slices of Parma prosciutto (optional)

Use a vegetable peeler to slice the asparagus spear lengthwise. (You can also use a mandoline, but be careful.) Repeat with all asparagus spears. Place the asparagus strips in a bowl. Add salt and toss. Place in the refrigerator for at least 2 hours. Gently squeeze the excess moisture from the asparagus strips.

Toss the asparagus with the arugula. Add cheese shavings. Drizzle balsamic vinegar glaze and olive oil over salad to taste. Toss.

*You can make this yourself by placing balsamic vinegar and a little light brown sugar in a saucepan and cooking it until it reaches a syrup consistency. (Be careful not to burn the vinegar and remember that it thickens as it cools.)

CHAPTER TWENTY-FIVE

The Other Side

THE LUBERON stands in stark contrast to all other places I have wandered in France. It is not the east side of Provence, the Côte d'Azur, with its azure blue, ethereal lightness, and bronzed inhabitants. Nor is it Normandy, with its apple orchards and grazing cows, the dramatic, thumping earth, and crashing cold sea. It is not Alsace, with its successive patchwork of light and green vineyards dotted with medieval castles. Instead, the Luberon is lush, abounding with dark green hills and valleys and trees with branches heavy with stone fruit. Fields of wheat, sunflowers, and lavender boast such enormity and beauty that it cannot accurately be captured with a camera lens or words.

I soar down the unknown two-lane road. Cyclists break from their spinning to refuel at fresh fruit stands on the side of the road, their bikes leaning against cherry trees. Every so often there is a singular farmer riding a tractor on the road with no hurry in mind. When I stumble upon Le Musée de la Lavande in Coustelle, an entire museum devoted to everything lavender, I feel compelled to stop. I learn how *lavande fine* is cultivated and that the oil is created by crushing the buds and then distilling them in a large copper still in the summer. The two-hour detour imparts knowledge and a few lavender products for my new *sdb*. Back on the road, I see Gordes from a distance crowning the top of the hill with the Vaucluse valley lying in green submission below. The 11th-century perched village is recognized as "one of the most beautiful villages in France" and, even from a distance, it takes my breath away.

My room overlooks the valley, and I open all three windows, inviting in the fresh air. But I do not stay in my room long, despite the welcome tray of regional goodies. Instead, I explore the compact village; at its center sit a stone statue of a soldier dedicated to "*la mémoire des enfants de Gordes morts pour la France 1914-1918*," and a castle with its imposing proportions, which has dominated the village for over one thousand years. Gordes has endured invasions, religious wars, plagues, earthquakes, and bombings, but as I walk around the town, I cannot tell. Unlike Rouen, where the noses on some statues remain broken, reminding you of its war-torn past, the statues in Gordes have their noses.

Cobblestone pathways hug the curves of the castle and hobble down the backside of the village. Well-fed cats and potted boxwood topiaries and pink geraniums decorate the hardscape. Boutiques and homes are painted in the familiar *provençal* pastels. Metal *bistro* tables and chairs sit in hidden pea-graveled gardens with terra-cotta pots bursting with tender herbs. I browse the markets and home shops and take the samples offered me. I am mad about the varieties of artisan honey—everything from dark *miels* of chestnut and rhododendron to much lighter *miels* such as lavender and thyme and buy a few jars of both light and dark. Across from the 18th century church is a *pâtisserie* where I sample and purchase *le gibassier*, a crisp cookie as large as my head made with olive oil, giving it a crunchy, fruity flavor, and *navettes*, small almond-shaped cookies flavored with *fleur d'oranger*, *anis* or *lavande*.

Knowing I can explore things more efficiently in my running clothes, I change and charge down the same main street, which brought me up the hill. One area on the side of the highway offers a perfect vantage point of the Gordes village, allowing my camera phone to capture it in its entirety. I am not alone in the discovery of this spot and share the space with an easel behind which stands a white-haired gentleman with a large straw hat and thick sandals. He looks away from his easel, only momentarily to glance at the village and dab his brush on his palette and then on the canvas, slowly and purposefully. He pays no attention to me nor the buses hauling tourists up the hill behind us. The Gordes cityscape on his canvas is all maroon, and it is beautiful. It would be lovely on a dish set.

At 9:30 p.m., the sun is setting, but not so quickly, and I understand its hesitation. It is difficult to put an end to a day filled with *provençal* sun, the calming smell of lavender and the cicadas' hum. The pea gravel crunches under the waiter's feet as he traverses the large outdoor *terrasse* and makes his way to my table set against an iron railing, the only thing separating my table from the valley below. He sets a glass of Châteauneuf-du-Pape on my table with a dish of olives and puffed pastry cheese sticks and brings me something warm for my shoulders. Twenty birds swirl above my head, getting in their last flight before dark, although their view cannot be much better than mine. The Romans were right: this is the land of the Gods, and perhaps that is why they claimed it as their own centuries ago.

SATURDAY MORNING I set out for the town of Apt, which is home to the largest open *marché* in the Luberon, a tradition started long ago as it is a halfway point for those living in the mountains and those living in the plains. I whiz through wheat fields in various stages of harvest and cherry tree orchards where more cyclists have parked their bikes underneath the trees and are relieving the branches of their heavy clusters. When I pass a sign for the Fromagerie de Banon, I slam on my brakes. *Comment?* Banon de Banon A.O.C.! The A.O.C. endorsement guarantees that the milk is from goats in the Provence *commune* that have grazed in particular areas and that the goat's milk was produced, manufactured, and ripened in the traditional way. Pulling my car off of the main highway, I follow the signs that lead me down a little road, surrounded by lavender fields. The factory is closed. But, just like with the cornfields in Alsace, I am compelled to be closer to my surroundings. The morning sun on my face, my senses suffused with the calming fragrance, I sit at the end of a lavender row on a mound of dirt, absorbing the abundance of beauty all around me. Life at this moment feels divine, and I believe I have found Xanadu—this former Roman land—that "romantic chasm" of which Coleridge wrote. That land of "fertile earth" and "thick pants" is *here* in erect purple rows exploding out of the ground right in front of me only to be harnessed by oil makers and appreciated by pleasure seekers like me.

The Apt market has overtaken the town's main road. Tables brim with summer fruits and vegetables and burlap sacks are filled with spices and *herbes de Provence*. Rows and rows of peonies are arranged by color. A vendor is selling *saucisson de chèvre* (goat), *de cerf* (stag), and *de sanglier* (wild boar); the latter is my favorite and I buy two. Several tables are devoted to small-batch tapenades and olives of every color and size. A few feet from the olives I discover *fougasse*, a light bread made with olive oil and cut (pre-baking) to resemble a leaf. This Grasse specialty is usually flavored with *herbes, fleur d'oranger,* or *lavande*. But here, it is uniquely made with whole, black cured olives and the salty, moist pieces combined with the airy bread make it the best *fougasse* I have ever had.

One woman has laundry-size baskets of culinary lavender sold by the kilo and two scoops of lavender are added to my *panier*. By the time I reach the cheese vendors, I have finished my *fougasse*. The cheese display is dominated, not surprisingly, with local goat cheese sold in various stages of ripeness—*mi-sec* (semi dry) or *cremeux* (soft). I discover *Banon fromage plié*, which uses the same folding and preservation process as the A.O.C. treasure but it does not have to be from Banon or even made from goat's milk. Both the A.O.C. and non-A.O.C. versions find their way into my *panier*.

Apt is known for its sugared fruit and fruit confit, and it would be culinary malpractice to leave without a jar or two. Finding it hard to choose, I select two preserved fruits and two jars of honey. The vendor tells me she has been selling honey and jam for twenty years, and she and I discuss the region and her experiences in the business of food. When I pay, she gifts me an additional jar of each.

It is said that a bundle of wheat from the summer's harvest when placed in your home will bring you luck. It is a *provençal* custom to which I was introduced in 2006 at the *Fête du Blé et de la Lavande* in Peille. One for traditions, I purchase a bundle for *l'appart* and then some *bio* flours—*seigle* (rye), *blé* (wheat), and *pois chiches* (Chickpeas)—in the name of wrist therapy. My *panier* must be carried with both arms because of its weight, but I make one last stop: a table filled with *provençal* tomatoes, second only to those my grandfather grew when I was a child, which I still remember to this day. The *tomates anciennes* and *cœur de bœuf*, large bright red tomatoes with creases on the sides which resemble a pumpkin and look like ruffles when you slice them, are my favorites. Vine-ripened, in the traditional sense (meaning they are ripened on the vine in the sun, not the store version of gassing the tomatoes "on the (cut) vine" in a warehouse to ripen them). The difference is a world of taste and zero deception. The vendor offers me one, and I bite into it as one would bite an apple. Tomato water and the caviar (seeds), drip down my removable cast. When I was little, we routinely ate grandpa's tomatoes sliced and served only with a pinch of salt. In Provence, they do the same but call it *salade de tomates*. We just called it sliced tomatoes.

The discovery of the Banon factory piqued my desire to match a village with a cheese. According to the signs, Banon is not far from Apt, so I follow the signs to the tiny village, the center of which is swarming with cyclists, not the cherry-picking kind, but the ones with shaved legs and tight pants. Parking is difficult to find because vehicles bearing bike racks and signs for the "Tour de Haute Provence" have taken over the tiny village with some type of ceremony taking place in its center. I park my car far out of the village and walk through the cyclists making a mental note that perhaps I should learn to ride a bike, maybe even ride in the French Alps some day (maybe when I can run without breaking my wrist).

My *fougasse* and tomato have worn off. I pass a few restaurants advertising daily specials such as *quiche au fromage de Banon*, and *farcis provençaux*. The restaurants are closed, but a wine bar, Les Vins au Vert, is open.

The walls in the homey wine bar are replete with shelves of wine and books. Stacked boxes of wine are well-placed throughout the room. A long communal table sits in the middle and a few smaller tables are scattered throughout the space, all of which are full. I take a place at the bar, which faces the kitchen. It is past lunchtime, but the owner, who introduces himself as Pierre, asks if he may bring me a charcuterie plate with bread, tapenade, and a mustard *purée. Oui SVP.* When I have finished that (which took no time at all), Sandrine, his wife, brings me a *café gourmand*, an espresso with a sampler of bite-sized desserts. When I am finished eating, I walk over to look at the wine selections. Wine is not my specialty, and I know very little of the regional wines. Pierre is removing wine from cases, and I ask him about local varieties. Selecting four, he then gifts me a bottle from the Côtes de Gascogne region that he and Sandrine are fond of, which he tells me I must try.

I retrieve my car and pull it in front of the wine bar. Pierre places the box of wine in the backseat and bids me a *"bon voyage."* Once again, I am soaring down the two-lane street, where more cyclists are spinning their way across the picnic paradise. When I come to a long thin road lined with rows of mature trees and surrounded by grass, I curiously follow it only to discover the little village of Villars. Another stop. Another camera moment. On the way back to Gordes, I stumble upon Le Village des Bories, consisting of 18th-century stone huts, which include everything from stone ovens to wine vats. Despite my delight in this discovery, I stay only one hour due to the heat and the fact I have cheese in the car.

Apparently I am the only single guest in the hotel. Couples (many newlyweds), small tour groups, and me. While I could dwell on how outwardly pathetic that may seem, I instead delight in the special treatment. Usually the first guest up in the morning (for a cappuccino before my run), the staff and I have become friendly. Today I am greeted with a *"Bonjour Chef."*

I run down the long hill upon which Gordes is perched, foraging lavender and wild fennel from the side of the road, and writing recipe ideas in my head inspired by my pickings. There are a number of campsites hosting metallic RVs, and I discover in my short time here that the Luberon is full of retirees, particularly Brits, exploring the region from campsite to campsite. Perhaps inspired by Peter Mayle and his books about Provence. This morning the campsites are as still as the hotel lobby, folded chairs and collapsed easels lean against the RVs awaiting the day.

I *déjeune* at Les Bories Hotel and Spa, where Michelin-starred Pascal Ginoux heads the kitchen and the lamb chops are roasted in a *cocotte* on a bed of fresh thyme. The waiter ceremoniously opens the *cocotte* table-side, releasing the aromas of roasted thyme and lamb into the air. The two-tiered cheese cart is a *fromagerie* in and of itself with jams and *gelées* for pairing. With encouragement, I select four cheeses, Le Sainte-Maure (goat cheese in the shape of a log with a piece of straw in its center), Fourme d'Ambert, and two regional *chèvres*, one rolled in herbs and the other with ash, recommended by the waiter who carefully cuts a slice of each one as if he is performing cheese surgery. He asks why I am taking notes of my lunch and I tell him. The unique flavor combinations (such as strawberries and rosemary in my dessert) I find inventive, and the creativity inspires my own ideas, which I write in my journal.

Walking back to my hotel, in the heat of the day, I conclude that two days is not enough time to explore all that I want to see and taste in the Luberon. I ask the hotel clerk if they are able to accommodate me for two more nights. They are, and they also help me switch my train ticket to Tuesday and make a late dinner reservation for me at Le Vivier, which they say is not to be missed.

Le Vivier is in L'Isle-sur-la-Sorgue, which lies within the two arms of the Sorgue river, thirty minutes from Gordes. The restaurant sits right on the stream Sorgue de Velleron, and my *terrasse* table provides a direct view of a large water wheel turning over and over on itself with a dozen ducks quacking and dipping their heads in the falling water. My melon gazpacho is divine. The pigeon breast stuffed with spinach and served *en croûte* (a traditional French dish that is making a comeback with younger chefs) is moist and flavorful. Not a drop of sauce nor flake of crust remains on my plate.

When the sun sets, I enjoy my espresso. The ducks are long asleep, but the water wheel continues to turn and the steady rhythm of the cascading water is melodic. A man offers me a wrap, which I accept, and when it falls on my nude shoulders, its weight has an ultra-luxurious feel and I ask him where I might find one like it (a perfect gift for my mother and grandmother). The gentleman writes down the name of the shop in town for me and introduces himself as Patrick. He and his wife own the restaurant. I compliment him on both the food and the restaurant itself. When I ask about a particular cheese I enjoyed, he gives me the address for the *fromagerie* in nearby Carpentras as well. As he writes, I tell him he is helping me on my Luberon culinary expedition and upon hearing that I cook, he enthusiastically provides me with restaurant recommendations in and outside of the village. He introduces me to his wife, Céline, and one of their daughters and the three of us continue to chat while Patrick telephones one of his chef friends to make me a reservation for tomorrow night. It turns out that the restaurant is closed tomorrow, but he writes down the information so I may go another time.

TODAY IS JULIA'S ninth birthday. Every year they are vacationing with their father and I miss her birthday. Although I rationalize that it is only "a day" and we can celebrate another time, to me it will always be more than just a day on the calendar, and it is no accident that I usually am on an adventure because the distraction of discovery keeps me positive. The nine-hour time difference prevents me from calling her now, so I drive to the Abbaye de Sénanque set in a base of a valley surrounded by lavender fields and mountains, just down the hill from Gordes.

Originally founded in 1148 as a home for Cistercian monks, the abbey was nationalized and then sold to a private individual during the French Revolution. The Cistercian monks repurchased it in 1854, and to this day they continue to run the abbey and rely on the honey hives and the lavender fields for their livelihood. I imagine Ava and Julia running through the rows of lavender, creating chaos in the quiet abbey and touching everything in the gift shop. They would love it. My visit is brief, and once the tour buses begin to roll in, I return to L'Isle-sur-la-Sorgue with my list of recommendations by Céline and Patrick.

The village itself is charming with its geranium-embellished bridges and water wheels and plentiful antique stores (the hotel staff says it is the third largest antique source in Europe). I wander through a few of them, naturally gravitating toward kitchen items. In one, I find an old silver carving knife and fork that I deem necessary for *l'appart*. Amidst the antiques stores I discover Jardin du Quai, a restaurant set in an outdoor garden replete with garden statuary set on a carpet of pea gravel. The food is uncomplicated *provençal* fare, specializing in fish, as fishing was the primary source of income for the village before antiques. My *entrée* is a tomato tartare with crab and the delightful addition of wasabi balls resembling green caviar add both novelty and zing to the dish. I befriend the waiter, Morgan, and the chef, Jeremi Fontin, and inquire about the source for the wasabi balls. Chef Fontin tells me without hesitation, and when he finds out that I cook he recommends a nearby knife store and asks where else I plan to visit. When I tell him I am thinking of driving up to Châteauneuf-du-Pape, he says that he has a friend who is President of one of the wineries. *Superbe.* He calls his friend so they know to expect me and gives me directions.

The recommended knife shop is not far and I find a few to add to my collection, including some beautiful wooden handled cheese knives with foldable blades. Then I drive forty-five minutes northwest where I am welcomed by an unsubtle sign and rows of stately castles and vineyards behind:

"ICI commencent les célèbres vignobles de Châteauneuf-du-Pape"

At Château Ogier Caves des Papes, Monsieur DURAND, with his thick dark hair and sweet smile, greets me. He introduces me to the sommelier who gives me a private tour of the facility and cellars and teaches me about the regional *terroir* and the effect it has on the wine. Sampling the various vintages, I select a few bottles and, to my surprise, I am gifted two as well, which will no doubt exceed my rolling suitcase capacity.

THE SUN IS setting when I finally return to Gordes. Le Clos de Gustave, another recommendation, is hidden behind the castle and the tables sit under the mature olive trees. Yet, I am not hungry (unsurprisingly) and the blanket of the evening sky reminds me of my girls. Back at the hotel, the joy of the last few days is distilled into the best moment: "Hi Mommy!" It is Julia.

That little voice. I break into my "Happy Birthday" song. She giggles with delight and when I have concluded my tone-deaf recital, she thanks me and tells me of the events that have been occupying their days. When I finally put my head on my pillow, my heart is much fuller than my stomach; I am ready to leave Gordes.

While I pride myself on efficient packing, and despite my expandable beach bags, even David Copperfield could not fit all of the wine, honey, jam, flours of different proteins, spices, walnut liqueur, melon liqueur, *saussicon*, among other food products and *trucs* into my bags. The seams of the bags are stressed, and they are so heavy my wrist cannot handle the load. I will have to drive back to Paris, rather than lug my new possessions through the train station. Ridiculous. My mode of transportation dictated by my culinary appetite.

Train ticket cancelled, I pack up the little car while the hotel makes arrangements for me to drop it off at Gare de Lyon in Paris. I decide to try one last time to visit the factory in Banon, but it is closed for lunch. I accept that I am just not meant to see the factory this time around, so I head back to Paris. Rain is forecast, and the anticipated nine-hour drive requires me to drive on the *périphérique* — "the belt" — the boulevard that loops around Paris. The thought is unnerving. The road passes through successive quaint towns with stops and roundabouts, which make me question whether I have taken a wrong turn, but they ultimately lead me to the A7, which is monotonous and with the rain, my view is uninspiring. After a few hours, I am no longer entertained by my own singing. The portable GPS beeps and the sound is making me crazy so I mute it. Traffic in Lyon leads to the A6 where I entertain myself by reading the signs for places I have either eaten or drunk — Chablis, Dijon, Mâcon Village — but have yet to visit. When I reach the belt, the boulevard ascends, giving me an unexpected full view of the westside of Paris; the sight of the Tower takes me by surprise but disappears as quickly as it appeared. The rain increases in intensity; the windshield wipers fly back and forth across my view. The GPS loses all signal, causing me a momentary panic, but the sights are now familiar — Porte Dauphine, Rue de Longchamp, view of the Tower — and I find my way home and even find a parking spot directly in front of my building. 9:30 p.m. Eight hours exactly, notwithstanding the Banon detour and the weather. *Pas mal!* I unload my treasures and place the wheat bundle on a table in the foyer for "good luck" but also to remind me of my weekend on the other side, where one experience led to another, all of it beautiful, and none of it planned.

I LEAP OUT of bed and reach Gare de Lyon without incident despite my paranoia of traffic or aggressive drivers and even manage to find a small above-ground gas station (challenging in Paris). Locating the rental car lot is another matter, however, and I circle the *gare* five times before I find an entrance to the parking spaces underneath where they are washing the rentals. I park the car in an empty spot and go inside to find the car rental office on the first floor. At 7:00 a.m. I am the first customer and I give the attendant the key and explain where the car is parked. She appears unconcerned and does not need to confirm that the car is in fact downstairs nor inspect it. Her nonchalant manner is almost disconcerting, but then again it is decidedly French. I run home along the Seine in the same gloomy weather I left five days ago. When I pass the Louvre, I think of Hemingway's *Movable Feast* wherein he tries to inflate F. Scott Fitzgerald's confidence in his manhood by encouraging him to compare his man parts to those of the statues in the Louvre. Everything in Paris reminds me of something I've read or seen. Paris is full of ghosts.

JUNE 21. The first day of summer is celebrated by the *Fête de la Musique*. The weather, however, has not checked the calendar. Yet, I do not mind as I am anxious to experiment with my new ingredients, and according to *Le Figaro*, the city-wide concerts do not begin until about 4 p.m. anyway. At the Casino I purchase *crème* and *œufs frais* and sign up for my *carte de fidelité*, which qualifies me for free home delivery and discounts, making me feel more official than ever. I stop at *le boucher* for a rack of lamb, which I ask him to *couper* into individual ribs. At *l'appart*, I cook with the windows open, only breaking for a quick run along the Seine.

When I return, *l'appart* is full of human noise. In the *sdb* I find Maria and two delivery men installing the washer/dryer machine.

One of the men explains to me how to work it and asks for some dirty clothes for a demonstrative wash. I reach for the laundry basket, and as I hand him some clothes, a *culotte* falls from the pile, draping itself across his work boot. All eyes focus on the black lace panty accessorizing his boot.

"*Pardon,*" I say and snatch it from view.

Maria smiles awkwardly. The men say nothing. The moment lasts an eternity, but jazz music from the *fête* streams in through the open windows and eases the awkward moment. He resumes his instructions, but I cannot focus on anything but my panty on this man's boot.

"EXCITING NEWS! You've been selected to be profiled in the *Breakover* pilot. Arianna [Huffington] and Nora [Ephron] loved your interview and are looking forward to featuring your story."

It is not a bad email to read first thing in the morning. The email is from Julie who works for the *Huffington Post*. She was referred to me by a mutual friend who thought I might be a good addition to their video series about women who have gone through various adversities and emerge in a positive way. I submitted a video a few months ago. Yet, despite my admiration for both women and the series, now that the piece is a reality, the thought of other people editing and clipping together my words and life to present it in a package that suits them makes me nervous. What if they get too personal? What if the focus is less on my cooking and more about my divorce? I tell Julie that I will think about it, and I do just that all the way to Christophe's office. But the lengthy walk to the 7th does not provide any real clarity on the pilot issue and proves just a prologue to an abbreviated and troubling meeting with Christophe. He reviews with me the recently issued additional report by the inspector. There are no answers to the humidity issue, and I fail to see much difference between the preliminary report and this one except it costs me more money.

"There is nothing for us to do," Christophe says.

Despite my adoption of the French *laissez-faire* attitude to the lawsuit, I am tired of hearing that "there is nothing to do." I am *américaine*. There *is* always something to be done. But the French do not see it that way. It is the *"c'est pas possible"* attitude, which means that there is nothing to do in the standard procedure in which we operate and we don't do the "out of the box" or "look for solutions" thing; we go strictly on tradition and routine and go down the list. It's the French way, and it is maddening and contrary to their creative and forward-thinking ideas exhibited in the arts.

When I leave Christophe's office, I walk to John and Mary's office, which is not far away to ask if they can contact the notaire about my deed as I have not made any headway in obtaining it from him (admittedly, the relationship is a bit strained due to the lawsuit). They are not in, but their assistant emails the *notaire's* assistant and receives an immediate response. The *acte authentique* was recorded on June 8 and it was sent to my home in Los Angeles. *La vente* September 30; deed recorded June 8. That is the French version of "a couple months."

"*Bonne fin de semaine,*" she says to me.

"*À vous aussi et merci encore,*" I reply.

I've heard "*bonne journée*" (have a good day), "*bonne soirée*" (have a good evening), "*bon après-midi*" (have a good afternoon), "*bon dimanche*" (have a good Sunday), "*bon week-end*" (have a good weekend), but "happy end of the week" is a new one for me.

I deposit my frustrated self at Les Deux Magots where I sit in the front row on the open *terrasse* with a book and notepad. It is an acceptable time for an *apéro* so I order a Kir. Under the Parisian gray, I listen to the musicians play in the square, exactly the distraction I need from the pilot and the lawsuit.

SATURDAY MORNING. I have taken to the *marché* tradition in my neighborhood with ease. Twice a week, successive white tents are erected in the center island on Avenue President Wilson. Today's market is larger than the Wednesday's. Joël Thiébault, known for his rare vegetables and greens, is considered *"TOP"* by Parisian chefs, and he has the most beautiful zucchini blossoms, rare greens for my salads, and purple and white flowering herbs (the chives are always the first to go). The *marché* tradition, however, is not merely about the fresh food, but the people, as it is an opportunity for neighbors to chat with other neighbors and with the vendors. After my zucchini blossom purchase, I visit the sausage vendor, who always greets me with a *"bonjour"* and *"ça va?"*

"*Bonjour. Ça va…La même chose, s'il vous plaît*," I say.

He prepares a paper sack of my favorite *noix saussion* in the 5-euro quantity. Next to him, the *cerises* and *fraises* are the most beautiful this time of year, and they are as plentiful as the peonies. I purchase a supply of all three and complete my *marché* ritual by stopping for other weekend necessities at the *boucherie, poissonnier, fromagerie*, and Monoprix, and although most of these things could have been purchased at the *marché,* I have my favorite places in the neighborhood for particular things. Using my various *cartes de fidelités*, the points and stamps accumulating and I *ça-va*-ing with local merchants.

Despite loving Paris, my palate has always been decidedly in the south. I work on my *pan bagnat* blog and three variations of a watermelon gazpacho. Putting to use all of the *pliable* (collapsable) kitchen equipment I purchased, and I hear my mother's voice "clean as you go," which was a great habit for culinary school where we were required to clean our stations every ten minutes. In my Paris kitchen, the "clean as

I go" habit is an absolute necessity or there is no room to cook.

My American phone quacks. It is Julie following up on her email. I convey my reservations and, in turn, she reassures me that the piece will be positive and tasteful. She goes on to tell me that because my story is so relatable, she believes it will help other women, and this is the comment that changes my mind. Although I will not receive compensation for my time, Julie promises to talk to the editor of the lifestyles page to see if I can contribute food articles and recipes at the same time the piece airs. So I put my faith in Julie's word and agree to do the pilot. Then the caveat: the pilot must be shot in Los Angeles by the end of July (which means the ten days I have in Los Angeles before the girls and I leave for Paris). In the meantime, she will Fed-Ex me a small camera, which I am supposed to talk into, documenting my activities here.

When JeF arrives, this time it is I gifting him things I bought for him in the Luberon. He is delighted and gives me a hug that envelops my whole body. The rain has diminished to a slight drizzle so we walk to Le Flandrin for Sunday brunch, which is packed despite the gloomy weather. Our Sunday brunch is long and leisurely and by the time we have finished, the drizzle has stopped. On the way home, I share with JeF my recent driving experience from Gordes to Paris. I am glowing with pride believing that JeF, who taught me to drive in Paris, will be impressed that I drove all the way to Paris, by myself, in the rain, in record time! He stops walking and asks me again about my time. He is not impressed.

"Lisa," he says in a strict tone that is French-serious scary, "How fast did you go? If you go 50 km/h over the speed limit … it is considered criminal. If they had stopped you, they would have taken you to jail."

My gaze focuses on him, waiting for him to start laughing or flash me that beautiful smile, but he is not joking. There is no smile nor dimples. My smile fades as he continues, "Lisa, there are cameras everywhere on the autoroute. I am sure they photographed you and the car. You were in a rental, right? Didn't the GPS beep?"

My pride devolves into a childlike panic. "*Comment?* The GPS? I turned it off," I say.

"What? Why would you do that?" he asks.

I begin crying. Cameras? Feeling foolish, I do not tell him that I muted the GPS because its incessant beeping annoyed me. My head is spinning, thinking of the parade of horribles that are sure to come my way as a French property owner. Am I going to have a criminal record? Will this affect my application for a *carte de séjour?* Will I be able to rent a car again or will I be on the most-wanted-foreigner speed violators list? Will this prevent me from obtaining a French license in the future? My head fails to hold a rational thought.

"You don't have a French driver's license; you most likely will be getting a fine in the mail," he says.

"What?" I say. "How much? And I begin blubbering like an idiot in the middle of the street. JeF covers my frame with a hug.

"It will be okay. You don't have a license here, so it will probably be nothing more than a fine," he says, then chuckles a little.

But his comfort does not comfort. The French are not comforting. They are too matter-of-fact about everything: "I know you're sick, but *c'est la vie;* we all die eventually." I watch French movies; there is never a happy ending, and in France, it just ends because that is how life is, and everyone is okay with that. *C'est la vie!* The conversation leaves me as damp as the weather. Maria has accepted service on my behalf, seen my underwear, and now I am convinced she is going to hand me bad news in the form of another summons or fine. My mother taught me to clean as I cook. She also told me not to speed. I should have listened to that as well.

CHAPTER TWENTY-SIX

The Gift of Movement and the Speed of Life

ON MY BALCONY, I sit in the quiet of the evening survey-
ing the life around me while contemplating my own. The man pulls
down the metal roll away shutter for the produce market and walks
to his white truck parked below me. The *brasserie, boucherie*, and Nat-
uralia (the *bio*, natural food store) are dark. Pedestrians walk in ones
and twos on the sidewalk toward their evening plans. The Place has
a steady stream of cars circling around it. Di Vino's *terrasse* is already
half-full.

The camera has not yet arrived; I am not disappointed. Now
that I am supposed to document my daily life, I have been contemplating that subject and I am nowhere near where I want to be, and, truthfully, I am unsure how to proceed. How is that uncertainty inspiring
to anyone? My own thoughts make me feel small. The French expression *le cul entre deux chaises* seems applicable. My ass *is* split between
two chairs. Two continents, actually. It seems overwhelming, trying to
figure out how to cultivate a future and a steady stream of income in
a country where I can be only on a part-time basis, particularly when
even born-Parisians who reside here full-time have difficulty finding
employment. Tackling such a goal as a single parent, at this stage in
my life and around a child-share schedule, the challenge seems ten-
fold. Then there is the sobering reality that by the time the girls graduate high school, and I can finally move to full-time status, I will be

older with less energy and opportunities, and they will be in college. The belittling contemplation on my balcony brings no solution to my two-continent conundrum.

I take to the Paris streets because the mere physical advancement of my befuddled bottom feels more empowering than sitting on it, and on the street I am surrounded with life. Lively chatter of dinner conversations escape the open windows above my head. At the Place a neighbor chats with a pizza delivery man while Blondie plays on his delivery *moto*. They break from their conversation and turn toward me.

"*Salut*," one says as I pass.

Three friends part ways at a car parked *on* the sidewalk, forcing me to walk in the street to get around it. They exchange kisses on all six cheeks with a "*bon ciao.*" Another new French expression for me.

The taxi line is a succession of green lights on Avenue d'Eylau, and they resemble soldiers standing at attention before the Tower. Café *terrasses* are full of smokers and wine drinkers. Immigrant trinket sellers circle the Trocadéro, shaking their large rings of miniature Eiffel Tower keychains. The odor of cooked sugar and crêpe batter permeates the air space in which toy planes swirl, while on the ground, battery-operated pink poodles advance forward and bark, causing both delight and annoyance. Street performers dance to Michael Jackson playing on a portable CD player in the center of a gathering crowd. In the *jardin* below, discussions unfold on benches between bites of *jambon* sandwiches. Lovers sip wine on blankets strategically placed in the grass among tripods readied for the perfect night shot of the flashing Tower, and the sidewalks of Pont d'Iena are full of people on their pilgrimage toward it.

I *flâne* along the side of the Seine, and even at this late hour there are many others doing the same. Singles. Couples. Groups. The lights from the dinner cruises reflect in the water. La Grande Roue rotates in the heart of the city. It is impossible to feel alone in Paris even when one is technically by oneself. When I reach the Musée D'Orsay, my phone vibrates in my pocket, and as I pull it out to answer it, I am distracted by the date: June 25. It was one year ago today that I found *l'appart.* I look back across the water toward the 16th. The distance created by my walk has given me a new perspective: the perspective of today. Time's place marker of my one-year anniversary fills me with gratitude, a sense of accomplishment, and the encouragement of positive things to come however uncertain they may seem now. *Bon anniversaire.*

TODAY THE SUMMER retail sales begin throughout Paris, a day which Parisians eagerly await for months. However, I avoid all retail temptation and head south to the suburbs to meet Carinne and JeF, where they are shooting a piece for Télématin, the French morning news show on Channel 2 on which Carinne provides simple recipes for viewers. In France, recipes are an important part of the daily news. In France, food is news.

I take the *métro* line until it ends and continue to walk in the unfamiliar suburb to the residence where the show is being taped. I should be able to watch the entire taping and still make my dinner with Mr. Monaco, who, despite his dislike of Paris, has Parisian clients so he occasionally abandons the comfort of the sunny Côte d'Azur for the hectic Parisian streets and the insular nature of Parisians. Julie asked me to record the things I do and places I visit and suggested I use my iPad until the camera arrives. So, as I walk, I talk into the iPad, describing the show and how I know JeF and Carinne. It feels incredibly lame, and I must look like an absolute narcissist as I am garnering unwanted stares from those with whom I cross paths.

I have not seen Carinne since her taping with Patrick Roger and, instead of Easter chocolate, today it is a barbecue theme and she is grilling sweet potato wedges with sardines stuffed with couscous and wrapped in (Canadian) bacon. Not a recipe that would generally work in America, but the French will love it. Carinne's bubbly personality is captivating, and she talks slowly, using her hands in a calm and deliberate manner and only at the appropriate moments. JeF mouths to me from behind the camera, "*Regarde Carinne...regarde ses mains!*"

I nod in agreement, noting that her demonstration style is the preferred method for filming and much in contrast to my waving hands and flapping arms.

At 5:3o p.m. the taping concludes. JeF offers me a ride into Paris on the back of his motorcycle. I hesitate. True, a *moto* is the fastest way to return to the city and JeF is a capable and experienced driver, but it is the belt, at the height of traffic, and while I have been on the back of his *moto* in the city before, it was not the belt and never without the aid of a calming glass of wine or Champagne first.

"*Tu viens?* You coming?" he asks

I accept because the alternative—hours in the stinky and crowded *métro*—is not appealing. More importantly, I do not want to be late for my dinner with Mr. Monaco, whom I am meeting at Di Vino (due to my time constraints and his distrust of French food).

The ride on the belt in stop-and-go traffic is not the self-confident experience of last week in my Mini, nor is it the cocktail-dress experience on the back of JeF's *moto* through the center of Paris in the early morning hours. Indeed, it is the first time I have experienced Paris with closed eyes. JeF weaves in between cars—fast, slow, stop, go—other motorcycles do the same. I tighten my grip around

JeF, but loosen it when I realize it may hinder his ability to drive. My heart races, and the speed of my own life flashes before my eyes. I am hoping to not lose a limb or have cigarette burns on my leg due to those ever-present left arms bearing cigarettes, hanging out the driver's window. After twenty minutes, I cannot take anymore and I ask JeF to drop me off at Porte de Saint-Cloud, where I catch the Line 9 home while I am still in one piece.

MR. MONACO is sitting at a *terrasse* table when I arrive. It has been some time since we have seen one another, and time has been gentle with him despite his claim of "aging badly." He stands to greet me and kisses me on both cheeks and then gives me a hug, which is simultaneously familiar and distant. He pulls out the chair for me, and I sit across from him and study his features as he speaks. He tells me of his work, his parents, and the shenanigans of little Martino, the two-kilo Chihuahua he gifted to his parents that delights the entire family. Mr. Monaco looks and behaves the same; his English has greatly improved. So, too, has my French, on which he compliments me. He tells me that he and his girlfriend purchased a second home in St. Tropez and are trying to start a family. Neither surprises me. As I listen to him talk, I cannot help but think of how different my life would be if we had continued our relationship. Ironically, if we had married, the outcome in the move-away case would likely have been different, because going to a foreign country to work or for a spouse somehow brings legitimacy—not whimsy—to a person's quest to live elsewhere. A dubious rationale, in my opinion, since I know that neither a job nor marriage guarantees permanence.

Mr. Monaco asks about my dating life. He knows of my up-and-down relationship with Prince. When I tell him it is off for good, he looks at me with a questioning glance.

"Lisa, you are too picky," he says, then adds, "poor bastard, trying to marry you is like catching the wind with a net."

Whether a passive-aggressive slight or poetic Italian sentiment, his English words sting because deep down I think there may be some truth to it. But maybe I do not want to be caught, at least not yet. And, in truth, being "caught" does not sound like the type of partnership I envision anyway.

"Lisa," he says, "you need someone to care for you."

"I can take care of myself," I retort.

"I know, but I would feel better knowing you have someone to watch over you."

Momentarily, I ponder his words. I fought him on the statement, but I know what he means. Everyone should have someone to look after them and vice versa, but all I can do is what feels truest to me.

"You don't have to worry about me. I am good. Promise. And, you know better than anyone that someone is already watching over me," I say. His eyes look at me, and we acknowledge, without words, the memory of what we shared in the Monaco hospital and how fortunate I am to be here now. "Tell me about your place in St. Trop. Is it close to your clients' home in the center? The ones I met?"

He knows me well and permits my deliberate subject change. We talk through all three courses and when my espresso and his macchiato have settled, we walk arm in arm toward the taxi stand. Despite the proximity of *l'appart*, he does not ask to see it, nor would I suggest it. We say our goodbyes and exchange cheek kisses followed by an embrace. I can feel it will be the last time we will see one another. Things have shifted; I can feel the marker of time. It is a wave that runs through my body, and I allow this chapter to close with sweet finality. I watch Mr. Monaco's large frame grow increasingly smaller as he walks toward the Tower and as I do, I make a wish that when my daughters fall in love, it will be with someone who possesses the character and generosity of heart and spirit of Mr. Monaco.

THE CAMERA arrives and with it a tax bill for its delivery. *Bien sûr.* I review Julie's instructions and go about self-consciously taping the various things I am doing in Paris my last few days here: shopping at my local *marché*, a Champagne class at Ô Chateau (where I discover smaller houses and make new Champagne-sipping acquaintances), and a productive visit to E. Dehillerin nearby. I tape additional food experimentation in my kitchen, which presents significant size challenges because I am forced to attach the camera by its flexible tripod to the ladder that I set in front of the refrigerator. The camera is aimed at a limited area of the counter where I prepare the zucchini and basil *soufflé* and eventually stuff the baked mixture into the fresh zucchini blossoms I hand-selected at the *marché*. Literally, I feel as if I am working in a box.

Julie gave me a list of questions that I am supposed to answer in a monologue diary-type style. I sit on the balcony at the day's conclusion and try my hand at talking into the camera. But even in the privacy of my own aloneness, I feel ridiculous and I stumble through my responses because it is unnatural for me to talk without doing something else at the same time or looking at another person. Playing it back, I receive confirmation that yes, indeed, I do look as ridiculous as I feel. I set the camera down and survey *l'appart*. Everything is ready for the girls' arrival: the kitchen is full of their favorite treats; the French games I found at my favorite toy store in the Marais are unwrapped and placed on the shelf with videos and books, in both languages; and fresh towels and linens are set out with their toothbrushes and favorite strawberry toothpaste. The dining room table is set for three. In less than two weeks I will return with *mes deux amours* and, although I am the adult, I am filled with childlike anticipation and joy.

THE MAN SITTING to my left in economy is wildly penning menus with ingredient lists, which catches my eye and I cannot help but ask: "*Vous êtes chef de cuisine?*"

"*Oui,*" he responds.

"*Moi aussi.*"

Lionel is a *cuisinier à la Présidence de la République,* which means he is one of the cooks for French President Hollande at the Élysée. A former "Top Chef" competitor, Lionel, like many French chefs, occasionally takes on private chef jobs to supplement his income. This week Lionel is serving as a private chef for a family in Newport Beach for one week with the aid of an interpreter. Having been in the reverse situation, I am empathetic to the learning curve. Differences in temperature, weight, and language can be overwhelming. Cuts of meat are different and many familiar products are not available. If you can find the product, its quality, consistency, and feel are different and all of that changes your cooking. And thus, the fun of cooking in a foreign land, adapting yourself to unknown circumstances and creating delicious food from the unfamiliar, is a Top Chef challenge seven days a week.

I warn him of the skinny white butter that literally pales in comparison, in consistency and flavor, to the yellow butter from Normandy he is used to. Langoustines, a French staple and on his menu in a risotto, are difficult to find (unless pre-ordered) and usually frozen. He asks about *pâte feuilletée* (puff pastry). I write down the English translation and suggestions of where to find the pre-made doughs and which brands I prefer.

That evening, Lionel emails me. He thanks me for my assistance and invites me to the Élysée for a kitchen tour and an introduction to his fellow chefs and colleagues the next time I am in Paris. The unsolicited offer is flattering and exciting. He closes by saying that my help proves that *"la cuisine est une grande famille."* The statement is as observant as it is correct. Cooks are nurturers by nature, with generous spirits, and there is an instant camaraderie when they find others with whom they share not only a passion for food but the desire to care for others. The kitchen *is* a big family.

WHILE LIONEL private-chefs in Newport Beach, I film the segment for the *Huff Post* in Los Angeles. The logistical arrangements were made while I was in Paris and, as luck would have it, both the Surfas Test Kitchen and the *Huff Post* production crew were available the same weekend the girls are with their father. So, despite my trepidation, I take the alignment as a sign that it is meant to be. Those who attended the June 9 demonstration were offered an additional opportunity to practice the recipes discussed and, to my delight, many responded favorably and no one seemed to mind the disclaimer that it would be recorded.

The first day of shooting is a brief few minutes at our home. The second day of shooting begins at 7 a.m. at the Venice Farmers' Market. The market is unknown to me, but I recognize some of the sellers and growers. Discreet the production is not: about ten people follow me with much too large a camera and far too many microphones, and someone seems to always be telling me that I am "out of range." Do, re-do, re-walk, and re-talk until they get "the shot" and/ or perfect angle. The repetitiveness is exhausting and feels stupid. I am a do-er. Not a re-do-er. Moreover, there is no escape; they film constantly, even in the car from the market to Surfas where the taped demonstration seems an orchestrated repeat and re-repeat for "the shot." Pull the tart out of the oven. Put the tart in the oven. Pull it out again. At the day's conclusion, the crew is fixated on the phrase "this is my kitchen," and I am requested to place my hands on the stainless-steel countertop in various stances, repeating the phrase over and over with various inflections in my voice. The only fun in this exercise is recalling when I have actually uttered the phrase. Day three of filming is a one-on-one interview format in my own kitchen. However, the questions range from my family and childhood to my divorce and what I am doing now. They are far more personal than I expected and, in my opinion, only marginally relevant. I dutifully respond to some, while others I decline to answer (pleased that I have grown from my French immigration experience). Julie gives me another camera with more questions, but I tell her that I have done all I will do. She agrees to work with what they have.

The taping left me feeling drained. As I fold the girls' summer clothes into efficient, compact squares and collapse their neon-flashing Razor scooters for the voyage, I reflect upon the experience. The filming when I interacted with vendors or cooked with volunteers felt natural, but the personal interviews and monologues were not for me. It is the human connection to others, the nurturing aspect of food— whether it be cooking or sharing—*that* is what I love about it. Food in and of itself is not the end game, not for me, but it allows me the opportunity to express myself and provide for others in a manner I enjoy. In this respect, the taping had value, even those self-conscious monologues. I close the suitcase and tuck the girls into bed, knowing that a good night's sleep may be too high an expectation for any of us. The excitement is palpable, and as I return to my own room, I can hear Julia giggling in hers.

TARTARE DE DAURADE
(Sea bream tartare)

Serves 2

    2 fillets of freshly-caught sea bream
    6 fresh raspberries
    1 tablespoon small diced green apple, peeled and cored
    1 tablespoon quality olive oil
    1 teaspoon fresh lime juice
    Pinch of *piment d'espelette*
    A/N quality sea salt
    ~1 tablespoon small fresh cilantro leaves with flowers
    Fresh almond slices (optional)

Using a very sharp knife, remove the fish skin (or ask your fish-monger to do it). Remove any bones. Dice the fish fillets into cubes (about ½ inch). Cut raspberries in half. Place fish cubes, raspberries, and diced apple in a bowl. Add lime juice and olive oil. Gently toss with a spoon. (It is important that the raspberries are very fresh, no mushy raspberries, or your tartare will turn pink.) Add salt (1 to 2 pinches) and *piment*. Gently toss.

Place bowl in the refrigerator for 30 minutes. When ready to serve, add the cilantro. Add almond slices if desired.

GREEN GAZPACHO

This summer soup is simple to prepare and it can be made in advance.
It is important to use the freshest ingredients you can find. (In August,
tomatoes and melons are at their peak.) I have included the yield
amounts for the primary ingredients due the variance of product size.
Do your final seasoning adjustment after the soup has been chilled.

Serves 6 to 8

> 4 ripe zebra tomatoes
> 2 cucumbers
> 1 white melon
> 1 small onion
> ½ avocado
> 1 teaspoon Xérès or sherry vinegar
> 2 tablespoons quality olive oil
> 1 garlic clove, minced
> A/N sea salt
> A/N freshly ground black pepper
> Fresh strawberries, sliced
> Sliced almonds, toasted
> Fresh basil leaves

Score the tomato skin with an "x" where the stem was attached to
the tomato. Repeat for all tomatoes. Place tomatoes in a saucepan of
boiling water. After 1 to 2 minutes, remove tomatoes with tongs and
place in an ice bath. Set aside. Once cool, peel the skins from the
tomatoes. Remove the seeds. Discard the skins and seeds. Dice the
tomatoes. (Yield about 6 ounces.) Place tomatoes in a bowl.

Peel the melon and the cucumbers. Remove the seeds. Dice. (Yield
about 6 ounces cucumbers and 1½ pounds melon.) Add to the tomatoes. Dice the onion. (Yield about 4½ ounces.) Add to the tomatoes,
melon, and cucumbers. Add the avocado, garlic, oil, and vinegar.

Purée all of the ingredients in a food processor (or use an immersion blender). Season to taste. Place in refrigerator for at least six
hours. Adjust seasoning. Serve very cold. (If soup is too thick, or you
want it even colder, you can purée it with a handful of ice cubes.)
Garnish with fresh strawberries, almonds, and basil leaves.

lappart

lappart

PART IV

CHAPTER TWENTY-SEVEN

Le Paradis

FRENCH AUTHOR Jules Renard said that if you add two letters ("A" and "D") to the word Paris, Paris is *paradis*. With the girls here in Paris—an "A" for Ava and a "D" for Dia (Julia's nickname) — Paris is *Paradis*, and Renard was correct.

"*Bienvenue chez nous,*" I say as I open the door.

Like horses out of the start gate, four sandaled feet sprint through the living room, around the dining table, and throw open the doors to the same balcony they enjoyed last August. Today, life below their toes is no less intriguing than it was then, and once they have satisfactorily observed all the activity in the street below, they leave the balcony and assess the changes in their Paris home.

"Wooow!" Julia exclaims.

"It is soooo different! It's great, Mom!" Ava adds.

They empty the contents of their suitcases all over the restored parquet and when *l'appart* has received their decorative touch, they join me in the kitchen seeking something to eat.

LE QUATORZE. The French day of independence. The fireworks from the Tower will begin at 23h when there will be the guarantee of a dark sky. Early evening we shimmy past the unconnected metal barricades in the 16th, past the food carts by the Seine selling grilled sausages cradled in baguettes and past the carts with every sugary, citric acid-coated jellied item a child can imagine. On Rue Saint-Dominque we meet Chloé and her children at Les Cocottes for dinner. All four children eat their meals with rapid enthusiasm and can hardly sit still while Chloé and I talk and finish our wine. When we leave the restaurant, we are swallowed by the river of individuals flowing from the street into the adjoining Champs de Mars, the large grass area that fronts the Tower. We land about thirty feet from the Tower's base with a prime view of the disco ball hanging from the first floor above, and I hold on tightly to the girls' hands. Standing shoulder to shoulder with strangers, in unison we sing and sway to the tune of Donna Summer's "Last Dance" and Madonna's "Holiday" while *les feux d'artifice* explode high above our heads and rain on the shoulders of the Tower. The girls are starry-eyed with grins to match. Bastille Day 2012.

WE ARRIVE in Saint-Jean-Cap-Ferrat and observe the changes that have taken place over the last year, which include more potted flowers in the village and installation art by the port. At the hotel, the owners are the same; their grandchildren have grown taller. Their son has a larger role at the hotel and greets us at the front desk. We stay in our usual room, *chambre seize*, with a view of the water and where I will enjoy my cappuccino for the next few mornings.

Days are lazily passed at Paloma Beach. Alice's sister and her family are visiting from New York so there are even more children with whom to collect sea glass in between visits to the ice cream stand. There are more adults with whom to share *rosé*. The kids discover a cove of sheltered water into which they jump from the rocks above. When they are not jumping off rocks, they ride an inflatable sitting contraption resembling a couch pulled by a boat via a rope. The couch bumps across the wakes; the more bumps, the better, and when they occasionally bounce out of the couch into the water, it only adds to the thrill of the ride.

Evenings are spent in the port village. We alternate dinner venues between the local eateries where the seafood is fresh and the authentic Italian pizza is baked in wood-burning ovens. The waitstaff and the menus have not changed since we began coming here. The town square hosts live music and the children's freedom of movement means that they sleep well. Our last night we even manage to catch an open-air piano recital at Chapelle de Saint-Hospice before returning home to Paris.

AVA HAS ELEVEN years today, as the French say. I have heard that the acquirement of the "double ones" brings with it a turning point: the end of childhood wonder before tween-dom, the slippery slope to the teenage years when their friends and hormones dominate. Occasional small moments foreshadow this impending maturation and separation. But for now, in this summer, Ava continues to think Mom is right and full of ideas, the bouncy house in the Bois is a delight, and the days are joyful even though her sister can be annoying.

After a day of shopping, exploring Parc Monceau with its pyramid and Corinthian pillars and visiting an exhibition of Egyptian Dynasties at the Musée Jacquemart-André, we walk from *l'appart* though the Trocadéro to the Tower. Dressed in their puffiest taffeta dresses with white cardigans draped over their shoulders, Ava and Julia admire their reflections in the mirrored doors of the elevator as we await its descent to take us to Le Jules Verne, Alain Ducasse's Michelin restaurant on the second floor, where we will celebrate this pivotal birthday as well as our new home.

Our window table faces the wings of the Trocadéro, providing us with a view of our neighborhood. The girls' dresses spill over the sides of their chairs and when the waiter drapes a cloth napkin across Julia's lap, her hands cover the blush on her cheeks. Another waiter hands us menus as we delight in locating our street and various points of interest in our neighborhood. Below our table, the viewing platform is filled with tourists, all of whom turn around and point their cameras upward to photographically capture the Tower's flashing lights at the top of the hour. Ava, the birthday lady, sits poised and thoughtfully asks me what she is permitted to order.

From our elevated vantage point, we watch the sun retreat in the west and take with it the light of day, illustrating why Paris is known as the City of Light. Although everything from the vegetables to the lobster is divine, Ava's meal is the favorite. Grand excitement comes when a tall waiter brings her a specially crafted dessert with a candle. She makes a wish and blows out her candle, but the birthday excitement is quickly outdone when something small and furry scurries across the floor on the opposite side of the dining room. "*Souris! Souris!*" Several tourists rise to their feet. Napkins fall to the floor. Cameras flash. Waiters hustle about the room with calm decorum to discreetly investigate while Julia, now also standing, announces in a voice that is not restaurant appropriate, "Mom, *it's Ratatouille!*"

We trace our steps back home. Julia skips across the bridge, laughing about the *souris* sighting and re-tells the tale. I show them how to read the blue plaques identifying the street name and the arrondissement.

"Who's that?" Ava asks as we pass the blue plaque for Georges Mandel.

"He was a politician. He opposed the Nazis and was killed during World War II. See, it tells you here, below his name it says when he lived and what he did. This is the date he died. 1944."

"Nazis were here?" Julia asks.

"Yes. They occupied Paris for a time. Actually, there is a famous photograph of Hitler and his officers taken right there," I say as I turn and point back at the Place du Trocadéro.

Then I point to examples of the American-ness in our adopted foreign neighborhood: Avenue President Wilson. Avenue New York. I show them the Benjamin Franklin statue and explain that he lived just south of that spot when the 16th was a suburb of Paris.

"Mom, how long will we keep this place?" Julia asks as we ascend the stairs to *l'appart*.

"Well, I have no intention of getting rid of it. When I die, it will belong to you two and you can decide if you want to keep it," I say as I open and close the door.

"Oh. I could live here? But that will not happen for a long time, right? You dying?"

"Probably not. But life is a gift and how long it lasts is not up to us," I say, knowing the truth in my own statement.

Taffeta dresses are exchanged for cotton nightgowns, and the bathroom nighttime rituals commence. Cool, fresh air from the open windows lends a calming note to the end of a busy day. When they climb into bed, I crawl in between them and together we settle in between the cool sheets.

"Thanks, Mom, for my birthday, "Ava says.

"You're welcome. Thank you for being my daughter." I kiss her forehead. Her whole face smiles in the moonlight. I kiss Julia as well.

"Mommy?"

"Yes, Dia?"

"I like it here in Paris."

"Me too, Dia. Me too."

OUR DAYS IN Paris begin with comforting regularity. A walk to a neighborhood *boulangerie* for a baguette or *pain au chocolat*. After our *petit déjeuner*, we explore our adopted city, me on foot while the girls speed ahead on their flashing little people movers. They soar over sidewalks and cross the bridges connecting both banks. As I trail behind, seeing their hair blowing in the wind, I see the warrior of time as if he is pulling them along, and they are laughing, not conscious of their fleeting childhood, but I know and I frame the image of the two of them in my mind. The double ones. We tackle our adventures by neighborhood: Saint-Germain-des-Prés, Île Saint-Louis, Le Marais. We visit museums, ice cream shops, parks, and boutiques. Some choices are more successful than others. La Maison de Victor Hugo—with its tiny furniture and dark family portraits—does not interest them, but nearby Place des Vosges with its monkey bars and same-aged children, is a hit. We pass Sunday with our neighbors in the Bois picnicking.

OUR LAST DAY in Paris begins with the girls' independent walk downstairs to the *boulangerie*. Julia is wearing the same tulle skirt she wore to Giverny and, indeed, all over Paris. I watch it bounce down the street from over the balcony rail. The domestic bliss is fleeting, however, because the moment the door opens, their arrival is punctuated with flying fists and psychological warfare in the form of name calling such as: "stupid," "idiot," "meanie," "little sausage," and my favorite, "fuzzball." The door slams.

"MOM!!!!" Julia yells.

Pain au chocolat squished in its bag. Baguette crumbs decorate the ebony floor. The constant bickering between the two has worn me down, and I have not even had my cappuccino. I stand up and slap my hand down hard on the table. They stop. The room is silent. Grabbing a notepad from the desk, I tear off two sheets and hand each girl a pen and a piece of paper.

"Write this down," I instruct them.

Then I dictate to them a contract of good behavior wherein they agree that they will not fight nor be unkind to one another. Penalty clauses are included should they breach. They write down my words and each one signs her copy. Ava post-dates her contract by a day.

"Nice try, missy," I tell her. "I don't think so."

She smiles smugly, and I place the signed contracts on the refrigerator door where all important domestic matters are placed.

After our third museum success (today, Musée des Arts et Métiers, which is accessed by one of my favorite Parisian *métro* stops with the same name), we walk to La Table Lauriston for dinner. We sit at the last open table on the *terrasse*. During our meal, Ava informs Julia that there is no Santa Claus.

"*Contract violation!*" I whisper to her.

Crying ensues. The next table must have heard the interaction because I hear a woman utter, "Ah ...." I am not even sure that Julia believes in Santa Claus anymore but learning that she now has an audience, she cries with gusto over the tragic news. And, when her table of sympathizers pass our table to leave the restaurant, they offer their condolences.

By the time the girls have finished their dessert, Santa and his questionable existence has been forgotten. As I wait to pay the check, I give the girls the key to *l'appart* and let them walk home. They are elated with the big-girl treatment and stand a little taller as they take the key and make their way down the street, negotiating who will punch the door code in the keypad and who will hold the key. Unbeknownst to them, I trail a distance behind, watching them experience a little of the independence I knew as a child, albeit in a different venue. I wait outside the door for a few minutes before I knock, and when I do, both greet me at the door, filled with self-satisfaction and already dressed for bed.

"Before you go to bed, you must leave your mark in the apartment," I tell them.

Julia's chocolate-brown eyes grow large and wild with wonder. When I hand them each a pencil, their smiles turn to puzzlement. I lead them to the bathroom and tell them that, in honor of our first summer in *l'appart*, I would like them to draw on the primed walls.

"*En garde... Prêt... Allez!*" I say, repeating the fencing terms we heard over and over at the Olympic games held just across the Channel.

They advance toward the walls, pencils drawn, and illustrate our Summer 2012—eating dinner at the Tower, the three of us holding hands in the city, and me running by the Tower. Although Henri will soon cover their artwork with mosaic, it is a secret the three of us will always have until it is discovered by who knows whom and who knows when. Until that time, I can immerse myself in these memories while soaking in clear, hot water.

Little Picasso and little Matisse fall asleep arm in arm. I pack their clothes for our return to Los Angeles and partially clear out the bathroom so Henri can install the mosaic. For the last time this summer, I sit on the balcony and take in the Paris night air. The street below is quiet. It is a crazy existence, living in two worlds and not completely settled in either my birthplace or my adopted home. After struggling to reconcile the two and categorize myself and where I belong, I realize as I sit here that I am not meant to be defined by or identify with only one; I am both. I have an American spirit with a French soul, and that is something that suits me just fine.

CHAPTER TWENTY-EIGHT

La Rentrée

IN FRANCE, *la rentrée* concludes *les grandes vacances* and signals the return to *la vie quotidienne*. Daily life. While France begins *les grandes vacances*, it is *la rentrée* for us as we fly back to Los Angeles. The return flight seems shorter than the outbound flight, although in reality the opposite is true.

I watch the girls settle into their movies and dive with enthusiasm into their airplane snacks as the large wings of aviation carry us to the new continent. They are significantly taller in their seats than they were six years ago when we began our adventures. The travel load lighter in every sense; I no longer struggle with car seats, *pliable* strollers, and bounties of luggage. Julia no longer sucks her two fingers. Every summer passes more quickly than the last. It is now relevant to me why my father used to sing "Time in a Bottle" when I was a child. I understand that unattainable desire to capture and hold things just as they are, the drawings under the mosaic. Everything becomes history and sooner than we think. This summer marked the finding and spreading of little wings.

La rentrée to-do list begins: autumn cooking jobs and classes in Los Angeles, personal goals, and the parent and school-related tasks that all make for a busy September. My list develops sub-categories, with a flow chart of after-school events and how to coordinate things with the limitations of time and traffic. Then there is that *carte de séjour* process to establish myself professionally in a country where I cannot yet live. I can focus on this now that the Paris nest is completed. Following up with that cooking school in Montmartre about a teaching position, other ideas for books. I begin writing recipes in which to showcase the Argan oil I discovered in the Luberon. I write a recipe for cannelloni made of thinly sliced cantaloupe stuffed with honey-ricotta cheese.

In my scribble fury, I drop my pen. As I reach down for it, I catch Ava's eye and meet her smile. I am transported to that morning at the breakfast table after the judge's ruling. The breakfast that made Paris part-time. Her features are the same but more mature, and the moment fills me with immeasurable joy because, as I look at her and her sister, I realize, in this very ordinary moment, that I have accomplished everything I set out to do. I created a home for us in France. I am giving them the opportunities I never had and exposing them to a life with a global perspective and an education beyond textbooks. I have a French kitchen of my own and I am cooking and learning about French traditions and foods. None of it is traditional or the way I envisioned. It certainly would not be many people's definition of success: a divorced mother of two who goes back and forth between two countries, the frequency and timing of her trips dictated by her child-share schedule (and budget), with no permanence in either place and no capacity to commit to normal working hours or a romantic relationship. Yet, I have created the life I dreamt of, the life I so badly wanted for the three of us. And most important to me, I did it without compromising the mother I wanted to be, and I kept my promise to them.

Julia pokes Ava for attention, and the sibling pestering that has both haunted and occasionally entertained me all this month resumes. As I watch their thumbs warring and elbows twisting, my gratitude for the present is met with unbridled optimism for the future. The to-do list with its flow charts before me becomes my *get-to-do* list. The future, whatever adventure it brings, and however far it may extend, seems bright, because I know in this moment that all the uncertainties of the past have collectively presented a clear today. I see in this moment, this epiphanic moment, that everything that has happened in my life and everyone who has been a part of my life, no matter how long they stayed, had purpose and were essential at *that* time, in *that* order, and those lessons that sometimes took years to understand were links to the next step. I am grateful for all of it. Without exception. For both the pain and the elation. The basement and the stairs. The sacrifices and those closed doors that led me to different paths I would not have sought but for losing control over everything so that I could rebuild with an understanding of acceptance and forgiveness, and appreciation for Giovanni and his credos and all of those years of planning and planting that he taught me and I did, and for Mr. Monaco who carried my lifeless body to the hospital and then selflessly released me so I could create the future I envisioned, and for those times that tested my courage and forced me to overcome my fears, and thank you for liking my cooking and for those four words because I had forgotten the woman I was and oh for that second chance at life and I watched you as you roared and to run and feel the wind on my face again and that little town that made me long for a life beyond those mountains to the cobblestone streets across the Atlantic where the little green men challenged me to run faster and farther with the smell of the melting butter and rising dough and the beautiful stone silhouettes against the rising sun and that sea that inspired me in that room with the paper crown hanging overhead and I was so fragile then but inside I felt so bright. Yes. And inside I was strong and I had a passion for life and living. Yes. And I was no longer going to be afraid and I was not going to wait and those little voices on the phone and that joy which filled that room and fill my every day. Yes. And the memories that no one will know or remember but me and that morning at the breakfast table. Yes. And those eyes those questioning blue eyes those brown eyes. Yes. The collective four that inspire me to try harder. Yes. And run farther. Yes. And it is the sum of all of this history that I am and they will be too. Yes. And I am grateful because all of it made me the woman I am. Yes. It is so clear the mother that I am. Yes. And I know all of it gave us Paris. Yes. It gave us Paris. Yes. Even if Paris is only Paris, part time. *Oui.*

Paris - Los Angeles - Saint-Jean-Cap-Ferrat,
2013-2014.

MELON AND HONEY-RICOTTA CANNOLI
WITH RASPBERRY *COULIS*

Serves 4

Cannoli
1 sweet, ripe cantaloupe
1 cup ricotta cheese
2 teaspoons quality honey, room temperature

Coulis
5 ounces frozen raspberries
2 tablespoons granulated sugar
½ teaspoon fresh lemon juice
A/N water
A/N fresh mint leaves

In a bowl, mix the ricotta cheese and the honey together. Set aside.

Place the raspberries, sugar, and lemon juice in a small saucepan over medium heat. Cook until the raspberries have liquified and the sugar has dissolved. Remove from the stove. Pour the raspberry liquid through a sieve to strain the seeds. Discard the seeds. Let the sauce cool. The sauce can be stored in the refrigerator to use later.

Cut the cantaloupe in half and remove the seeds. Lay the cut side of the cantaloupe flat on a cutting board. Cut off either side (right and the left) about ½ inch. Cut off the melon rind. Square off the rounded side of the cantaloupe and lay the flat surface on a mandoline. Slice the melon (thin enough that the slices are pliable) until the slices begin to have a hole in the center. (With the sides of the melon that are too small to slice, save for another use.) Repeat the process with the second melon half. Set aside. It is best to cut the melon before service rather than storing it sliced.

Place a tablespoon of the ricotta-honey filling in the center of one melon slice. Roll the melon like a cigar. Serve with raspberry *coulis*. (If the *coulis* has thickened, add a little water to make it sauce consistency.) Garnish with small, fresh mint leaves.

SEARED TUNA ROLLS WITH MICROGREENS

Serves 2

> 1 heaping tablespoon *Persil de la Mer*
> 1 teaspoon golden sesame seeds
> 1 teaspoon black sesame seeds
> ½ teaspoon kosher salt (or black Hawaiian sea salt)
> ½ teaspoon freshly ground black pepper
> 6 ounces Albacore tuna, sushi grade
> A/N olive oil
> 1 teaspoon yuzu juice
> 2 pinches *piment d'espelette*
> 2 handfuls of microgreens
> 1 ripe avocado
> 2 Persian cucumbers
> 1 jalapeño, optional

Combine the *Persil de la Mer*, sesame seeds, salt, and pepper in a large bowl. Press the top of the tuna fillet into the mixture. Turn the fillet over. Repeat.

Place a nonstick pan over a high flame. Once pan is hot, add olive oil (you only need about 1 to 2 teaspoons). When oil is hot, add tuna fillet. Sear for 2 to 3 minutes. Using tongs, turn over and sear the other side. Remove fillet from pan with tongs and set aside on a plate. (You can sear the tuna in advance and store in the refrigerator in an airtight container.) Tuna is best served cold.

Peel the cucumbers and remove the seeds. Cut the cucumbers and avocado *julienne* (matchstick-size). Set aside. Place microgreens in a bowl. Combine *piment*, yuzu juice, and olive oil (to taste) in a separate bowl. Combine and add to microgreens.

Slice tuna into strips about ⅛ inch thick (2 to 3 inches long). Lay one tuna slice flat on a cutting board. Place 2 to 3 avocado strips on the center of the slice. Add 2 to 3 cucumber strips and a pinch of the dressed microgreens. Roll the tuna slice, enclosing the greens and fruit. Serve immediately (or the yuzu juice will wilt the microgreens). Serve with thin jalapeño slices. (Optional.)

Paris

UN PEU PLUS …

The IRONMAN race in Nice, France, is a 2.4-mile swim in the Côte d'Azur, followed by a 112 mile bike ride in the French Alps, and finishing with a full marathon, looping back and forth from the Promenade des Anglais to the Nice airport in the humid summer heat.

An IRONMAN was never on my hospital to-do list. However, once I completed that list, I wanted to create a memory of strength to balance my memory of fragility. For me, I wanted to harness the optimism I felt in my hospital room and physically embrace the limitless sea that I looked out upon.

So, in August 2014, after the girls and I returned from Paris, I signed up for the IRONMAN in Nice. The goal scared the hell out of me. Objectively, it was a whimsical thing to do. I had never done a triathlon. In fact, my swimming skills did not extend past a modified dog paddle and plunging my face in the water actually gave me anxiety. Moreover, I had never clipped into a bike and did not know the difference between a road bike, a mountain bike, or a tri bike. The months of training to swim, bike, and run were a struggle of time and energy.

Nine months later, in June 2015, I returned to Paris with a road bike. Days before I was set to depart to Nice for the race, my wallet was stolen from my purse while JeF and I dined on Di Vino's *terrasse*. Everything, including my *carte de séjour*, was stolen. Filing a police report and trying to replace the stolen items was a triathlon in itself. Without a driver's license or credit card, I could not retrieve my rental car to drive the cycling route before the race. Catching a cold did not help. *C'est la vie.*

Nevertheless, on June 28, 2015 — on a hot, beautifully sunny Sunday in Nice—I participated in, and completed, the race. As the familiar sea passed underneath the five scars on my stomach, I thought of my hospital stay. I thought of the wonderful things I learned and the people I met who helped me achieve this goal. I thought of the extra time I had been granted. The first thing I did after the race was Skype with my daughters who were in Los Angeles with their father. The pride and love exhibited on their faces is something I will never forget. The girls' father congratulated me, too. Now I have an IRONMAN medal to go with my paper crown, and in the process, I experienced the iron in me that I always knew existed because it exists in us all.

ACKNOWLEDGMENTS

When I began my search for Parisian real estate, a friend suggested that I take copious notes and document my experience. "You could turn it into a book," she said. I took her advice.

Nearly two years after *l'appart* was purchased, in the summer of 2013, I secured a part-time position at a cooking school in Montmartre in Paris. My *carte de séjour* in place and my suitcase packed, a few weeks before I was due to arrive in Paris, the school informed me that my services were no longer needed; one of its part-time chefs decided to work full-time, eliminating my position. I arrived in Paris with no job. With an empty schedule for a few weeks and the Parisian rooftops to inspire me, I sat at my desk and culled through journals, notes, and receipts, and began writing.

The writing of this book was neither a labor of love nor cathartic. However, I knew it was a unique phase in my life and, for that reason, I felt compelled to write about it. Writing about my hospital stay was painful to mentally relive. Trying to write a few hours a day in between other projects made the process laborious. Initial drafts (and there were many and they were quite large) were, in truth, awful. Discouragement set in. But, there were a few people who saw its potential and it was their encouragement and constructive comments that kept me going. As such, I would like to extend my sincere gratitude to Brenda Barton, Alison Petrocelli, Patricia Benson, Céline Guillou, Leslie Steiner, David Steiner, Marcie Greene, and Samy Ayari. A huge thank you to my editor, Monona Wali, whose counsel made this book what it is. Thank you to Maryam Bozorgmehr, Courtney Kearns, and William Baumgart who provided critical edits and comments. Thank you to Judith Crane, my copy editor, for your attention to detail. Thank you Rebecca Nevitt and Tony Manzella for making my photographs beautiful.

To everyone mentioned in this book, whether under an alias or actually named, my life is infinitely better for knowing you. Thank you. Although mentioned infrequently in the book, I would like to thank my parents for making me the woman I am today. I love you.

Lastly, to my daughters, Ava and Julia, I am grateful for every moment I have had with you. The opportunity to raise you and watch you blossom into the strong, wonderful young women you have become has been a privilege. I enthusiastically look to the future, eager to witness what you both do with your gift of life and blessings of talent, smarts, and heart. My love for you is infinite and without condition or exception.

LBM